David Plummer, PhD

One of the Boys
Masculinity, Homophobia, and Modern Manhood

D0207077

One of the Boys
Masculinity, Homophobia, and Modern Manhood

HAWORTH Gay & Lesbian Studies
John P. De Cecco, PhD
Editor in Chief

The Empress Is a Man: Stories from the Life of José Sarria by Michael R. Gorman

Acts of Disclosure: The Coming-Out Process of Contemporary Gay Men by Marc E. Vargo

Queer Kids: The Challenges and Promise for Lesbian, Gay, and Bisexual Youth by Robert E. Owens

Looking Queer: Body Image and Identity in Lesbian, Gay, Bisexual, and Transgender Communities edited by Dawn Atkins

Love and Anger: Essays on AIDS, Activism, and Politics by Peter F. Cohen

Dry Bones Breathe: Gay Men Creating Post-AIDS Identities and Cultures by Eric Rofes

Lila's House: Male Prostitution in Latin America by Jacobo Schifter

A Consumer's Guide to Male Hustlers by Joseph Itiel

Trailblazers: Profiles of America's Gay and Lesbian Elected Officials by Kenneth E. Yeager

Rarely Pure and Never Simple: Selected Essays by Scott O'Hara

Navigating Differences: Friendships Between Gay and Straight Men by Jammie Price

In the Pink: The Making of Successful Gay- and Lesbian-Owned Businesses by Sue Levin

Behold the Man: The Hype and Selling of Male Beauty in Media and Culture by Edisol Wayne Dotson

Untold Millions: Secret Truths About Marketing to Gay and Lesbian Consumers by Grant Lukenbill

It's a Queer World: Deviant Adventures in Pop Culture by Mark Simpson

In Your Face: Stories from the Lives of Queer Youth by Mary L. Gray

Military Trade by Steven Zeeland

Longtime Companions: Autobiographies of Gay Male Fidelity by Alfred Lees and Ronald Nelson

From Toads to Queens: Transvestism in a Latin American Setting by Jacobo Schifter

The Construction of Attitudes Toward Lesbians and Gay Men edited by Lynn Pardie and Tracy Luchetta

Lesbian Epiphanies: Women Coming Out in Later Life by Karol L. Jensen

Smearing the Queer: Medical Bias in the Health Care of Gay Men by Michael Scarce

Macho Love: Sex Behind Bars in Central America by Jacobo Schifter

When It Is Time to Leave Your Lover: A Guide for Gay Men by Neil Kaminsky

Strategic Sex: Why They Won't Keep It in the Bedroom edited by D. Travers Scott

One of the Boys: Masculinity, Homophobia, and Modern Manhood by David Plummer

Homosexual Rights of Passage: A Road to Visibility and Validation by Marie Mohler

Male Lust: Power, Pleasure, and Transformation edited by Kerwin Kay, Jill Nagle, and Baruch Gould

Out of the Twilight: Fathers of Gay Men Speak by Andrew R. Gottlieb

One of the Boys
Masculinity, Homophobia, and Modern Manhood

David Plummer, PhD

Harrington Park Press
An Imprint of The Haworth Press, Inc.
New York • London • Oxford

27.95

Published by

Harrington Park Press, an imprint of The Haworth Press, Inc., 10 Alice Street, Binghamton, NY 13904-1580

Cover design by Marylouise E. Doyle.

Library of Congress Cataloging-in-Publication Data

Plummer, David, 1957-
    One of the boys : masculinity, homophobia, and modern manhood / David Plummer.
       p.   cm.
    Includes bibliographical references and index.
    ISBN: 1-56023-973-5 (hc. : alk. paper).—ISBN: 1-56023-974-3 (pbk. : alk. paper).
    1. Homophobia. 2. Homophobia in children. 3. Boys—Psychology. 4. Men—Socialization.
5. Masculinity. I. Title.
HQ76.P53 1999
305.9'06642—dc21
                                                              99-34431
                                                               CIP

To all of my family,
especially my partner, Brian Tunks

ABOUT THE AUTHOR

David Plummer, PhD, MD, is Associate Professor in the School of Health at the University of New England in Australia. In addition he is a sexual health physician and health sociologist. He has authored a number of papers, chapters, and books on sexuality and health. He was the first National President of Australia's national top non-government AIDS body, the Australian Federation of AIDS Organizations (AFAO). Dr. Plummer is also an executive member of Australia's top governmental AIDS advisory body, the Australian National Council on AIDS and Related Diseases (ANCARD), which advises the Federal Health Minister.

He founded and has served as co-editor of *Venereology: The International, Interdisciplinary Journal of Sexuality and Health* for over ten years. Dr. Plummer has special interests in public health, marginalization and health, Aboriginal sexual health, sexuality and aging, and the impact of gender on health. He has been involved in international program development in Australia, Papua New Guinea, and Indonesia.

CONTENTS

Acknowledgments

This work is based on research undertaken at the Australian National University and funded by the National Health and Medical Research Council.

Thanks to the young men who generously gave their time to recount their stories.

Special thanks to Brian Tunks for his endless support.

Thanks also to Robert Kosky, Dorothy Broom, William Walters, Michael Ross, John Ballard, Victor Minichiello, Chris Puplick, Matt Gillett, Dan Sybaczynskyj, Jennifer Hickey, and Bruce Forrest.

Introduction

Homophobia is widespread, takes diverse forms, and has far-reaching behavioral and social consequences. Instead of people viewing homosexuality with simple disinterest, a number of studies have confirmed that antihomosexual bias is extensive and often deeply felt. The extent and intensity of homophobia invites inquiry into the significance of biases about homosexuality, particularly when homosexuals are so often portrayed as weak individuals belonging to a marginal minority that poses no obvious threat.

This study investigates the development of homophobia and the meanings and significance people associate with it. It is concerned primarily with antihomosexual bias experienced by males. Detailed life histories were collected, focusing on how the informants came to understand sexuality. Subjects described their own experiences as well as how sexual issues were handled by their peers. Interviews were analyzed according to key themes that emerged from the data. Themes include the relationship between homophobia and masculinity, the processes involved in becoming homophobic, the effects of homophobia on masculine self-concept and identity, and the impact of homophobia on intimacy, sexual expression, and relationships. Findings were then used to elaborate on existing theories that attempt to explain homophobia.

The ways in which terms referring to "homosexuality" are used during childhood and adolescence are the key observations of this research. The term "poofter" comes into currency almost universally during primary school and is considered to be among the most negative of terms that can be applied to another boy. Significantly, for the first few (crucial) years of use, "poofter" and similar terms do not have explicit homosexual connotations and many young boys have no understanding of homosexual identity and practice. Instead, these terms take diverse meanings and are applied to boys who are different—particularly those who are softer, academic, less team sport oriented, less group oriented, who differ significantly from the standards of other boys or who are less restrained by gender roles. Prestigious team sports take a central role in defining and enforcing homophobia.

This study finds that homophobia serves to define a key repository for ideas of "not self," "difference," and "otherness" during the processes of forming adult male identities. As sexual maturity approaches, the notion of "poofter" evolves, becomes more specific, explicitly sexual, and is eventually embodied in the male homosexual. A recurring pattern is that homophobia commences, crescendos, peaks, and then in early adulthood, it starts to dissipate (although never completely). This process, called "homophobic passage," coincides with the passage of young males from childhood to adulthood and appears to play an important role in the formation of the modern adult male self.

Chapter 1

The Homophobic Puzzle

Homophobia is a fascinating puzzle. Even though it is neither universal nor uniform, homophobia is extremely common and has been identified in many modern societies (Hendriks, Tielman, and van der Veen, 1993). Far from provoking simple disinterest, homosexuality typically attracts considerable attention and homophobia is often deeply cathected and can culminate in extreme violence. Studies from around the world have shown that homophobic violence frequently follows well-documented patterns and that people who engage in violence share a range of characteristics. In contrast, the extent and intensity of homophobia seems to be "at odds" with the apparent principal target—in the case of Western homosexual males—who constitute a small minority and are stereotypically portrayed as emasculated and weak. Further, although homophobia appears to be an important, widespread phenomenon, the term was coined only recently (less than twenty-five years ago) and it attracts comparatively little research. This work is concerned with addressing these issues, with elucidating the processes that underwrite male homophobia, with adding to our understanding of how homophobia comes about and why it exists, with tracing the meanings that homophobia invokes, and with defining its relationship with masculinity.

DEFINING HOMOPHOBIA

Since it was first used, the meaning of the term "homophobia" has evolved considerably. "Homophobia" was introduced into the literature by George Weinberg in 1972 in his milestone publication *Society and the Healthy Homosexual.* At the time, he defined homophobia as "the dread of being in close quarters with homosexuals" (Weinberg, 1972: 4). This definition is consistent with formal criteria in the psychological literature for a phobia (American Psychiatric Association, 1994; World Health Organization, 1992). However, since 1972, the use of the term has shifted to include meanings that are considerably broader than Weinberg's original sense—which is rarely used now even in scholarly writing.

Homophobia is a problematic term, particularly when taken literally. In a 1991 review, Haaga notes that contemporary usage includes "a wide range of negative emotions, attitudes and behaviours toward homosexual people" (Haaga, 1991: 171). These characteristics of homophobia are not consistent with accepted definitions of phobias, which Haaga describes as "an intense, illogical, or abnormal fear of a specified thing" (1991: 171). Five key differences distinguish homophobia from a true phobia. First, the emotion classically associated with a phobia is fear, whereas homophobia is often characterized by hatred or anger. Second, a phobia generally involves recognition that the fear is excessive or unreasonable, but homophobic responses are often considered understandable, justified, and acceptable. Third, a phobia typically triggers avoidance, whereas homophobia often manifests itself as hostility and aggression. Fourth, a phobia does not usually relate to a political agenda, while homophobia has political dimensions including prejudice and discrimination. Finally, unlike homophobia, people suffering from a phobia often recognize that it is disabling and are motivated to change.

The lack of consistency between the contemporary usage of homophobia and the criteria used to designate true phobias is also reflected in the *Oxford English Dictionary. The New Shorter Oxford English Dictionary* (Brown, 1993: 1254) defines homophobia as a "fear *or hatred of* homosexuals and homosexuality" and a homophobe as "a person who is afraid of *or hostile to* homosexuals and homosexuality" (emphasis added). Even in Weinberg's original writings, homophobia is used to refer to widespread social occurrences and to a broad range of antihomosexual bias and is considerably broader than his initial definition allows. For example, he variously refers to homophobia as "hostility," "revulsion towards homosexuals," "the desire to inflict punishment as retribution," a "prejudice," a "pattern of attitudes," and "part of the conventional American attitude" (Weinberg, 1972: 3, 4, 8, 18, and 132).

In an attempt to resolve these inconsistencies, Haaga suggests that the use of the word "homophobia" be restricted to its literal meaning, and those phenomena characterized by antihomosexual bias, which are not true phobias, be reclassified. To support his argument for restricting the use of homophobia and to designate other words for associated nonphobic phenomena, Haaga argues that the term "does not accurately depict the phenomena generally subsumed under homophobia" (1991: 172) and that the term preempts an etiological theory. Various authors have offered alternative terminologies including "homoerotophobia" (Churchill, 1967), "antihomosexual prejudice" (Haaga, 1991), "homonegativism" (Hudson and Rickets, 1980), "homosexism" (Hansen, 1982), "homosexual taboo" (Marshall, 1994), "homosexual bias" (Fyfe, 1983), and "heterosexism" (Neisen, 1990). Unfortunately, the alternative terms also imply etiological frameworks of their own; none of which can be assumed to accurately define homophobia, nor to suggest adequate explanations. Furthermore, all terms seem to reflect a desire to collectively refer to the phenomena generally subsumed under the term homophobia, phobic or not, rather than to fragment homophobia.

The uncertainty about how homophobia is to be defined is important for this project because it affects which literature can be drawn upon and the area to be analyzed. Clearly, "homophobia" in its literal sense is an unsatisfactory term. However, rather than attempting to quarantine homophobia to its literal sense, contrary to its general usage, it is advantageous to accept and analyze the meanings reflected in its broader contemporary use despite its etymology. There are a number of reasons for this. First, this is a study of homophobia in everyday life, and it makes some sense to use terms that accord with everyday usage. Second, this project is interested in describing and exploring antihomosexual bias generally, and it is appropriate to use a definition that captures a broad range of phenomena (including true phobias). This avoids making assumptions about etiology as narrower, more precisely defined terms might. Third, there is no generally accepted alternative term, probably because this area has a short history and does not have an extensive theoretical literature to draw on. It may also reflect how poorly we understand homophobia, and consequently, our language is ill equipped to describe it. For the purposes of this project then, "homophobia" will be used imprecisely, to encompass a broad range of situations and processes characterized, at least in part, by antihomosexual bias. It should be understood that in this context homophobia is a provisional term not to be taken literally. The meanings ascribed to homophobia will emerge as this work unfolds.

CLARIFYING THE TERMS OF REFERENCE

Difficulties with defining homophobia are not confined to whether or not it is a true phobia. The term involves implicit reference to homosexuality, which also has inherent definitional problems. There has been considerable debate in recent years over whether "homosexuals" are universal across different cultures or whether "the homosexual" is an identity that can only be legitimately discussed in relation to modern Westernized cultures. It is argued that it is only possible to talk tentatively of homosexuality prior to the mid- to late nineteenth century because the word "homosexual" only entered the German language in 1869 and English in 1892 (Halperin, 1990: 15). Prior to that time, the concept did not seem to exist—sodomy and nonprocreative forms of sex were of concern, but these acts are not the sole domain of homosexuals. Halperin makes the additional point that it may even be inappropriate to speak of "sexuality" prior to this. He argues that although sex existed, the cluster of phenomena that we refer to as "sexuality" may not have been thought of collectively, or as "sexual" until more recently (Halperin, Winkler, and Zeitlin, 1990: 5). In contrast, it is possible to talk of antihomosexual bias prior to the introduction of the term "homophobia" in 1972, since "antihomosexual bias" only requires the formulation of the concept "homosexual." A case can be made that antihomosexual bias existed prior to the introduction of the word homosexual, if it can be shown that sodomy laws were exercised differentially and primarily against sodomy between males (Weeks, 1991: 17; Dollimore, 1991: 239). (In fact, it will be argued that homophobia is a necessary prerequisite for the formulation of the "heterosexual" and "homosexual" dichotomy.)

Acts of male-male intimacy have different meanings and follow different patterns in different cultures. Therefore, patterns of bias against these acts might also vary, or be absent. For example, Herdt reports that ritualized male-to-male insemination was an obligatory rite of passage for all young men in parts of Melanesia (Herdt, 1993: 6-7 and 61-65). Halperin and Dover explore the culturally valued homoerotic practices between men (*erastes*) and boys (*eromenos*) in the ancient world (Halperin, 1991: 37-53; Dover, 1989). Watanabe and Iwata describe the special place that homoeroticism played in traditional Japanese culture, particularly for the Samurai warriors (*Wakashu/Shu-do*) and the Buddhist monks (*Chigo*) (Watanabe and Iwata, 1989). These examples are of interest because if bias against male-male intimacy existed at all, it must have been quite different from modern forms so these culturally important phenomena could be accommodated without provoking antihomosexual hostility. The details of each of these cases are quite different, and they are culturally and racially unrelated. It is also notable that the societies where these practices arose have changed. As Watanabe notes, in modern Japan, homosexual behavior has become highly stigmatized and hidden, and is considered alien. He articulates a prevalent modern Japanese attitude: "The Western vice that we Japanese have never known is invading our country" (Watanabe and Iwata, 1989: 121 and 12). These findings suggest that social factors play a powerful role in generating homophobia, and a hiatus or absence of homophobia in certain situations is evidence of its nonessential nature. Thus, although modern surveys in Westernized cultures have found that homophobia is frequent and adheres to identifiable patterns, the historical and cultural evidence reminds us that we cannot assume this is due to an innate human predisposition to antihomosexual bias, nor is it culturally invariable. Indeed, these findings of historical and cultural variability prompt us to look at modern social arrangements to see if we can identify how contemporary patterns of antihomosexual bias are generated, transmitted, and enforced.

A further problem is that sexual difference is often portrayed as dichotomous, opposite, and symmetrical and this representation influences the operations of homophobia and how it is analyzed. Man, woman, boy, and homosexual are different, but it is illogical that a man is simultaneously the *opposite* of a boy, a woman, a transvestite, and a homosexual. Sexuality and gender systems are founded on nonsymmetrical differences and the difference between man, woman, and child is not one of "equally opposite symmetry." There is no intrinsic reason why the opposite of heterosexual is homosexual or perversion, except when opposite values such as good and evil become attached to these categories. Even within contemporary Western culture, ambiguities concerning homosexual acts and homosexual identities are common, and they have become particularly obvious in HIV/AIDS social research (Altman, 1992: 32-42; Dowsett, 1994). This ambiguity manifests as a gap between people who feel "authentically homosexual," many of whom have had enjoyable heteroerotic experiences, and those people who feel "authentically heterosexual" but sometimes seek out homoerotic experiences. Similarly, a paradox arises in the difference between societies where there is homosexuality, homophobia, and people who feel "authentically homosexual," and those societies where there are homoerotic cultural arrangements but it is not possible to identify a class of people who could be described as "homosexuals." Dichotomies that we view as naturally opposite and symmetrical may not be essentially so, but are positioned that way because of cultural values that are attached to them (Weeks, 1985: 86-87). Likewise, categories that seem unnatural, unbalanced, and asymmetrical appear that way because of the values that serve to define them and their relationship with one another. It will be argued that a principal repository of these "cultural values" is homophobia, which plays a crucial role in creating and maintaining asymmetrical, seemingly natural oppositions.

In Western culture, homophobia is regularly directed at men who are "effeminate." Many researchers have therefore assumed that homosexual men are "womanly" and that homophobia is primarily disapproval of men who act like women. However, homophobia also targets men who aren't obviously effeminate, and transgression seems to occur when same-sex gender conventions are not observed rather than when characteristics of the "opposite" sex are expressed. Thus, there are differences between homosexuals, transvestites, and transsexuals, although they might all be accused of acting like the "opposite sex"; leathermen, "muscle Marys" (gay bodybuilders), and drag queens differ markedly in how effeminate they are. Furthermore, homosexual relationships are one of few where sex roles are not anatomically preconfigured and there is a potential for symmetry and role change. Although it may be true that homophobia can target men (and boys) who are not "conventionally masculine," this should not be equated exclusively with being "feminine" or with the female gender (Pringle, 1992: 82). Perceptions regarding being "masculine" or occupying a "female sex role" are highly culturally variable (the dominant males of two centuries ago made a practice of wearing wigs, powder, beauty spots, and flamboyant "drag" that looks decidedly "gay" now). Just as homophobia often occurs independently of known details of a person's sexuality, this project has identified aspects of homophobia that do not seem to be directly related to gender. Consequently, the process of interpreting this research becomes tricky and requires continual and conscientious reevaluation of prevalent concepts of sexuality and gender.

A number of theorists have equated homophobia with heterosexism or attempted to subsume it under the umbrella of heterosexism (Altman, 1992: 44; Neisen, 1990). This is not satisfactory. Heterosexism and homophobia do overlap, but they are not the same. By conflating them, homophobia is subjected to stronger, competing, sometimes homophobic agendas and the characteristics that differentiate it are at risk of being submerged. Heterosexism also seems inadequate because it suggests that homophobic dynamics arise from intergender considerations, but male homophobia can be considered just as much an intragender phenomenon ("between men"). Furthermore, heterosexism explains certain social arrangements that affect homosexuals, but it lacks a satisfying framework to fully explain the *passion* that permeates homophobia. Last, heterosexism suggests that homophobia primarily has a sexual basis (unacceptable sexual preference). Although it may be difficult at this stage to see homophobia in any other way than sexual, the possibility that homophobia has its origins in nonsexual processes must be kept open until the evidence is reviewed.

This project is concerned with homophobia—not homosexuality. However, many people who knew this was a study of homophobia seemed to read it as a study of homosexuality and wanted to talk about homosexuality and its origins. This is an interesting paradox, one that was sometimes hard to avoid: homosexuality and homophobia often seem to be conflated. This paradox seems to recur in a popular belief that homophobia is perpetrated by homosexuals who haven't accepted their own homosexuality. This is inconsistent with homophobia being a widespread social prejudice that exceeds the minority of people who are homosexual who are being held responsible. Perhaps the attractiveness of this belief has its origins in homophobia as a wish to make homosexuals responsible even for their own persecution. Alternatively, a controversial proposition is that most perpetrators are heterosexual but are suppressing/repressing more universal homoerotic impulses (perhaps kept in check by homophobia). However, regardless of whether they are suppressing/repressing homoerotic impulses, the majority of homophobic people are and remain heterosexual, and despite earlier reservations about "heterosexism," it is meaningful at this level to relate homophobia to heterosexuality rather than blaming the victim. As Jonathan Dollimore writes when he paraphrases Norman Mailer, "anyone who has succeeded in repressing his homosexuality has earned the right not to be called homosexual" (Dollimore, 1991: 46).

This leads to a further question: although the apparent target of homophobia is "the homosexual," is he, perhaps, not the principal target? Again, if homosexual males are a small and stereotypically "weak" minority, then the extent of homophobia in this culture and the amount of energy put into it seem disproportionate. Is it the case that the energy behind homophobia actually arises because of what homophobia means or does for the majority? In view of these possibilities, it is necessary for the reader to keep an open mind as to the exact operations of homophobia. This is difficult because the culture we live in seems to be deeply impregnated with homophobic conventions, undoubtedly infiltrating the views of the writer and readers of this work.

THE "EPIDEMIOLOGY" OF HOMOPHOBIA: STUDIES OF HOMOPHOBIC VIOLENCE

Homophobic violence constitutes the tip of the homophobic "iceberg." However, studies on homophobic violence provide a useful foundation for investigating homophobia because violence is comparatively easy to define, is increasingly well documented, has major ramifications, and offenders' statements often provide un- equivocal evidence of homophobic motives.

As a class, gay men and lesbians are at greater risk of harassment, violence, and murder, regardless of whether the motive of the of- fender is known. In addition, studies that include motives for anti- homosexual violence show that homophobia plays a role in most of the increased violence experienced by gay men and lesbians. A survey commissioned by the New South Wales Police Service in 1994 studied the experiences of gay men and lesbians who attended an outdoor gay event known as the "Mardi Gras Fair Day" (San- droussi and Thompson, 1995). This event attracts 22,000 people who constitute a broad cross section of Sydney's homosexual men and women. Two hundred and fifty-nine gay men and lesbians agreed to be surveyed and the response rate was estimated to be 80 percent. The survey found that both gay men and lesbians were at least five times more likely to experience verbal harassment in a twelve-month period than the "general community" had ever expe- rienced. It was also found that the 139 gay men in the sample were at least four times more likely than the general Sydney adult male population to experience an assault in a twelve-month period. This was reportedly an underestimate because, unlike the gay cohort, the comparison group—the general Sydney adult male population—in- cluded both threatened and actual assault and domestic violence. The survey also found that 57 percent of respondents had experi- enced some crime/harassment in the past twelve months and that just under half of these (27 percent of the total) had experienced more than one type of "incident." Thirty-three percent of respond- ents reported three or more separate incidents in the past twelve months.

The frequent experience of harassment and violence is not con- fined to a few surveys or to one city. Similar findings have been found elsewhere. In 1994, the group Gay Men and Lesbians Against Discrimination (GLAD) published the results of a survey of Victo- ria's gay and lesbian population (GLAD, 1994). The sample of 1,002 people (492 women and 510 men) was recruited through diverse channels, including 500 surveyed at venues and events, 350 via mailings, and 150 during public meetings. Three thousand surveys were distributed and the response rate was therefore around one in three. In this survey, 70 percent of lesbians and 69 percent of gay men reported having been verbally abused, threatened, or bashed in a public place "on the grounds of sexuality." This includes 11 percent of lesbians and 20 percent of gay men having been physically assaulted ("bashed") and 2.6 percent of lesbians and 5.5 percent of gay men reported being physically assaulted by the police.

Further evidence for the widespread and serious nature of antigay violence comes from analyses of murder cases in New South Wales. Sandroussi and Thompson (1995) report that since 1990 there have been twenty-two murders in New South Wales that "appear to be gay-hate related." This information is echoed by Tomsen (1993), who reports that between 1989 and 1993, there were seventeen gay murders documented by the New South Wales police and that this constitutes one-quarter of all "stranger murders" in New South Wales during this period. In another paper, Tomsen reports that between 1988 and 1994, there were twenty-four cases of murder "in which the victim's sexuality formed the evident basis for a fatal attack" (1994: 3) and again that this figure constitutes about one quarter of all "stranger murders" in New South Wales in the same period. In 1997, Tomsen expanded these findings to thirty-one murders in the ten years to 1996 (Tomsen, 1997: 38). In addition, violence between men who are known to each other also includes attacks where sexual preference is an important factor.

Similar data are available from Britain and the United States. In a study of 400 gay teenagers in London, Trenchard and Warren found that more than 50 percent had been verbally abused, 20 percent had been beaten up, 10 percent had been "thrown out of home," and many had been sent for medical treatment because of being homosexual (Trenchard and Warren, 1984: 151, quoted in Mac an Ghaill, 1994: 167). Berrill reviewed twenty-six studies of antihomosexual violence and victimization in North America (Herek and Berrill, 1992). Of these, the seven most recent major surveys, covering most of the United States and Canada, reported broadly similar results to those from Sydney and Melbourne. The seven studies were conducted between 1988 and 1991, and each study included sample sizes of 234, 1,363, 234, 291, 721, 542, and 395 respectively (3,780 responses; 2,000 male; 1,379 female; 401 sex not specified). Results for the two largest samples (1,363 and 721 men and women combined) found that between 84 and 87 percent of respondents had been verbally abused; 45 to 48 percent had been threatened with violence; 25 to 27 percent were targets of "objects"; and 19 to 20 percent reported having been punched, hit, and/or kicked because they were gay or lesbian. Higgins quotes a report from the Hollywood division of the Los Angeles Police Department that sexual preference was a factor in ten of forty-two murders in that precinct (similar proportions to the New South Wales data) (Higgins, 1993: 264).

Characterizing Antihomosexual Incidents

While the number of incidents of violence experienced by gay men and lesbians is substantial, the patterning of the violence is also revealing. The people most frequently associated with antihomosexual violence share a number of important similarities, and the violence they engage in follows predictable patterns both in Australia and overseas.

The "Lesbian and Gay Anti-Violence Project" in inner Sydney monitors incidents of antihomosexual assault and publishes the results in their *Streetwatch* reports. The project relies on self-reporting, and only those incidents considered serious enough to be reported are recorded. These reports do not provide an accurate indication of the incidence of attacks, but they do provide a useful database of the characteristics of antihomosexual violence. The *Count and Counter Report* (Cox, 1994) in the *Streetwatch* series documents 184 incidents: ninety separate incidents between November 1991 and June 1992 and ninety-four separate incidents between July 1992 and June 1993. Physical assault was reported in 110 of the 184 incidents. Forty of these were defined as serious injury (multiple injuries, broken limbs, or major wounds) and fifty-five were less serious (bruises and cuts). Seventy-four cases (76 percent) involved injuries to the head; forty-three (44 percent) injuries to the torso; twenty-six (27 percent) injuries to the limbs, and one with injuries to the groin. Ninety of the attacks involved no other weapon apart from fists and feet; ten involved knives; and twenty involved objects such as clubs, bottles, and stones. Only 1.1 percent of the 1992 cases and 6.4 percent of the 1993 cases included robbery.

The sex of the offenders was recorded in 169 of the incidents. One hundred and forty-six incidents (86 percent) were by males only; a further twenty (12 percent) were mixed; and only three (2 percent) were by females only. The person making the report estimated the age of offenders. The estimated average age of offenders in 113 cases (61 percent) was under twenty-five, and in 144 (78 percent) cases, it was under thirty. The report noted that there was an inverse relationship between the average age of the offender and the number of offenders involved. Of the 177 incidents for which the number of offenders was known, 126 (71 percent) of the incidents involved more than one offender; ninety-five (54 percent) involved three or more assailants; and twelve incidents involved more than ten. Of the 184 incidents, only thirty-two (17 percent) involved assailant(s) who were known to the victim (Cox, 1994).

Details indicating reasons for attacks were recorded. These were divided into "subjective" and "objective" indicators. Of the 152 reports for which the perceived motive was recorded, 143 (94 percent) felt that it was related to sexual preference (including four cases in which this was related to HIV status). The words spoken by the offender at the time of the attack were recorded as an objective indicator of reasons for the attack. It should be noted that in many studies showing evidence of homophobia, it is not possible to conclude whether homophobia precipitated the attack or whether the attacker used it to legitimize the attack (in either case, homophobia is still involved). In 144 of the 184 incidents (78 percent), the assailant spoke. Of the 144 people spoken to during the assault, 104 (72 percent) reported antihomosexual or anti-AIDS (nine cases) comments. The analysis found a correlation between the perceived motives for the attacks and the objective indicators (Cox, 1994).

These Australian findings are similar to those from the United States. Berrill cites a "profile of a gay basher" compiled by the San Francisco group "Community United Against Violence" (CUAV) as "a young male, often acting together with other young males, all of whom are strangers to the victim" (Berrill, 1992: 30). In a study of 418 offenders by CUAV, 54 percent were twenty-one or younger, 92 percent were males, and 57 percent involved multiple offenders. In another study by LeBlanc, published in 1991, of 1,363 victimized respondents, the offenders were identified in 661 episodes. Ninety-two percent of these episodes involved male offenders only and 4 percent were mixed. Of the 587 people who reported being attacked by strangers, 42 percent said the offenders were "adolescent" and 45 percent were in their twenties. Of the 646 cases where the number of offenders was recorded, only 22 percent were by individuals and 56 percent were by three or more (Berrill, 1992: 30).

Berrill (1992) also reviews the type of attack. Of the seven antihomosexual victimization surveys in the United States between 1988 and 1991, with sample sizes ranging from 234 to 1,363, four surveys report "verbal abuse" in between 79 to 91 percent of the cases; four report "threats of violence" in 37 to 48 percent; five report "property violence" in 14 to 27 percent; five report "targets of objects" in 21 to 28 percent; six report being "followed or chased" in 13 to 41 percent; four being "spat upon" in 7 to 15 percent; seven being "punched, hit, and kicked" in 9 to 24 percent; and six report the use of a weapon in 7 to 10 percent.

Comstock quotes Flemming, a physician giving evidence about the emergency room of a San Francisco Hospital before a hearing of the San Francisco Board of Supervisors, as saying that antihomosexual attacks are

> vicious in scope and the intent is to kill and maim . . . weapons include knives, guns, brass knuckles, tire irons, baseball bats, broken bottles, metal chains, and metal pipes. Injuries include severe lacerations requiring extensive plastic surgery; head injuries, at times requiring surgery; puncture wounds of the chest, requiring insertion of chest tubes; removal of the spleen for traumatic rupture; multiple fractures of the extremities, jaws, ribs, and facial bones; severe eye injuries, in two cases resulting in permanent loss of vision; as well as severe psychological trauma. (Comstock, 1991: 46)

For obvious reasons, surveys cannot capture antigay murders, but as we have seen, these probably account for one-quarter of "stranger homicides" in New South Wales. There is growing evidence in Australia, the United States, and Europe that antigay murder is frequently characterized by extreme violence (beyond what is required to simply kill the person). Berrill quotes Melissa Mertz, Director of Victim Services at Bellevue Hospital in New York City, as saying, "Antigay murders are often marked by extreme brutality. They frequently involved torture, cutting, mutilation, and beating and show the absolute intent to rub out the human being because of his sexual preference" (Herek and Berrill, 1992: 25).

Miller and Humphreys published a study of fifty-four murders between 1973 and 1977, titled *Lifestyles of Violence: Homosexual Victims of Assault and Murder.* They found that

> an intense rage is present in nearly all homicide cases involving gay male victims. A striking feature . . . is their gruesome, often vicious nature. Seldom is the homosexual simply shot. He is more apt to be stabbed a dozen or more times, mutilated *and* strangled and in a number of instances, stabbed or mutilated after being fatally shot. (Miller and Humphreys, 1980: 184)

They noted that a disproportionate number of murders involved stabbing: 54 percent of their sample compared with 18 percent of all reported homicides in the United States at that time. Comstock quotes Kiel on a study of autopsy findings published in 1965 as saying, "multiple and extensive wounds are not uncommon in the fury of the antihomosexual murder" (Comstock, 1991: 47).

These findings are collaborated by recent cases in New South Wales (NSW). A summary of evidence from thirteen recent cases provided in a discussion paper from the NSW Attorney General's Department also reveals patterns of extreme violence, some involving multiple stabbing and a combination of bashing and stabbing (New South Wales Attorney General's Department, 1996).

Evidence Concerning Traditional Safe Havens

Refuges that are usually available to people who have suffered violence seem less willing to offer shelter to people who have experienced antihomosexual violence.

Schools are generally viewed as safe havens for children to be educated and to grow. Yet studies that examined school experiences consistently identified a significant proportion of people who experienced antihomosexual harassment at school. For example, 18 percent of female and 20 percent of male respondents to the GLAD (1994) survey reported harassment during their education. The younger the respondent, the more likely he or she was to report harassment: 47 percent of respondents under the age of twenty and 21 percent of those between twenty-one and twenty-nine. Several studies reviewed by Berrill reported antihomosexual "victimization in high school or junior high school" in the United States. A study of 721 people (461 male and 260 female) in Pennsylvania in 1988 found that 49 percent of respondents experienced antihomosexual victimization. This was echoed in four earlier studies: 33 percent of 167 people in Philadelphia in 1985; 38 percent of 213 people in Wisconsin in 1985; 37 percent of 323 people in Maine (high schools only) in 1985; and 37 percent of 2,074 people in eight major cities in the United States in 1984 (summarized in Berrill, 1992). Similarly, Comstock found that 29 percent of 104 males and 17 percent of fifty-three women experienced antihomosexual violence at school (Comstock, 1991). The *Schoolwatch Report* documents the results of a survey of 152 people, conducted mainly in New South Wales between 1992 and 1994 (Griffin, 1994). In this study of antihomosexual victimization experienced by students, student teachers, and teachers, 59 percent reported verbal harassment; 21 percent reported threats of violence; and 18 percent reported physical violence. Seventy-seven percent of incidents occurred between 1990 and 1994. Fourteen of the twenty-seven respondents who experienced physical antihomosexual violence at school reported three or more such incidents. Of respondents, 81 percent reported students and 11 percent reported teachers as the offenders in incidents that they considered their most serious.

The family also frequently failed to provide safe haven. Berrill summarizes six separate U.S. studies between 1984 and 1988 that recorded antihomosexual abuse and violence occurring in the family (Berrill, 1992). These studies were from Vermont (n = 133; 58 male; 75 female), Philadelphia (n = 734; 323 male; 411 female); Maine (n = 323; 176 male; 147 female); eight major U.S. cities (n = 2,074; 1,420 male; 654 female); Pennsylvania (n = 721; 461 male; 260 female); and the District of Columbia (n = 395). They found 41 percent, 19 percent, 38 percent, 34 percent, 22 percent, and 24 percent, respectively, of familial verbal abuse related to the subject's homosexuality, and the second, fourth, fifth, and sixth studies reported familial physical abuse related to the subject's homosexuality in 4 percent, 7 percent, 5 percent, and 8 percent respectively.

When interpreting these findings, it should be borne in mind that homosexual men and women disclose their sexual orientation selectively. Martin explored the reasons for this in his paper "Learning to Hide: The Socialization of the Gay Adolescent" (Martin, 1982). Even the decision to disclose selectively reflects on the safety or perceived safety of the family environment. In *Young and Gay: A Study of Gay Youth in Sydney,* Bennett (1983) reports family disclosure and family reactions of young people in Sydney in 1983. Of 387 young people interviewed, regardless of disclosure, 136 (35 percent) reported having observed favorable family responses to homosexuality and 251 (65 percent) reported nonaccepting or very negative family reactions. When this was cross-tabulated with disclosure, 129 reported that their families were not aware of their homosexuality and 258 that their families were aware, and that those who had observed more favorable reactions were more likely to have disclosed. It should be noted that this study recruited young people from the gay community and therefore may overestimate the number whose family is aware compared to those who are "in hiding."

Another feature of the problems normally associated with safe havens is the difficulty in accessing police services. The GLAD Survey (n = 1,002) found that 22 percent of lesbians and 33 percent of gay men reported difficulties with the police, including 2.6 percent of the women and 5.5 percent of the men reporting physical assault by police (GLAD, 1994). Nine of the studies summarized by Berrill included data on being "victimized by police." Between 8 percent and 30 percent of people reported police victimization. The rates were 20 percent (23 percent males; 13 percent females) and 16 percent (20 percent males; 11 percent females) in the two largest studies (n = 2,074 and 1,363, respectively) (Herek and Berrill 1992: 21-22). The *Count and Counter Report* from Sydney includes ninety-five incidents that were not reported to the police (Cox, 1994). One reason given was that the incident was not serious enough to report, but reasons also included "the report would not be taken seriously" (thirteen cases); the "police would be hostile" (seventeen cases) and the assault was by a police officer (seven cases).

All cases were considered serious enough to make a full report to the Lesbian and Gay Anti-Violence Project.

Social Dimensions of Antihomosexual Bias: The Law and Public Opinion

The purpose of this analysis of antihomosexual violence was to focus attention on important observations that form the foundations of this project. First, antihomosexual violence and harassment is common. Second, it has been shown to occur in strikingly similar patterns "independently" on at least two continents. Third, it is often associated with extreme reactions, which suggest that it is deeply felt by many young men. Fourth, it occurs against a background of antihomosexual bias in key institutions that would ordinarily provide safe havens. Thus, although antihomosexual violence might have initially been viewed as random, aberrant behavior, closer inspection shows it to be highly patterned and is typically a group activity. These observations raise questions about the social "nature" of antihomosexual violence and to what extent homophobia is officially sanctioned.

The Third Pink Book is published as a regular "survey of the social and legal position of gay men and lesbians in the vast majority of countries in the world" (Hendriks, Tielman, and van der Veen, 1993: 249). The third edition systematically catalogs and analyzes the legal status and public opinion of homosexuality in 202 countries. In terms of social acceptance, *The Third Pink Book* reports that the majority of the population is in favor of equal rights for gay men and lesbians in only eleven (5 percent) of the 202 countries surveyed, and that a reasonable minority is in favor in forty-seven countries (23 percent), including Australia, while in 144 countries (71 percent) there is virtually no support at all. This situation is reflected in Australian public opinion polls. In 1993, the majority of the population favored equal rights for gay men and lesbians in only three jurisdictions (South Australia, New South Wales, and the Northern Territory) and a minority in the Australian Capital Territory, Queensland, Tasmania, Victoria, and Western Australia (Hendriks, Tielman, and van der Veen, 1993).

Of the 178 countries where legal data are available, homosexual behavior is illegal in seventy-four (42 percent) countries and not illegal in ninety-eight countries (55 percent) (Hendriks, Tielman, van der Veen, 1993: 250). It is important to note that "not being illegal" should not be equated with being socially acceptable or legal. In many countries where homosexuality is not classified as illegal, there are different ages of consent for heterosexual and homosexual sex. Significantly, although most societies stereotypically portray women as more vulnerable, the age of consent for male homosexual sex is usually higher. Furthermore, as we will see, in jurisdictions where homosexuality is legal, and even where there are antidiscrimination laws, there are often mechanisms to "legally" exercise discriminatory treatment. At the time of the survey, only six countries, plus parts of Australia, Canada, and the United States, had laws that protect homosexuals against discrimination, while most countries where homosexual behavior is not illegal provide no protection. Paradoxically, although protective laws are often viewed as a sign of a progressive society, the existence of such laws implies that there is sufficient prejudice in a society to justify its regulation.

The Australian legal situation is complex but it reflects the issues raised in the previous paragraph. Acts "against the order of nature" and "acts of indecency between males" were completely illegal in Tasmania until April 1997 and continue to be criminalized in Western Australia in early adulthood (below the age of twenty-one; Godwin et al., 1991). The age of consent in the other states differs from state to state and differs within the state for male homosexual and heterosexual sex in New South Wales (eighteen for male homosexual; sixteen for heterosexual), the Northern Territory (eighteen for male homosexual; sixteen for heterosexual), Queensland and Western Australia (twenty-one for male homosexual; eighteen for heterosexual). The ages of consent for heterosexual and homosexual sex are the equivalent (sixteen) in the Australian Capital Territory, South Australia, and Victoria. There is legal protection from discrimination in several states/territories and New South Wales also provides protection against vilification. However, even in jurisdictions where discrimination is prohibited, many regulations provide for the differential and discriminatory treatment of homosexuals, for example, in relationships, wills, pensions, taxation, court cases, and superannuation.

A substantial number of countries enshrine antihomosexual bias in their laws and regulations. In Australia, this only started to change in 1975 when South Australia became the first state to decriminalize homosexuality. Yet despite changes in the law, there is considerable scope for bias within the framework of the law. We have seen that police are sometimes involved in antihomosexual harassment. We have also seen that in one-quarter of "stranger homicides" in New South Wales, sexual orientation plays a central role. Yet Tomsen notes that despite this, government reports on violence in Australia give "scant reference, and then only in the form of a tokenistic afterthought, to antigay violence," adding that "if this group has featured at all in the study and analysis of crime in Australia, it is as offenders breaching public order and morality with their sexual practices" (Tomsen, 1993: 209).

Bias has also found expression in court cases and jury verdicts of people tried for homicide in which the victim's sexual orientation was an issue. The best-known example of this has become formally named the "Homosexual Advance Defense." This defense relies on the jury being swayed more in favor of accused men when they allegedly "acted in self-defence or under provocation in response to a sexual advance made by another male" (NSW Attorney General's Department, 1996: 6). This is not a formal, legally recognized defense, but concerns arose about the adverse influence of these allegations on the outcome of trials after a number of recent murder cases in New South Wales, Victoria, and South Australia. In these cases, alleged homosexual advance by the victim seems to have influenced the proceedings and resulted in an acquittal or lesser conviction.

These concerns prompted an official inquiry in New South Wales (NSW Attorney General's Department, 1996). The inquiry reviewed thirteen cases from the period 1993 to 1996 in which an allegation of a homosexual advance was made. As a result, a number of recommendations were made: (1) the law should not treat a homosexual advance "as an act of provocation to any lesser or greater degree than . . . a comparable sexual advance upon a woman"; (2) on the issue of sexuality, that "the person's background is not of the slightest relevance, with no prejudice against the deceased or the accused on the basis of sexual orientation"; and (3) an accused person who is "abnormally or exceptionally sensitive to behaviour which may be regarded as provocative is not permitted to escape the full responsibility for causing the death of another person" (New South Wales Attorney General's Department, 1996: 4-5). The "homosexual advance defense" has also been described in other jurisdictions, including the United States, where it is also known as the "Homosexual Panic Defense" (Comstock, 1989).

Social Dimensions of Antihomosexual Bias: Health Care

Antihomosexual bias is also endemic in health care institutions (Plummer, 1995). This has special importance because victims of antihomosexual assault might turn to health workers for assistance. This is also the domain of the "caring professions," and as a rule, caring professions are not formally charged with enforcing discriminatory practices.

In 1994, the American Association of Physicians for Human Rights (AAPHR) published a report titled *Anti-Gay Discrimination in Medicine: Results of a National Survey of Lesbian, Gay and Bisexual Physicians* (Schatz and O'Hanlan, 1994). The report published the results of a survey that was sent to 1,311 gay, lesbian, and bisexual members of the association in February 1994. By mid-March 1994, there were 711 replies (54 percent response rate), including 118 medical students and 583 physicians from fifty medical specialties and forty-six American states. Of the responses, 255 were from women and 441 were from men.

Concerning antihomosexual bias by colleagues against gay, lesbian, or bisexual patients, 91 percent of respondents reported knowing of situations in which patients were subjected to antihomosexual bias; 88 percent reported having personally heard colleagues make disparaging remarks about gay, lesbian, or bisexual patients; 67 percent reported knowing of patients who had received substandard care or been denied care because of their sexual orientation; and 52 percent reported having observed colleagues providing reduced care or denying care to patients because of their sexual orientation. Furthermore, 5 percent of respondents reported suffering significant discrimination because their patients are perceived to be gay, and 4 percent because their patients are perceived to be HIV positive.

The report also documents antihomosexual bias experienced by the health professionals themselves. Of the respondents, 59 percent (56 percent of physicians and 67 percent of medical students) indicated that they have suffered discrimination, harassment, or ostracism from colleagues because of their sexual orientation; 34 percent of physicians and 54 percent of medical students reported being socially ostracized; and 34 percent of physicians and 51 percent of medical students reported being subjected to verbal harassment or insulted by their medical colleagues because of their sexual orientation. Further, because of sexual orientation, 17 percent of physicians reported being refused "medical privileges," denied employment, educational opportunities, or promotion, or were fired; 17 percent reported being denied referrals; 11 percent reported being denied a place in, or discouraged from entering, a residency or fellowship program; 5 percent reported being denied acceptance into a medical school; and 5 percent reported being denied a loan, credit, or insurance.

These findings were despite most respondents selectively disclosing their sexual orientation: 21 percent of respondents reported that less than 10 percent of their colleagues knew of their sexual orientation, and only 22 percent reported that more than 90 percent of their colleagues knew. Of respondents, 67 percent agreed that physicians would jeopardize their practices if colleagues learned of their sexual orientation and 64 percent did not agree that gay, lesbian, and bisexual physicians are accepted as equals in the medical profession. In response to the question "Have you ever been punched, kicked, beaten, or assaulted because of your sexual orientation?", 12 percent of medical students and 14 percent of physicians answered that they had. Of those who had, 19 percent were male and 5 percent were female.

In Australia, the only large systematic survey to examine antihomosexual bias among health professionals is the GLAD survey of 1,002 men and women in Melbourne (GLAD, 1994). This study found that 17 percent of men and 16 percent of women experienced some form of antihomosexual discrimination in medical and dental services. This included inadequate or inappropriate treatment (13 percent of women; 12 percent of men), breaches of confidence (5 percent of women; 6 percent of men), and being refused treatment (2 percent of women; 3 percent of men).

THE SIGNIFICANCE OF HOMOPHOBIA:
EVIDENCE FROM TWENTIETH-CENTURY PUBLIC LIFE

Analysis of homophobic events from the mid- to late twentieth century and the homophobic discourse of people in public life reveals an extensive catalog of rationales and justifications for homophobia that is characterized by certain recurring themes.

Against Tradition: God, Nature, and the Order of Things

Powerful recurring public discourse focuses on the "potential" of homosexuality to cause chaos and disorder. In this discourse, the liberalization of homosexuality is equated with social chaos. For example, in a party room discussion on decriminalizing homosexuality George Brown, the British Secretary of State for Economic Affairs (1966), echoed Edward Gibbon (1789) in the *History of the Decline and Fall of the Roman Empire*. Brown stated, "this is how Rome came down. And I care deeply about it—in opposition to most of my church . . . you will have a totally disorganized, indecent and unpleasant society. You must have rules! We've gone too far on sex already" (Higgins, 1993: 194).

Thirty years later on the other side of the globe, the Parliament of the Australian State of Tasmania had its own debates on decriminalizing homosexuality. Several members of parliament including John Loone, Member of the Tasmanian Legislative Council (MLC), echoed the sentiments expressed by George Brown. Loone is recorded in Hansard as saying that Tasmania's laws need "a clear provision that makes it a penalty to encourage and lead people into homosexual activity, because at the moment these two clauses—122 and 123—are the only barriers against further moral decline. That is why so many people want them wiped out. If we remove them, if homosexual activity becomes legal, all sorts of floodgates can open" (Morris, 1995: 93).

Anything that invokes fears of disorder could be seen as a direct challenge to the forces of order (classically nature or God) and much of the discourse on homophobia relies on religious imagery for its authority and occult imagery to discredit homosexuality. In a speech to the Tasmanian House of Assembly, Ron Cornish (MHA) claimed that the law "can restrain sexual perversity. Even if it cannot restrain such bigotry or perversity, it ought to try. Further, even if it can do nothing else, the law ought to identify evil for what it is" (Morris, 1995: 84). This linkage between homosexuality and evil was also used by the Honorable George Brookes, MLC, "Do not let them sully our state with their evil activities" (Morris, 1995: 105). Similar imagery can be found in the British discourse of the 1950s in a statement by British Judge Tudor Rees (1955) that homosexuals are affected by an "unconquerable demon" (Davenport-Hines, 1991: 300). And when it appeared that the United Nations might intervene in Tasmanian politics, the Honorable George Brooks (MLC Tasmania) seemed to use simultaneous homophobia, xenophobia, and an oblique allusion to hell: "I would hope the State Government would tell the United Nations to go to buggery" (Morris, 1995: 104).

Disease is an extension of negative metaphors concerning nature, and much discourse—even by advocates of decriminalization—refers to homosexuality as a disability. In 1965, Lord Arran, who led the parliamentary campaign to decriminalize homosexuality, described homosexuals as "the odd man out, the ones with the limp" (Davenport-Hines, 1991: 290). Others were not so benign: Frederick Bellenger, a member of the British House of Commons in 1958, in an extraordinary statement that succinctly combines revulsion, filth, abnormality, disease, dissemination, "flaunting it," the occult, death, chaos, the fall of civilization, and the homosexual as an animal, described homosexuals as "a malignant canker in the community, and if this is allowed to grow, it will eventually kill off what is known as normal life. . . . I believe that human life would eventually revert to an animal existence if this cult were so allowed to spread that, as in ancient Greece, it overwhelmed the community at large. . . . I am repelled by the dirtiness of some of those whose conduct is exposed to the public gaze" (Higgins, 1993: 188).

Hygiene is purity and prophylaxis against disease and it is not surprising to find it used as a counterpoint for the "transmissibility" and "filth" in homophobic discourse. The direct inference of hygiene is to the links between homosexuality and anal sex and this seems to be a potent concern. But here again, by equating homosexuality with anality, the argument relies on logical "slippage" to be convincing. Davenport-Hines points out that numerous surveys indicate that anal sex is a feature of heterosexual sex too (p. 323) but does not seem to have the same stigmatized association. He also reports surveys that show that a substantial proportion of gay men don't engage in anal sex, but this conveniently goes unnoticed (p. 294). Nevertheless, in the popular mind, homosexuality is equated with "the sexual use of the anus, usually filled with rotting excretory matter, evoked . . . the iridescence of decay" (Davenport-Hines, 1991: 323). Hygiene is, however, more than personal practices; it is a code for public health and a statement of the health of a society or race. Sexual deviance was frequently portrayed as a "stain on the nation" and the regulation of purity was the domain of the health sciences. In Australia, as in most of the English-speaking world until the 1960s, this was explicit in the names for family planning and sexually transmissible disease (STD) clinics. Until then, STD clinics were called "sexual hygiene clinics" and the Family Planning Association was the "Racial Hygiene Association" (Siedlecky and Wyndham, 1990: 215). STD was also a feature of antihomosexual sentiment, and nowhere is this better illustrated than in the histories of syphilis and HIV.

Discourse that relies on disease and hygiene invites a search for causes and remedies. This is a field that still attracts considerable popular and professional interest, and regular reports in the medical literature concern research into neurological, genetic, and hormonal "causes" for homosexuality. Biomedical theories about causation inevitably lead to attempting treatment. Perhaps the best known of these were conducted in the German concentration camps during World War II, described by Gunter Grau (Grau, 1993). Davenport-Hines records similar practices in Britain, which were also not uncommon in Australia, that included the injection of androgens/ estrogens, psychiatric treatment, and physical and chemical castration (Davenport-Hines, 1991: 293). Homosexuality can only be conceptualized as a condition to be treated as long as it is perceived to be discontinuous from "normal" sexuality (as "otherness") and has sufficiently negative connotations. The resilience of homophobia is reflected in the nature versus nurture debate, for which homophobia positions itself to underwrite either outcome. Regardless of whether homosexuality is thought to be due to a biomedical event or to result from upbringing, either case can imply abnormality and

be an invitation to attempt "correction." Homophobia injects caus-
ative significance to a dichotomy that wouldn't be an issue if homosexuality were seen as normal and had no "cause."

Against the Future: Family, Race, and Reproduction

Disorder also has a counterpoint in continuity. Continuity has
spiritual dimensions in the afterlife and eternal life; social dimensions in the survival of cultures, races, and family lines; and for the
individual, in reproduction. Homophobia has exploited each of
these levels by imbuing homosexuality with symbolic significance
as the antithesis of spiritual, racial, family, and individual continuity
(the relationship between homophobia and heterosexism starts to
emerge in this kind of discourse).

Homophobia has allied itself with the authority of nature, evolu-
tion, and biology. For example, in a statement to the British Parliament concerning homosexuality, the biologist Lord Stamp (1977)
said, "the breakdown of the procreative function of man can only be
regarded as unnatural" (Davenport-Hines, 1991: 329). Implicit in
his statement is the assumption that homosexuals are nonreproductive, and that being nonreproductive is a breakdown of nature that
has serious implications for society. There is no recognition that
populations "naturally" accommodate nonreproductive members or
that the world is oversupplied with people.

The Tasmanian debate also saw the biological metaphor used in a
more agricultural vein by the Honorable Hugh Hiscutt, MLC, who
is recorded in Hansard as saying "If we had a bull like that (homosexual) I know where he would end up if he would not serve the
females—he would be in the mall tomorrow among those 8,000
sausages" (Morris, 1995: 105). Clearly, if you are not actively heterosexual, you have more value in the slaughterhouse where you
can be reconstituted as Freudian small goods.

Reproductive states seem to occupy a hierarchy of acceptability,
in which homosexuality rates poorly. In view of the profound taboos against incest noted by Freud and numerous anthropologists, a
comment to the House of Commons by William Shepherd, MP, in
1958 is highly revealing: "Incest is a much more natural act than
homosexuality" (Higgins, 1993: 188).

The reproductive unit in society is often depicted as the "nuclear family." This seems to be as much a symbolic notion as reality, and there is a considerable literature that documents that the nuclear family is a relatively recent development in social arrangements (Gilding, 1991). While the state of the nuclear family is not the concern of this project, the positioning of the homosexual as being opposed to the family is. The theme that homosexuals are antifamily is another potent area for public officials and it features in British and Australian materials (Morris, 1995: 35). This is apparent in statements concerning the family as a unit where it is not only assumed that homosexuals don't belong to families, but that they don't have any commitment to them. This attitude is also built into public statements concerning the problematic relationships with each of the separate family roles: homosexual men are failed or untrustworthy fathers, woman haters, and child molesters. Rather than homosexuals being antifamily, it would seem that the political notion of "family" will not accommodate its homosexual members. The "failed father" theme is illustrated in the feminization of male homosexuals and the possibility that they have been weak and led astray. As Lord Macleod said, about homosexual law reform in the British Parliament in 1977, "young men will be led up the garden path who might otherwise shortly be married and happy" (Davenport-Hines, 1991: 329). Jack Breheny, Devonport Town Councillor and ex-state parliamentarian, emphasizes the "feminization" when he said he didn't have anything "against the poor unfortunate creature who is born more effeminate than others—is a misfit in life . . . some people are born murderers, but you wouldn't want to condone murder, would you?" (Morris, 1995: 33). This negatively valued "softness theme" recurs in comments by Breheny: "all the pansies in the country were using the AIDS Council as a front for propaganda for their filthy practices" (Morris, 1995: 32).

Substantial material aligned homosexuals with women, both as allies as well as by "feminizing" gay men. This may be an effect of gay men and women being positioned as the opposite of "real men," in which case, logic demands that they be conflated. In contrast, there was also material on the "woman-hating" status of homosexual men. Perhaps the most illustrative example of the woman-hating theme comes, not from Australian or British material, but from

Lesley Hazelton in *The New York Times*, on May 15, 1986, when she wrote that homosexuality "threatened me because I saw in it a satirical mirror of femininity, the very kind of femininity that feminism struggled against: a precocious little-girlism, giggly and fey and cruel. There was a hate of women behind it, and I felt it . . ." (Higgins, 1993: 265). This statement illustrates the classic stereotype of the effeminate homosexual and ascribes it to homosexuality in general. Furthermore, instead of frivolity, she reads the stereotype with a sense of personal affront, even though it allegedly parodies the femininity she rejected (thanks to feminism), and instead of seeing blurred gender roles where boundaries have lost rigid meaning, she reads cross-gender intent that is deeply disrespectful to her. Alternatively, her statement could be read, as she admits later, as her own projected homophobia because it stereotypes and reads malice into an enactment of conflicting expectations of gender. The woman-hating theme can be seen again in the Tasmanian material where a Presbyterian minister, writing in the *Sunday Examiner* newspaper (April 9, 1988), talks about homosexual men "being repulsed by the thought of having relations with the opposite sex" (Morris, 1995: 39).

However, the most comprehensive catalog of all of the homophobic discourse we have discussed came in a submission by the British Law Society to the "Wolfenden Committee"; it proclaimed that homosexual law reform would (1) discourage marriage; (2) be a disincentive to have children; (3) may damage the state if "they should get too strong a hold"; (4) contaminate others, particularly the young; and (5) spread venereal disease (Davenport-Hines, 1991: 318).

Against Society: Antisocial, Treacherous, and Criminal

Threatening the "order of things" is not always accidental, and when this is depicted as a challenge to God or nature, then evil, disease, and death become the consequences. In contrast, when "free will" is invoked, then betrayal, sabotage, and criminality become the "free will" equivalents of corruption, decay, and disease. Shortly, we will examine the propaganda value of homophobia and the fear (in the post-World War II world) that homosexuals are treacherous and a threat to state security. This anxiety was not confined to the United States, but extended to the U.S. allies and beyond, and the preoccupation with sexual deviance became such a problem that the British Cabinet set up an inquiry called the "Committee on Homosexuality and Prostitution" (1954-1957). For many, this was such a confrontational and impolite name that they referred to it euphemistically as the "H and P" or "Huntley and Palmers" inquiry. It eventually became known after the chair, Baron Wolfenden, as the "Wolfenden Committee."

In an interesting example of how homophobic discourse is appropriated from one field to another: The British Medical Association (BMA) submission to the "Wolfenden Committee" reflected concerns about loyalty and national security. The BMA submission contained "medical evidence" that male homosexuals encouraged public hostility by placing their loyalty to one another above their loyalty to the institution or government they serve (Davenport-Hines, 1991: 320).

While the fear of betrayal probably resonated at a number of levels—ranging from family domestic arrangements to international politics—there was a degree of truth beneath the "paranoia" (as Davenport-Hines calls it). Homosexuals probably had understandable reasons for being disaffected with their social position, and their vulnerability due to stigmatization was apparently widely exploited by blackmailers. Davenport-Hines reports the former Attorney General and Lord Chancellor Jowitt as saying that 95 percent of blackmail cases between 1929 and 1932 arose from allegations of homosexuality (Davenport-Hines, 1991: 297). In 1951, it was revealed that two British diplomats, Guy Burgess, who was homosexual, and Donald Maclean, who was bisexual, had worked as soviet spies and fled to Russia. Even if sexuality was not a major factor, these events reinforced the link between homosexuality and betrayal in the public mind.

Homosexuality has been linked to criminality in a much broader sense for years. Buggery (with men, women, or animals) was a capital offense in Britain from the 1530s, and male-to-male sexual acts were specifically criminalized in Britain in 1885 (Weeks, 1991: 17). Years after decriminalization, the link persists. For example, in a statement to the British Parliament in 1977, Countess Loudon described homosexual acts as "a crime against society" (Davenport-Hines, 1991: 329).

Homosexuality and "Otherness"

In 1993, *The Third Pink Book* reported that "the 53 countries where homosexual behaviour is illegal, where there is no social support for gay and lesbian rights, and where no gay and lesbian movement exists are predominantly Islamic, formerly communist or have been part of the former British colonial empire" (Hendriks, Tielman, and van der Veen, 1993: 251). *The Third Pink Book* also reports that the overall status of gays and lesbians is "proportionally the worst in Africa and the best in Europe" (but there has been a rapid growth in the number of developing and former communist countries that now have gay and lesbian rights movements) (Hendriks, Tielman, and van der Veen, 1993: 250). What *The Third Pink Book* fails to make sufficiently clear is that the relatively liberal situation in Western Europe is by no means clear-cut, and if recent history is any guide, then the status of homosexuals is generally very tenuous there too.

Several studies have documented the rapid reversal of fortunes of homosexuals in Germany during the 1930s and 1940s (Haeberle, 1991; Plant, 1986; Grau, 1995; Heger, 1980). Although in 1929 the Reichstag Committee on Criminal Law recommended the deletion of the German law against homosexuality (known as paragraph 175), the Nazi takeover of Germany in 1933 saw the immediate widespread persecution of homosexuals. During that year, the first German homosexuals were sent to concentration camps, and between 1933 and 1945, between 50,000 and 63,000 men in Germany were convicted for homosexuality and between 5,000 and 15,000 were sent to concentration camps (Haeberle, 1991: 375). However, homophobia wasn't only the province of those in power. Heger describes how inmates in concentration camps also didn't accept homosexuals. Inmates "were described as the scum of humanity, who had no right to live on German soil and should be exterminated. . . . But lowest of the low in this 'scum' were we, the men with pink triangle" (Heger, 1980: 32-33). The pink triangle was stitched to the uniform of inmates to identify homosexual internees.

Cases from extraordinary periods such as World War II, must not be allowed to obscure a more general problem: homophobia is not confined to particular political systems or to times of war. If anything, the mid-twentieth century appears to have unleashed a homophobic potential that was already widespread, and a case can be made that the twentieth century has witnessed more homophobia (at least for men) than any other period in history. In the mid-1930s, the Russian Communists under Stalin also recriminalized homosexuality and commenced widespread repression and persecution (Karlinsky, 1991: 361; Plant, 1986: 39). In addition, the postwar American and British allies were homophobic. Plant describes how "some American and British jurists of the liberation armies, on learning that an inmate had been put in a camp for homosexual convictions ruled that judicially, a camp did not constitute a prison," and they were sentenced to complete their prison terms after liberation (Plant, 1986: 181). The stigma of homosexuality prevented many who were sentenced for homosexual offenses from returning to their families or a supportive peer group after the war, and unlike other groups, none of the homosexuals were entitled to compensation. Neither did postwar governments readily reject the homophobic programs of the Nazis. Paragraph 175 was not repealed in West Germany until 1969 and in East Germany until 1967 (Plant, 1986: 181).

Homophobia continued to be an important political issue after the war for the "liberal democracies" of the United States and Britain. For example, Senator Joseph McCarthy and the "House of Representatives Un-American Activities Committee" orchestrated the "witch hunts" and purges of homosexuals from public positions during the 1950s (Comstock, 1991: 8). Davenport-Hines describes how at the same time the military and police in Britain conducted systematic purges of the military and civilian population (albeit less theatrical than in the United States). In 1954, the British Admiralty issued new fleet orders on "the horrible character of the unnatural vice" and ordered officers to "stamp out the evil" (Davenport-Hines, 1991: 300-310).

In the modern Western world, antihomosexual bias seems to be resilient and persistent and it permeates the "social fabric." The common thread in these diverse twentieth-century cases is that "the homosexual" is readily and credibly portrayed as the common enemy. In each case, the power of attributing homosexuality to the enemy was used in propaganda against the other regimes: Stalin and the Western Allies equated homosexuality with the rise of fascism, the Nazis viewed homosexuals as the enemy of the German people, and the Americans saw homosexuals alongside communists and traitors during the "cold war" (Karlinsky, 1991; Comstock, 1991). This pattern is not confined to male homosexuality, and some influential studies have described how marginalized women in the sixteenth and seventeenth centuries sometimes came to be transformed into witches (the "other") and then persecuted (Barstow, 1994; Hester, 1992).

This tendency can also be identified in recent public discourse: although they might once have been equal members of society, homosexuals forfeit that status and become alien. Reminiscent of earlier arguments, contemporary discourse continues to allude to homosexuals as foreign, subhuman, monstrous, or animalistic. The Honorable Robin Gray, Premier of Tasmania, exploited xenophobia when he said that he "welcomed everybody to Tasmania except homosexuals" (Morris, 1995: 105). The idea of two separate classes of people was encapsulated by Doone Kennedy (Lord Mayor of Hobart, Capital of Tasmania) in a televised statement advocating "one law for heterosexuals and one law for homosexuals" (Morris, 1995: 105). Homosexuals were even portrayed as less than animal in a statement by Jack Breheny, Devonport Town Councillor and ex-Tasmanian parliamentarian, who felt the "greatest disgust for the filthy people who indulge in filthy practices that no one else in the animal kingdom would" (Morris, 1995: 32).

Interestingly, although much discourse discredits homosexuals as emotional and unstable (being racked by the emotions of the female "other"), many homophobic statements also contain strong emotive elements such as anger and revulsion. The Honorable Richard Archer, Tasmanian MLC, said that the police need to "track down and wipe out, like murderers, drug addicts and deviant AIDS carriers . . . when I hear a Minister of the Crown making reference to the decriminalization of homosexuality I feel sick in the guts—when I hear these people (homosexuals) talking about human rights, my blood boils" (Morris, 1995: 105). Davenport-Hines (1991: 323) documents that British Lord Chancellor, Kilmuir (1961) refused to sit at cabinet meetings where the "filthy subject" was discussed. Of course, whereas homosexuals are portrayed as excessively emotional, the powerful emotions in these statements are ones that are respectable for men in authority.

Homosexual Transmission: Homophobic Quarantine?

A dominant feature that spans Nazi, British, and the recent Tasmanian debates is the fear that homosexuality is transmissible. There is a rich vocabulary in this area, and this suggests it is a potent and meaningful issue and important to explore. Not all of the rhetoric is in the form of "sophisticated" germ theory, but all of it carries the implication of being a progressive process that can spread: taint, decay, corrupt, pollute, recruit, convert, pervert, contaminate, malignant, pestilence, open the floodgates, overwhelm. Even statements such as "choice" and "lifestyle" allude to the possibility that people may become homosexual, presumably under the "adverse" influence of some external factor. The belief that homosexuality is transmissible was explicit in some academic research. Gunter Grau documents a case of doctoral research at the University of Marburg in 1936 that purportedly traces epidemics of homosexuality (Grau, 1993: 226). British Judge Sir Roland Oliver also articulated concerns about transmissibility in 1954: ". . . once vice got established, it spread like a pestilence, and unless held in check, spread indefinitely" (Davenport-Hines, 1991: 308). It is understandable how this rhetoric dovetails, with the association between homosexuality and fears of social chaos.

Countess Loudon expressed this sentiment in the British Parliament in 1977, again: "are we to encourage the infectious growth of this filthy disease by giving the authority of Parliament to the spreading of corruption and perversion among a new generation of young men? . . . you cannot be a homosexual alone, which inevitably leads to the corruption and perversion of others, which is a symptom of the disease" just like "an attack of cholera, such an outbreak must be contained and isolated" (Davenport-Hines, 1991: 329). And again in the Tasmanian debate, Jack Breheny, Devonport Town Councillor and ex-State parliamentarian, is quoted as saying that the supporters of decriminalization are "just trying to recruit new people to replace the ones they were losing through death from AIDS" (Morris, 1995: 32).

The paradox of these statements is their implication that homosexuality would seem to be intrinsic, possibly even natural, because anyone is vulnerable to becoming homosexual (presumably even the most vehement opponent). Thus, we find the concern for protecting young men, not so much from sexual assault, but from information that might influence their sexual orientation: the homosexual "lifestyle should not be encouraged or promoted to those who are young or vulnerable" (Ray Bailey, Tasmanian MLC, in Morris, 1995: 97). The implications of these arguments extend further, portraying homosexuality as deeply seductive, even addictive, and homosexuals as uncontrollably predatory (Davenport-Hines, 1991: 319). This seductiveness is revealed by Sir Compton Mackenzie (1956): "if the fruit were not so severely forbidden, then fewer would be tempted to indulge" (Davenport-Hines, 1991: 318). In the Tasmanian debate, these themes are repeated with subtle variations. John Loone, Tasmanian MLC, sees homosexuality as an unnatural alternative that apparently comes naturally for all men unless diverted by the law: "Where will we draw the line if we begin to sanction and to approve by silence, a practice that is patently unnatural, debasing and unhealthy; where will it end? Men and rivers are alike: they both become crooked by following the path of least resistance" (Morris, 1995: 93).

Sir Laurence Dunn (Chief Metropolitan Magistrate in London from 1948) described male homosexuals as "harpies" and the "lowest of the low," and he too alludes to the seductive nature of homosexuality by simultaneously using predator, hunger, and addiction metaphors when he says homosexuality "is admitted by all, save addicts, to be an evil. To countenance homosexual practices in private is playing with fire. Appetites are progressive and a homosexual sated with practices with adults, without hindrance, will be far more likely to tempt a jaded appetite with youth . . . it would be disastrous to give further tacit encouragement by altering the law" (Davenport-Hines, 1991: 305). Notice, too, how he manages also to exploit the images of fire, evil, disaster, pedophilia, and the dangers of doing nothing—of "passivity." British Lord Chief Justice Goddard reiterates these themes. If male homosexuals "are adults, they are, I believe, invariably addicts," and "it is such a horrible and revolting thing, and a practitioner is such a depraved creature, that he ought, in my opinion, be put out of circulation" (Davenport-Hines, 1991: 316). Statements by the Bishop of Rochester (1957) concur with this view: a law is needed "to protect men from being made into homosexual addicts and then let loose on the world with their predatory corruption" (Davenport-Hines, 1991: 320). A key feature of these statements is the loss of control that a homosexual is said to have—or rather the loss of control that young men can anticipate once they experience homosexuality ("taste the forbidden fruit"). So while homosexuality can be seen as disorderly, and as willful and malicious, it is also positioned as uncontrollable, predatory, and transmissible—an insatiable appetite, an addiction—and this justifies intervention with legal restraints and social containment.

Homosexuality As an Intractable Negative Quality

Homophobic public discourse frequently relies on equating the homosexual with "otherness" and homosexuality with disorder. These elements contain a common implicit factor that needs to be made explicit: *homophobia attaches intensely negative connotations to any argument concerning homosexuals or homosexuality.* Some of the examples described in the previous section suggest that the negative value placed on homosexuality is so powerful that it persists even when arguments are illogical or contradictory. David Halperin makes a similar observation when he notes that homophobia is often resistant to reason and is able to retain its negative qualities even if the rationalizations used to justify homophobia can be proven to be unreasonable. He observes how new (often logically opposing) reasons can be adopted to support homophobia if the original justifications are discredited (Halperin, 1995: 37-38). The literal meanings of homophobic terms and their associated rationalizations appear to be fluid and superficially adherent to more resilient and permanent underlying phenomena. We will return to the "slipperiness" and multiplicity of homophobic meanings and their capacity for contradiction and paradox in the final chapter.

While law reform might have had its basis in social justice, Davenport-Hines observed that in Britain even the supporters of law reform did so in very negative ways. In public discourse in

Australia and Britain, it appears to be important for politicians to distance themselves from any personal knowledge of homosexuality, and advocates of law reform generally left homophobia unchallenged, preferring to appeal to other social justice issues. In Tasmania, one failed attempt to reform the law had decriminalization integrated into public health legislation concerning AIDS. The subsequent remedy to this failed attempt at decriminalization was for the federal government to enact privacy legislation that neutralized the state laws. In Britain, Davenport-Hines shows how law reform came about because of values of individual privacy instead of a specific commitment to social justice and tolerance for homosexuals (Davenport-Hines, 1991: 326).

In this section, we have seen how positive or neutrally valued occurrences take on deeply negative connotations when associated with homosexuality. It says a lot about homophobia that an extraordinary array of rationales has been generated to justify people's antihomosexual bias. Most justifications are powerful because they align themselves with cherished institutions and beliefs, and homophobia ostensibly seeks to defend the integrity of these (homophobia is ostensibly on the side of God, nature, and the law). This alignment places homophobia on the "moral high ground" and largely beyond question and logic, and modern homophobia is empowered by appealing to seemingly ancient and fundamental truths. The counterpoint of homophobia is chaos and the end of society, as we know it. This also implicitly carries a profoundly negative connotation—because social change can be equated with improvement and progress. But, while the threat that societies pose to their homosexual members seems to be considerable, the actual threat that homosexuals pose to society remains nebulous.

Chapter 2

Swearing Allegiance

The detailed descriptions compiled by this project constitute a rich source of data to explore homophobia. Just as studies of anti-gay violence used statements made by attackers to confirm the links between homophobia and violence (Cox, 1994), certain key words and phrases are used in the present study to identify how homophobia is deployed, how males become homophobic, and what its effects are. A useful starting point is references to homosexuality (including colloquialisms such as "poofter" and "faggot"), and a principal task of this chapter is to extract these references and catalog them. A strength of collecting detailed life histories is that data are compiled in a chronological framework that enables the concurrent mapping of homophobic words, their evolving meanings, and the processes associated with their use (Layder, 1993; Minichiello et al., 1990). To paraphrase Bob Connell, rather than attempting to define gender and sexuality as objects for analysis, this project is particularly interested in evaluating homophobic processes and how they influence the constitution of these objects (Connell, 1995).

In these "postmodern" times, we are regularly reminded that meanings are multiple. This is certainly true of the data reported here, and only some meanings can be examined. The most obvious are meanings that are explicit, and these constitute the core of the analysis. However, *implicit* meanings—when statements draw upon underlying assumptions for their significance—are also important. For example, statements can implicitly appeal to complex notions of good, God, order, or nature, or they can rely on dichotomies that are assumed to be "essential." Some of the assumption that are used to invest homophobia with authority are not fully recognized by the speaker; their significance is lost in the history of the arguments being used. Arguments that hold homosexuality responsible for the "fall of the Roman Empire" are an example. These exploit assumptions about the dangers of homosexuality and its role in the fate of civilization to add authority and legitimacy to homophobia, but they have little connection to historical analysis. The notion of implicit meaning also raises questions as to whether this project examines the unconscious. To the extent that assumptions which aren't fully comprehended can be drawn upon for homophobic purposes, this is arguably the case. But the unconscious is a disputed concept, and it is unnecessary to introduce formal concepts of the unconscious, when it is sufficient to demonstrate implicit meanings. The question of the relationship between this analysis, the patterned operations of homophobia, and the unconscious will be left to the reader.

HOMOPHOBIC MEANINGS

English has a rich vocabulary referring to homosexuality, some of which will be cataloged in this chapter. Probably the most commonly used colloquialisms for homosexual males are "poofter" or "poof" and "faggot" or "fag." These forms are widely used in the English-speaking world and all of them appear in *The New Shorter Oxford English Dictionary* (Brown, 1993: 2288 and 906). Descriptions of how these words are deployed are useful to trace when and how young people become homophobic and what significance is attached to them.

Tracing the use of words such as poofter initially appears to reach an impasse because many respondents reported that when they were young, words referring to homosexuality were largely meaningless. For example, subject U21* recalls that he first heard the word "poofter" in primary school, in about

> grade five or six . . . . I don't think many people . . . knew quite what it [poofter] was. (U21)

---

*Each participant was allocated one of thirty nonidentifying alphanumeric codes starting from A1 through Z26 and then from AA27 to DD30. Where both the interviewer and the participant are quoted, they are introduced as "D:" and "S:", respectively.

But further exploration raised questions as to whether words such as "poofter" really were as meaningless as was first assumed, even in their earliest use. Subject J10 reflects this uncertainty when, although he says that poof "didn't mean anything," his comments raise the possibility that "poof" did indeed have significance for him—even if it wasn't the same as his adult understanding:

> [poof] didn't mean anything. It was . . . the way it was used, it was a derogatory term. (J10)

This was elaborated by U21 who acknowledges negative (but not homosexual) connotations, and that it referred to certain recognizable characteristics:

> . . . and knew the characteristics of the people who were called poofter, and therefore knew that it wasn't the type of thing you'd want to be called because you'd be in their group. (U21)

Subjects reported that they started to use terms such as poofter and faggot from a very early age. Most reported using homophobic terms in primary school and all of them recalled starting well prior to puberty. Similar observations have been made by Barrie Thorne: "by fourth and fifth grades 'fag' had become a widespread and serious term of insult" (Thorne, 1993: 154).

> "Poofter" would have been [used] really early on. In fact, I can remember poofter when I was about six. . . . We had some guys when I was in primary school—they were at high school next door—and if you did something that was deemed to be slightly effeminate . . . they'd sort of say "Oh, you poofter!" (I9)

This statement suggests that early exposure to homophobia can be traced to older children. A similar statement was made by Z26, whose brother introduced him to the word "poofter" when he was six or seven. The following statement confirms the very early experiences of a young man who is now gay:

> Oh God, when did people start calling me a poofter? Really early on in the piece. . . . Oh, probably from about third grade. (Y25)

There was a striking consistency between the accounts from young men regardless of their adult sexual identity.

Further evidence that the early use of terms referring to homosexuality was far from meaningless comes from establishing the circumstances in which these terms were applied, and in reference to whom or what. For example, from the beginning, it was clearly inappropriate to use the term "poof" in reference to girls:

> I can't ever remember calling a girl a homo or a poofter. They just wouldn't, didn't come into it. (BB28)

In contrast, several accounts indicated that girls could use homophobic words against boys:

> **D:** Was it [poof] ever said against girls?
> **S:** Not that I can remember. . . . Oh, girls would have said it about a boy. (CC29)

As subject T20 puts it, poofter was a "boy's word."

These indications show that terms such as "poofter" refer to male characteristics and have negative meanings for boys even from their earliest use. However, although these meanings are rich and powerful, they apparently don't refer to homosexuality:

> **S:** I think it was a good way of hurting people . . . it was a really good way. . . . I didn't think of, like you know, homosexuality or anything else. It's just like "You poof!" you know?
> **D:** Are there any better ways of hurting . . . young men, boys?
> **S:** No. I don't think so. You call them poofter. (DD30)

It is hard to overstate the depth of negative meaning for young males associated with terms such as poofter. Comments by CC29 are typical of the responses of subjects concerning the power of the poofter label to devalue:

> . . . [poofter] was probably *the* worst thing . . . it pretty much carried the connotation that you weren't worth much *at all*. (CC29)

At least for the first few years boys use words such as poofter to refer to something else—something different. And although there is no question that these meanings refer to a "poofter," it seems that in early childhood, being a poofter is not the equivalent of being homosexual:

> **D:** So if it wasn't sexual, what did these things mean about a person?
> **S:** Different.
> **D:** Different?
> **S:** Or you lost your temper with them and you'd yell at 'em. You needed something to say. (E5)

The initial use of "poofter" to refer to "different" was confirmed in most of the interviews. K11 offers a similar view on what poofter meant at primary school:

> . . . something different. They don't understand what it means. They just use it because they've heard it somewhere else. This word equals this person, therefore I will use this word to equal this person. (K11)

While uncertain about the kind of difference poofter refers to, G7 also seems clear that it refers to being different:

> I'm inclined to say maybe those that are racially slightly different . . . because they are different. And we know kids can be right little sods and make things blatantly obvious. . . . Those that are different and/or don't conform. (G7)

Interestingly, the term "sod" according to *The New Shorter Oxford English Dictionary* (Brown, 1993: 2933) is probably a derivation of sodomite!

Eventually, words such as poofter do acquire unambiguous homosexual meanings. This was generally found to occur in the first years of high school, close to puberty and with older peers as mentors. This contrasts with the first few (formative) years of their use, in primary and early secondary school, when they had precise and rich meanings that were nonsexual.

CATALOGING HOMOPHOBIC MEANINGS

An array of meanings for words such as poofter and faggot was mapped by studying the way boys use these words. Furthermore, homophobic words were found to evolve over time, and successive layers of meaning became folded into them. This eventually includes explicit references to homosexuality, but homosexual meanings are added late in a complex process, and important events occur prior to the "homosexualization" of homophobia. Also, early meanings given to poofter are not discarded and replaced by new meanings as children get older. Instead, meanings accumulate and earlier ones persist alongside newer meanings, even when they are contradictory (for example, faggots are too close to women and are women haters). These evolving meanings seem to parallel boys' development. Thus, as time passes, poof can mean crybaby, "girl," nonfootballer, and homosexual. There also appears to be an important retrospective shift in the meaning of precursor words. On the one hand, boys are generally exposed to and start using "poofter" during primary school and this word supersedes and subsumes the negative connotations that are associated with being called a "crybaby." On the other, an older boy who cries can be called a crybaby and this comes to have allusions to being a poofter. The term "onion skinning" was coined during this study and refers to a process of successively accumulating overlapping layers of meaning in terms such as poofter.

Being a Baby

The link between being a baby and being a poofter frequently arises in the interview data. In particular, this association seems to relate to unpopular aspects of babies, such as crying, sooking,* being vulnerable, and being immature. The following quote illustrates how peer pressure from other boys is directed against being a crybaby:

> . . . if you are a boy and you cry in the playground, other boys will call you a crybaby. Yyou don't want to be humiliated, so you realize that this is not an acceptable thing to do. (I9)

---

*Sook is a colloquialism meaning timid, soft, and/or cowardly.

The next extract by the same subject starts to suggest the links between being a crybaby, being a sook, and being a poofter:

> **D:** What other terms of humiliation would be used?
> **S:** Ah, "sooky bubba" I suppose. I don't know if that's still used by kids these days, but it certainly was when I was small. Yeah "sooky bubba," "crybaby," probably "poofter." (I9)

And again from another viewpoint, the link is unequivocal:

> . . . if you were a poofter then you were the most likely one to burst into tears. (H8)

Further elaboration showed how crying was also interlinked with being a "girl" and being weak, soft, and "wussy" ("wussy" will be shown to be a more subtle form of homophobia.) Even though the following statement refers to a "presexual" use of the term, the meanings associated with "poofter" in early high school now appear to be more elaborate and specific:

> I'm fairly sure that the initial associations [of "poofter"] weren't so much sexually oriented. It was a case of . . . meaning you were a bit of a girl . . . you were weak and wussy and liable to cry. (H8)

In addition to identifying a relationship between crybaby, sook, and poofter, many of the interviews give a clear indication of a hierarchy among terms. In this case, as in most, poofter was the worst:

> Poofter was worse. Because it also carried [the idea that] not only are you lacking in the courage area or the toughness area, you lack in *every* area. Whereas sook and crybaby [meant] you're not being tough enough, whereas poofter meant you're hopeless, you're right off. (CC29)

Being Soft and Weak

Being "soft" was regularly associated with being a poofter, and this usually provided a counterpoint to toughness that was configured as a key characteristic of "hegemonic boyhood." Ellen Jordan talks of "the power of the warrior discourse to grip the imaginations of little boys" as definitive of many masculine attitudes (Jordan, 1995: 82). As with many of the analytical categories in this catalog of boyhood homophobia, the walls are not rigid and one set of meaning flows into others. For example, the meanings attached to being soft resonated with being vulnerable, unmasculine, academic, unsporting, weak, a "wimp," a pansy, a fairy, and a baby:

> The wimpier kids that would cry. . . . If you would see a kid crying, fallen over or something like that: "Poofter!" because he'd showed a softer side, definitely. (T20)

These images are reiterated by H8 and here again, the continuity between them is apparent:

> . . . crying certainly wasn't something . . . that . . . you did . . . certainly at high school you didn't cry. That was just a peer thing, you know. It was more a softness inferred with that, or weakness inferred with that. (H8)

Fighting was a way of proving strength, toughness, and masculinity, but perhaps more important, it was a test of whether your boyhood was "suspect." This applied whether you were a pacifist and refused to fight or whether you lost. Even the style of fighting was significant:

> Like when they had a fight and they got beaten, they were considered a poof. Or if they started [to] get out their claws and started scratching people, biting people, they were called a poof. If they didn't punch they were a poof. (DD30)

Being a Girl

Many writers on gender have recognized the gendered component of homophobia, although it is often read as the feminine characteristics of homosexuality. As Rosemary Pringle observes, "The one area where sexual theorists treated gender as central was with reference to homosexuality where a lot of clichéd assumptions were, and still are made about the connections between 'gender' and sexual preference (masculine/feminine and active/passive)" (Pringle, 1992: 81-82). One homophobic device used to discredit the male target is misogyny, by attributing female characteristics to him. In this group of meanings there are sissies, girls, and effeminacy. These also connect to notions of weakness and being "wimpy." Note also in the following statement how the sequential addition of meanings to the evolving idea of poofter is evident (onion skinning) and how misogyny is not perceived to be the entire story:

> Being weak or girlish, yeah . . . being weak and girlish or wimpy or whatever. And then that was halfway to a meaning and then . . . the gay connotation coming into it, I remember that. (U21)

Just as poofter didn't always have homosexual connotations, not everyone who was called a poofter was thought of as gay. Here is an example that also illustrates the theme of misogyny:

> **D:** What about people being picked on for being sissy?
> **S:** . . . I never thought of them as poofters, I probably called them poofters, but I didn't think they were gay. (F6)

Being Unmasculine

Being unmasculine is not equivalent to being feminine. This relates to the conceptual difficulties introduced in Chapter 1 concerning constructed dichotomies that are, in reality, more arbitrary. Robert Connell notes that "'Masculinity' does not exist except in contrast with 'femininity'" (Connell, 1995). However, given that masculinity exists, then being unmasculine stands in contrast to more than femininity. For example, the previous section found that being unmasculine included being babyish. Therefore, masculinity contrasts with immaturity. Being unmasculine also depends on how masculinity is defined or, more important, how masculinities are defined. An additional complication arises because concepts of masculinity can be readily identified in descriptions of boyhood and are active and highly influential well before "maturity."

A feature of modern theoretical writing is that defining masculinity is difficult. However, one way (perhaps the only way) that masculinity is defined is negatively—by marking what is unmasculine. This was articulated by subject V22 in a discussion late in the interview about masculine stereotypes:

> **S:** . . . I'm tempted to say that it's [masculinity] almost defined negatively as well.
> **D:** Yes, what do you mean?
> **S:** And there's things like you *don't* cry . . . you *don't* have emotions. You *don't* talk about your emotions. . . . What is expected of masculinity was more subtle than what was expected *not* to be part of masculinity. (V22)

Being less masculine or unmasculine is linked to sexuality and thereby with homophobia. In this example, masculinity is equated with toughness and this is used as a yardstick to equate lack of masculinity with being a faggot:

> . . . It was just . . . yeah, lack of masculinity or something. You know, it wasn't necessarily you had sex with men; it's . . . you're not as tough as us, so you're a "faggot." (L12)

In the next extract, homophobia is explained as a justification for reacting adversely to difference and to not being male. The respondent articulates the link between sexual orientation and being a poofter (in case there were doubts whether a poofter had anything to do with homosexuality!). Here, different types of women are employed in contrast rather than in analogy to poofters. The implication is that women get more leeway for not being conventionally feminine, than men who don't fit conventional male roles:

> Poofter bashers go 'round bashing up poofters because they can't handle the fact, the situation that other people are different from them. They can't handle the fact that there are people who are not heterosexual. Especially men. Men? [deeper voice parodying masculinity] "Yeah well, men don't do that sort of thing." It's not macho. It's not male. (G7)

Homophobia is not simply a matter of whether the target is masculine or unmasculine, nor is masculinity ever absolutely present or absent. There are degrees of masculine legitimacy that appear to relate to an individual's level of "social credit." The next section examines a situation in which a cumulative loss of credit can earn a person the label of "poofter," and Chapter 5 will show how gaining credit in competitive sports can cause that label to disperse.

Being Academic

Academic achievement is also associated with being viewed as a poofter. Similar findings have been made in other studies where peer culture associates academic achievement with low status "ear'oles," "nerds," and "brainiacs" (Willis, 1977: 149; Kinney, 1993). For the participants in this study, being a poofter is stereotypically associated with academic achievement, being emotional, and being unmasculine. This contrasts with analyses of masculinity in academic settings, where rationality and intelligence are said to characterize hegemonic masculinity and emotionality belongs to the female domain (Lloyd, 1984):

> . . . if they were more intellectuals and academics, they were always deemed as the fags or things like that. (F6)

Similar observations were made on this matter irrespective of the sexual orientation of the subject. As one gay participant put it:

> . . . a bit too knowledgeable or something like that. That sort of marked them as a poofter and they just would see that as a sign of weakness. And they would sort of pick on them for that. (X24)

Another gay informant described characteristics that were used as indicative of being a poofter:

> . . . being a bit daydreamy . . . singing and dancing. Being smart for God's sake! (V22)

There are several possible explanations for these apparently contradictory findings. Works such as Lloyd's focus on philosophy and academia, not on school-ground culture. On the school ground, physicality is central to defining "hegemonic boyhood" and being studious is equated with not being physical. This explanation finds support in other studies (Willis, 1977; Connell, 1983; Kurdek, 1988; Selzer, 1992). Messerschmidt reports that "the lads perceive office jobs and 'bookwork' as 'sissy stuff,'" adding that "real men choose manual, not mental labor" (Messerschmidt, 1994: 92; the association between masculine physicality and team sports has been reported by Messner and Sabo and will be explored further in Chapter 5; Messner and Sabo, 1990; Messner, 1992). Academic achievement can be seen as conforming with adult authority at the expense of peer group loyalty, and not being part of the group is suspect and characterizes poofters (also noted in Messerschmidt, 1994: 92). The next extract shows how being favored by teachers can attract homophobia:

> ... if you were ... teacher's favorite sort-of-thing, you were a poofter. It was used a lot, a real lot actually. (N14)

"Crawling" to teachers also attracted the epithet.

In addition to being smart and having special relationships with teachers, certain types of academic endeavor consistently attract homophobic criticism. Singing, dancing, theater, playing the piano, and religious studies were all suspect. In addition, doing well in core subjects intended for both boys and girls (history, geography, language) was more suspect than doing well in subjects normally seen as male oriented (sports, technical trades). CC29 reflects this when he explains who might be targeted with words such as poof:

> ... not achieving ... in the boys activities ... doing particularly well at something, that everyone had to do, but it was considered a bit girlie, waste of time, like square dancing or parent craft or something like that. If you did well in that, you'd get that criticism. (CC29)

Many of the interviews revealed a continual tension between conforming to peer expectations or to adult authority. The latter was suspect.

Being Special

Being "better" than other boys is also of importance to homophobia. Being good at team sports or being "physical" protected boys against homophobia, especially when it accorded with peer group expectations. In contrast, boys who were better in things that were not stereotypically masculine or in pursuits that were not peer based, risked attracting homophobia. The association between homophobia and being "better" encompassed a range of examples. In one case, having a velour "special jumper" made by his mother was stigmatizing. Although it was the correct colors, the jumper was sufficiently different from standard school clothing not to be overlooked by the other boys. In this case, the implication was not that it was more feminine, but that it could be read as attempting to be a little bit better and to stand out from the rest of the boys:

> . . . I hated that jumper. (CC29)

Q17 found that homophobic harassment from his brothers was made worse because he was believed to be getting special treatment at home:

> . . . they always felt that Mum was spoiling me because I would stand up to them I suppose, or I was getting away with things they didn't get away with as firstborn. I was getting privileges they didn't get when we were a poorer family. (Q17)

V22 also suggests that homophobic teasing in his home was associated with him being smarter and talented and that this was associated with an element of prestige:

> . . . it was kind of meshed in with also being . . . smart and talented and things as well, which most . . . the rest of the family didn't have labels for . . . To an extent there was an element of prestige that went along with the teasing. (V22)

Looking and Acting Different

Elaborate peer group codes govern most aspects of appearance on the school ground, and a boy whose appearance differed from what was sanctioned by his peers risked homophobia.

> If you did something flamboyant, you got the label "poof"
> straightaway from nearly everybody. . . . Flamboyant means
> doing something stupid with your clothes or something stupid
> with your sports technique or having some flash sports bag or
> bright colors or something like that. (CC29)

Homophobia could be used to mark almost anything that was
irritating or unacceptable. Here, AA27 describes how being "gay"
can be used against anything where difference and negative value
coincide:

> . . . it's not a sexuality thing. If it looks a bit different, looks a
> bit tacky, pathetic, or anything like that, it's "gay." (AA27)

Homophobia can also be exacerbated by "antisocial" behavior,
and in the following example, a form of "social credit" seems to be
playing a role:

> It wasn't because they were . . . identified as being gay or
> anything, I think faggot was a euphemism for . . . punching
> bag . . . it certainly didn't help when people did an antisocial
> thing like stealing money or smelling bad . . . that only exacer-
> bated it. (P16)

In this case, antisocial behavior also implies that the target has
offended group expectations or is outside group influence and control.

Based on peer codes, boys could detect "poofters" by observing
characteristic nonsexual behaviors (being labeled a poofter typically doesn't depend on evidence of sexual practice). Accusations
were frequently made according to how boys talked, walked, and
looked:

> **S:** . . . you knew who was a poofter and who wasn't, you could
> hear it, you know.
> **D:** You could hear it? In a voice?
> **S:** Yeah. You could see it in how they dressed. (BB28)

The way some boys deported themselves (mincing or uptight),
how they moved, how they held their wrists were all subjected to

homophobic scrutiny. In the following quote, BB28 tries to describe the characteristics of a school acquaintance who was labeled a poofter:

> . . . it's just like the "Fast Forward Air Hostess" [a camp television characterization], the air hostie with the little moustache and he walks around, you know, really rigid . . . . (BB28)

The boy whom this statement referred to didn't have a moustache, so this actually relates to the way he deported himself. How a boy speaks is also important:

> Not everyone got called a faggot, but, it was more prevalent for people who were sort of fairer and more softly spoken. (P16)

As well as the style of speech, speech content also has homophobic significance. For example, among other things, Q17 describes how "not using abusive language" can contribute to being labeled.

Homophobia was also attached to relatively minor physical differences, including skin color, hairstyle, dress code, and physical build. Being fair skinned, slight of build, having blond, curly, or dyed hair and going through puberty late can all be considered "poofterly":

> . . . something out of the ordinary, like dyeing their hair, that would be considered really poofy. (DD30)

Not surprisingly, significance was also attached to appearances that in this culture are more often recognized as feminine. For example, pink is traditionally associated with girls, and a boy who wears pink takes a substantial risk:

> Oh, you know, you little faggot, you've been wearing pink. (L12)

The effects of homophobic labeling of these physical traits during childhood can be sustained. One subject described how he still wears his hair very closely cropped as an adult because of being teased about his hair as a primary school child:

> I've got curly hair and it's blond . . . and thinking that'd be right, boys are supposed to have dark, straight hair. . . . Now as you can see, I cut it right off because I despise it so much, and I used to get teased about that in early primary school, very early primary school. (O15)

Another participant described that how a boy's hair was parted could make him vulnerable to accusations of being a poofter. Note how there seems to be a role for social credit here again. An accusation of being a poofter was more likely when a combination of signs were present rather than only one:

> You were already hearing some funny things about your hair . . . probably not your "poofy hair" but your "part" in that sort of sing-songy voice and then if you didn't make some sort of showing somehow, you would be "that sort of boy." (CC29)

The same subject also describes how this appears to be a response to boys who are felt to conform too much to external authority figures, and not sufficiently to the authority of the peer group. There is a peer group expectation that

> . . . you should have the hair *you* want, and *you* should want what *the boys* want. (CC29)

Predictably, the concern with the homophobic significance of hair even extends to this (heterosexual) hairdresser as an adult:

> And people were thinking that because you were a hairdresser, you were a fag. And, I tried to detract from that image, and as much as I thought if anyone ever thought that I was, you know, I'd probably feel upset. (F6)

For boys in boarding school, there was little opportunity to escape peer scrutiny and the pressure to conform was continuous. For example, scrutiny extended to items of personal grooming:

> . . . the worst accusation was that you were a faggot or a poofter, and the guys that got called faggot or poofter were

anyone that was in a position of weakness basically. I remember one guy who used a hair drier, and that was it! He cooked his goose! There was no redemption for him! (P16)

Even the brand of an item of personal grooming had homophobic significance:

> **S:** Oh, I remember getting teased at one point about having Cleopatra soap and had to destroy that pretty quickly. Someone almost caught me out. . . . My cover was nearly blown . . . [laughs] 'cause, it was such a girlie thing to have.
> **D:** And why did you let yourself have it in the first place?
> **S:** Oh, what was I thinking? What was I thinking? I dunno. . . . I was impressed by the ad. It had Cleopatra bathing in ass's milk or something. I thought it was just so cool, I'll buy this. But of course in a boarding house situation that was like "you bloody fag." You know, unless you're using Sard Wonder Soap you've got to be out of it. So, there was a couple of times there, that and the pansy episode, where I just nearly, blew my cover. But I managed to do some pretty good damage control. [laughs]. (P16)

In fact, the damage control must have been good, because he later became school captain, although, as we will see, P16 believes this was only possible by temporarily suppressing his homosexuality.

Not Belonging

Belonging to peer groups and conforming to their expectations was important at school, and poofters were characterized as not belonging or not conforming. The homophobia associated with being independent of peer involvement ("the in crowd") is described by T20 when he relates what characterized poofters:

> The ones that weren't playing sport . . . more interested in collecting bugs, reading. . . . The one's that weren't in the "in crowd," were. The ones that weren't doing what everyone else was doing. (T20)

The association of homophobia with the lack of team commitment, in this case letting the team down, is clear in a similar statement by U21:

> Poofter would be . . . you're letting the side down or . . . you're
> not . . . one of the team or . . . you're being weak or . . .
> something like that. (U21)

He takes this theme one step further, by aligning poofters with
desertion or betrayal of the peer group:

> . . . if someone did something which they weren't happy with
> . . . particularly something which was against conformity . . .
> which is against the group . . . like leaving early or saying that
> you had to go and look after your sister. . . . "Why don't you
> stay and be one of us?" If you'd try and bail out you'd get
> stuck with "Don't be a poofter!" (U21)

Here again, group betrayal (of the standards of masculinity) is significant:

> Dobber is definitely unmasculine. (W23)

Betrayal is a theme we have already touched on in Chapter 1 and in
the work of Davenport-Hines (1991: 300-320).

Homophobia is a powerful instrument of peer group politics and
it can be exploited to rearrange positions in the peer hierarchy.
Skillful use of homophobia can be used to control the group and to
rise up in the "pecking order":

> . . . and if you can insult someone and get a better grab on
> them, then you're one up on the pecking order. And so homo-
> phobia is great for the pecking order. (A1)

In contrast, people who were unpopular risked attracting homophobic harassment, which was exploited by peer group politics to
marginalize boys:

> . . . most kids certainly don't want to be loners at that age . . . it
> [being labeled a poofter] . . . wasn't only used directly . . . it

was like back stabbing, you know. You could keep someone
out by . . . marshalling against them by telling everybody and
by you know, reinforcing with your friends that this person's
taboo or this person is an outcast. (U21)

Sports

In many respects, sports are a more formalized and codified
variation on the peer dynamics described previously. The importance of sports for masculinity has long been recognized, and the
deeply homophobic dimensions of sports are being increasingly
well documented (Messner and Sabo, 1990; Messner, 1992; Parker,
1996). The present research confirms a number of associations
between sports and homophobia that have been noted overseas, and
the data on sports in this project proved extremely rich. Sports
provide a clearly defined "microcosm" of peer dynamics and are
examined in detail in Chapter 5.

Sports engage with homophobic dynamics at numerous levels. If
a boy doesn't play sports or avoids sports, he is considered a poofter. Some sports, such as football, are prestigious, and success in
these sports usually brings redemption. In the "Cleopatra Soap
case," P16 described how he engaged in some effective damage
control: he took up football. He felt this was a key factor in eventually becoming school captain. He also felt that if people had known
he was gay, he would not have become captain. Perhaps these are
one and the same thing, since if you don't play football you risk
being called a poofter.

The type of sport is also important; the most prestigious/least-
suspect sport is football:

> . . . if you didn't achieve at footy, if you lost at the footy, you
> were a poofter. (N14)

Others sports were ranked below football, although this ranking
varied a little from school to school. For example, soccer was prestigious in some schools and suspect in others. At the bottom of the
ranking were certain games belonging to girls:

> . . . if a boy played [certain games], he was a sissy. Games like
> elastics and skipping and that sort of thing. (Y25)

Expectations for boys in sports were high, and doing your best or achieving a placing was not sufficient to protect a boy's reputation:

> If you came third in a race, "Oh, you poofter." (N14)

Also, not participating in team sports, being a loner, letting the team down, or being a "spoil sport" were also factors:

> . . . playing handball and someone took the ball away, then you know you'd say, "Oh, you poofter!" (W23)

Sexuality?

A recurring pattern is that although words such as poofter were deployed meaningfully from their earliest use and according to complex codes, they were frequently not used to signify homosexuality. Perhaps this is not surprising, since the use of homophobic terms starts and gains considerable significance prior to sexual maturity. And when they acquire homosexual connotations, homophobic words already resonate with many of the accumulated (nonsexual) meanings that remain familiar to adults. However, homophobic vocabulary does eventually acquire homosexual references and all informants acknowledged making links between homosexuality and words such as poofter and faggot. Subjects clearly differentiated between nonsexual/presexual homophobic references and homophobia that had homosexual connotations. Evidence supporting these observations was also reported by Mac an Ghaill, who writes, "the label [poof] had several shifting meanings; sometimes it is used with an explicit sexual connotation, while at other times it is used as a general term of abuse. The notoriety and frequency of the use of the label caused much distress to the students throughout their schooling as a major source of derision of their growing sense of their sexuality" (Mac an Ghaill, 1994: 165).

The following example illustrates the presexual use of homophobia:

> I don't think it was ever meant as a sexual remark to another person. I always think it was made as an insult, to someone, but not fully knowing what the term meant. (F6)

The second example illustrates the nonsexual use of homophobia even when the sexual dimension is understood:

> . . . Usually the people who got labeled "fags" were there from day one [and it] was usually because of their appearance. Not because they were staring at all the dicks. (P16)

Many subjects also acknowledged a transition from presexual homophobia to homophobia that had sexual connotations:

> I think there was . . . a transitional phase, where poofter actually became an insult meaning you're a homosexual. (V22)

Similarly, I9 was able to date the time of that transition fairly accurately to around the age of thirteen. On the other hand, H8 implies a transition when he describes how homophobia had different meanings at school compared to when he was in the defense forces:

> . . . in school I think it was much more the emotional aspect . . . whereas in the [defense force] it was very much a sexual aspect. (H8)

It is also worth reiterating that even when poofter was used in a deliberately sexual way, it was rarely, if ever, based on any evidence of sexual preference and the target might not even have been gay.

EVOLVING HOMOPHOBIC MEANINGS: "ONION SKINNING"

Cataloging the meanings associated with words such as poofter provides an opportunity to explore some of the interrelationships between homophobic words and the conventions that govern their use. It was found that homophobic words start to circulate well before puberty and are used extensively and meaningfully prior to acquiring explicit sexual references. They were also demonstrated to have powerful negative connotations at all stages. An important issue is whether these observations can be explained as reflecting the general lack of specificity of swear words, which are largely interchangeable. The data on this point are rich, and a progressive and cumulative "onion skinning" of homophobic meanings can be demonstrated that is quite distinct from other slang terms that boys use as insults. Data reported by Thorne also support these observations in the United States (Thorne, 1993: 166).

Homophobic terms are interrelated by sharing meanings. In this first example, the implied similarity between poofter, fag, and the earlier more respectable word "pansy" illustrates a tendency for these words to be conflated:

> . . . I think being called a poofter or pansy or fag or something like that would have been the words to avoid for sure. (X24)

Shared meaning is suggested, but there are important nuances that distinguish how the different words are used. In introducing the previous quote, the term "more respectable" was used quite deliberately. Despite their shared meaning, poofter is clearly a much more loaded word:

> **D:** . . . Do you think that pansy was just a more polite form of the same thing?
> **S:** Yeah. It was. Definitely. Because, like I said, it wasn't accepted to use that word [poof] at home. And if we ever used that word at home we would have got a belting definitely. (Z26)

Z26 was brought up in a strict religious household and restraints on using "poofter" are because it is an unspeakable word, not because of sympathy for homosexuals.

It is also possible to demonstrate succession between words, that one word absorbs the meaning of the other and then succeeds it.

> . . . pansy was just a much earlier term. . . . I don't think pansy really was used by secondary school time. (V22)

V22 went on to confirm the close links between pansy, poof, and girlie.

Almost identical patterns can be demonstrated with other words such as sissy, nancy, weak, and wuss. Here is an example where sissy and poofter are conflated along with an allusion to a later homosexual layer of the "onion skin":

> Although the word [poofter] was in use, I don't think I had any conception of what gay meant. . . . It was more a sissy. (N14)

"Girl" shows the same phenomenon and again the chronological shift in meaning is implied:

> Girl indicated that you'd be much the same sort of thing [as fag or poof in primary school]. (K11)

Here is an example for "nancy" and not being tough:

> . . . actually "poofter" would be—if I had called someone that—it would have been a sort of "nancy" sort of . . . not tough. (M13)

Here again is an example using what seems to be a fairly acceptable popular "new age" word "wuss":

> I remember it [poofter] taking on . . . a meaning sort of along the lines of wuss, as well. (U21)

Similar observations were made with "camp," "queer," and, by a subject who grew up in New Zealand, "ponce." There was even an indication that poof had a successor in "fag":

> . . . "poof" was a fairly common term, and that did lead on to "fag" probably sort of [in] late high school. (H8)

But by this stage, poof and fag had sexual significance and could be used interchangeably rather than poof being superseded. Instead of being a successor, the choice between using poof or fag seemed to depend on the age of the respondent, schoolyard codes, and the influence of American culture, where fag is usual (Brown, 1993: 906).

At certain stages, a range of words that have a relationship with poofter (e.g., pansy, sissy, wimp, weak, wuss) can be used interchangeably as meaning is passed progressively from one word to another. The successor, poofter, becomes a much larger word as it retains the meanings of the words that preceded it while also acquiring new associations. Earlier quotes demonstrate how the precursor is incorporated into the larger meaning of the successor. In addition to meaning being passed progressively, it is also cumulative. This phenomenon persists into adulthood. For example, adults can still use "poofter" to suggest that a person is weak, even after it acquires its sexual "layer." In contrast, in the absence of innuendo or other indications, it is not as straightforward to imply that a person is homosexual by saying he is weak.

Importantly, the evidence does not indicate that words such as poofter are random or meaningless insults occurring simply because boys don't yet know what a homosexual is. On the contrary, there is a clear, almost palpable idea of what a poofter is, even when he is not homosexual! But what about the reverse possibility: whether other, or perhaps all, swear words used by boys are tied to homophobic processes? One clue comes from the relative intensity of feelings associated with insulting words. In this case, there is a very clear differentiation between homophobic words and other swear words:

> I mean, sure you can handle walking around being called a loser or a dickhead or a wanker or something but . . . . Oh no, poofter's a bit larger, you don't want that hanging over your head. (BB28)

In the next example, depth of feeling is also apparent, but in addition, there is an indication that the words are being used against clearly differentiated classes of people:

> . . . it was like it was categorized too . . . bastard was a male word used against males . . . cunt was for females, fuck was for both basically . . . mole was for girl, rag was for girl, you know, poofter was the only really challenging thing, and I mean if you really really really wanted to offend somebody, you called them a poof. (DD30)

While this quote illustrates how insulting words target specific classes, the next excerpt also illustrates that different meanings are associated with those classes. There is also a further indication of the stigmatizing power of homophobic labels in the absence of homosexual meaning:

> "dickhead" was a term that you could . . . palm off without too much hassle. . . . I think "wanker" probably was a bit as well. But "poofter" had a certain amount of stigma attached to it that was sort of hard to shake off. It was sort of the implied weakness. "Dickhead" sort of was a bit more naive, a bit stupid . . . and "wanker" was more "you know, you're an egotist," and those kinds of insults were not that much of a worry. (H8)

"Onion skinning" refers to the accumulation of meaning and the evolving relationships between groups of words that, in this case, have a shared association with homophobia. These words carry complex and specific meanings virtually from the first time they are used. The early use is probably the result of first observing others (particularly older peers) use these words. Meanings constantly grow and evolve as key words accumulate successive layers of meaning. Poofter and faggot are "larger" words (stronger and more meaningful) than their precursors and ultimately they incorporate references to homosexuality. Although some of the precursor words are discarded because they are superseded and are no longer as useful, the powerful meanings they once carried persist in the new word, which effectively becomes a "megaword." This does not appear to reflect a lack of competence with swear words (something that young people rarely suffer from) or their indiscriminate use. The meanings they exploit are highly specific and the different clusters of swear words are clearly associated with different meanings and classes of people. The "homophobia word complex" or "homophobia complex" (what has been rather clumsily called "words like poofter") is in a class of its own and is arguably the most intensely negative for boys and quite different from other swear words and insults.

THE POWER OF HOMOPHOBIC WORDS

Data from this project indicate three main ways that young males are exposed to homophobia and learn its implicit negative value:

through observation, by deduction, and by being personally targeted. It is notable that direct targeting is not the only (or necessarily the most important) way that most boys experience homophobia. First, as Gonsiorek writes: "Rejection by peers need not be experienced directly to be felt keenly. Many gay and lesbian youth observe the treatment of peers and clearly understand what could happen to them if they appear to be, or are known to be different" (Gonsiorek, 1993: 473). The present study supports Gonsiorek's observations:

> I saw what the blatantly, obviously, obvious gay guys, who weren't labeled gay, who weren't seen as homosexual but . . . they were termed sissy or effeminate. . . . And they got abused quite a lot, and were on the outer all the time. Didn't achieve very much, weren't popular, had some major problems at school, fitting in anywhere academically or sport[wise] or, you know, . . . they just didn't fit in. And they were hassled so much, like every day, in the end they even became hassled by the teachers, you know, because they weren't achieving anything. And there was no way I was going to let myself . . . let that happen to me. (N14)

Second, young people are alerted to the importance of homophobia and its significance is reinforced by deducing it from the reactions of others:

> . . . a contributing factor is just watching people go quiet if you mention boys together. (AA27)

This and the following example illustrate how silence can be meaningful. A pervasive background level of homophobia at school or home easily renders such a silence noticeable, and a refusal to contest it imparts a special status to homophobia:

> [homosexuality] was never talked about, by . . . teachers . . . never, never talked, never told about it . . . thereby implying, I suppose, it was not the thing to do. Then you end up presuming that it's dirty, disgusting, horrible, and everything else to go with it. And you can't even contemplate it without going about and bashing somebody. (G7)

Third, the importance of homophobia can also be learned through direct homophobic targeting. Subject A1 demonstrates this:

> **S:** . . . when I was about eight, I think. I was very distinctly and abruptly told that I was a pansy. [laughs]
> **D:** At the age of eight?
> **S:** Yeah, and that it was unacceptable for me to be that way . . . girls were supposed to be pansies and boys were supposed to act according to the boy laws [laughs]. I couldn't work it out. [laughs] . . . was forced to basically walk a certain way and act a certain way. That was the way it was supposed to be done if I didn't want to, you know, get slapped across the back of the head, punched . . . so I found out very quickly. (A1)

All subjects indicated there was considerable cost associated with sustained targeting for being a "poofter" during childhood, and they all experienced the fear of being labeled. Barrie Thorne observes that "teasing, a prevalent form of criticism among kids, has powerful emotional and behavioral consequences for gender relations" (Thorne, 1993: 53), and Mooney and others report that very young children rapidly learn how effective teasing can be "as a means of torment" (Mooney, Creeser, and Blatchford, 1991: 103). The negativity and intensity of feeling associated with homophobic labels is apparent even before they become specifically associated with homosexual meanings. This book will return to this issue repeatedly (often implicitly), but there are three aspects that reflect the intensity of feeling associated with the "homophobia complex" that will be considered here: the frequency of homophobic references; the intense impact of homophobic references; and factors that act to modify the intensity.

Homophobic Intensity

Poofter and faggot play a powerful role in peer groups because they have such intensely negative associations, and this pattern prevails no matter where the participant went to school; whether it was in the country or the city; regardless of how long ago the person left school; and whether the school was private, public, or coeduca-

tional. Here is the view from a country coeducational government
school:

> . . . it was a word, and it wasn't actually an act associated with
> a word. It was quite a harsh word, that would just hit people in
> the face and they wouldn't think, "Right, poofter: homosex-
> ual" . . . they'd just think poofter: word: they're degrading me:
> hit them in the head. (T20)

This is the (heterosexual) view of a government coeducational
school in a capital city:

> **D:** OK, so calling somebody a knob sucker or a poof was
> enough to provoke attack?
> **S:** Yeah. Well, that was the horriblest, meanest word that I
> probably knew. (Z26)

And this is the view in a Catholic boy's school:

> I mean that poor kid who was labeled that [poofter] in year
> seven. I'm sure his ego was totally deflated by it. 'Cause to
> have it . . . to have, the ultimate humiliation in lower secondary
> school is to have your sexuality questioned. That's the ultimate
> in front of other people. (BB28)

Finally, two views from a government coeducational school background:

> . . . it was just that yeah, "poof" was probably the hardest one
> . . . the most insulting. (H8)

And:

> . . . poofter would have to be the top. Like that would provoke
> the most out of everybody. (DD30)

The impact on the informant also features prominently in the
interview material. In the following example, the intensity of homophobia is apparent from the protracted nature of the harassment and

how the informant "hated" it. Here, a young gay man recounts how his peers had labeled him before he ever had sex and even before he had recognized his own homosexuality:

> I used to be the local "poof" for some reason . . . they used to call me that and they used to chase me and I couldn't stand them. I hated it . . . primary school and high school and it went on, and on, and on for years. (O15)

Even in the absence of direct homophobia, all subjects indicated the considerable risks they perceived to be associated with being labeled. In the next example, B2 responds to being asked what would have happened if he were "openly gay at school":

> You would've just copped hell. You know, you probably would have been . . . bashed, you would have been embarrassed, you know, it would have almost been public humiliation full stop. I mean God knows what your parents would have done to you if they had found out. . . . Nothing short of being flogged within an inch of your life. (B2)

The intimidating power of homophobia is also acknowledged independent of specific events in the next example:

> . . . [poofter] was the worst thing you could be called. I can't think of anything else that would have made me feel worse. (T20)

Similarly, for this heterosexual participant who has played professional football and has since joined the police force, these words had a special intimidating quality:

> . . . Knob sucker and poofter for sure, would be what you would use to another boy to really hurt him. And I would hate to have been called a poof or a knob sucker. Without even knowing what a knob sucker was! (Z26)

Homophobic Frequency

At its peak, boy's peer and school-ground culture is saturated with homophobic references. Although this does not seem to be the case in the classroom, an enormous amount of extremely powerful homophobic dynamics is compacted into those short times when students are out of earshot of teachers, in the schoolyard and before and after school. The following quote illustrates how homophobia is an integral part of playground vocabulary for almost everyone, even boys who eventually become gay:

> I remember getting in trouble for it by the teachers. Because I started using it as well. Because everyone was using it, and it just became part of our vocabulary at school. It was our playground talk. (N14)

It was generally reported that most people are targets of homophobia (some more than others) at some stage in their school years and that homophobic accusations were expected to be challenged. For example, suggestions that a person was "poofterly" invited a beating:

> I think everyone was [called a poofter] . . . maybe only once until they thumped that person. (U21)

And this saturation is not confined to the spoken word:

> . . .'cause you'd see it written up in all different forms. In . . . the toilets and the sheds and things like that. . . . It featured a lot in graffiti and . . . then I was thinking of the drawings, there were often erections drawn up on toilet walls . . . and people's names written up against poofter as well. So it was quite visible and you heard it as well as saw it. (N14)

The interviews revealed that homophobic references generally become increasingly frequent until they peak at about school year eight. At its peak, being exposed to homophobic references is a daily occurrence for boys:

> Oh, every day. It [poofter] was a very popular word. (N14)

Also, in most cases homophobic talk was heard many times per day regardless of whether the school was Catholic, Protestant, or government and whether the student left school quite recently or some years ago. This is the view of a (heterosexual) student, age eighteen, who completed his schooling at a prestigious Catholic boy's school only a few weeks before the interview:

> **D:** How many times [per day] would you have heard [poofter]?
> **S:** Oh yeah. Two, three, four, five. Something like that. (BB28)

The following is the observation of a (bisexual) subject, age twenty-two, who went to a coeducation high school in the country:

> . . . just a rough number, you'd probably hear that [poofter] about fifteen times in a day, at least. Thrown around in different contexts. . . . It was a loaded term. So that would be the one that was the most cutting. . . . I can't think of another word that would be as offensive to another boy. (T20)

Next, the experience of a gay man, age twenty-four, from a coeducational government school in Canberra:

> **S:** In high school, it just sort of accelerated.
> **D:** So, in high school at its peak, how often would you have heard it?
> **S:** Oh, God. Oh. Probably twenty or so. Twenty, thirty [times per day]. (Y25)

There was some variation in when the frequency of homophobic references peaked (ranging from year five to year twelve), as the following examples illustrate. Here is a conversation with a (gay) participant, age eighteen, who went to a Catholic coeducational school:

> . . . the peak was year eleven and twelve . . . the word faggot, gets popped up, oh at least once a sentence. . . . Oh, oh, oh, it's uncountable, like I said every sentence. . . . Not literally, but it just happened constantly. A figure on it? Oh, over fifty. Yep. (AA27)

The next observation comes from a (heterosexual) participant, age thirty, who attended a government coeducational school. His observation is consistent with the previous ones made by gay subjects, except that he located the peak much earlier:

> **S:** Oh. Twenty, thirty times at least. That [poof] was *the* word you know. Or the one that stands out basically anyway.
> **D:** And what class would you have been in? What age? Would that be primary or secondary school?
> **S:** No, that would have been about fifth class. (Z26)

So while the number of times that "poofter" was reportedly used is only a very rough guide, young men consistently recall it as being very frequent at its peak.

Modifying Factors

Although homophobic accusations are frequent and often severe, there are factors that mitigate and regulate the impact of homophobia. The role of "social credit" has already been touched on. Although a single event could lead to sustained stigmatization, a combination of occurrences is more likely to result in labeling, as the status of the boy becomes progressively more tenuous. Conversely, a boy with status might be able to resist labeling that would ordinarily stigmatize someone else. Credit can avert stigma or it can be used to rehabilitate a damaged reputation. Being physical (fighting or playing sports) is one way of accumulating credit. In Chapter 5, it will be shown how R18's reputation was redeemed following success in a swimming championship. This phenomenon is also encapsulated by I9, who says:

> Normally, if they were good at sports, "queer" didn't have quite the same effect. (I9)

Similarly, taking an accusation as a challenge that had to be defended with a "thumping" was illustrated by U21 (in the previous section). Or, in this case, finding someone to "bash up" seems to be a way of accumulating credit:

> I wanted to prove that I wasn't the most wimpy, so I attacked and bashed this kid up. (Q17)

At the time of participating in this project, Q17 was gay and this example raises an important point. Examples of gay men who attempted to deflect homophobic accusations by directing homophobia at others were identified. But the strength of homophobic dynamics meant that homophobia was a useful of way of gaining status for everybody. Homophobia is a widely practiced group process, and although some participants in homophobic harassment became gay, the majority who were involved were not.

Just as the status of the target modifies the impact, subjects report that the context of accusations such as "poofter" is also important. Differences were noted depending on how the words were used, such as whether you used the shorter or longer version:

> Actually, there was a slight difference between poof and poofter. Poof was funny, someone funny, someone girlie, but they were okay because they were making you laugh. Poofter was bad. (CC29)

In many situations, poofter was used as a fleeting insult, often as a device to regulate a situation. The following quote differentiates between permanent homophobic labeling and when homophobia targets an unacceptable action:

> You often get called poofter for . . . being, you know, a bit soft . . . in one action you did. But some people would get called poofter all the time, he *is* a poofter. Not he's being a poofter, he *is* a poofter. (U21)

So homophobia can transiently target behaviors and characteristics, or in certain cases, homophobic labeling can be sustained and boys can find it difficult to escape. When this happens, being a poofter becomes part of the boy's school-ground identity. In Eric Rofes's words, "In the eyes of youth culture, sissy boys function as gay youth even before the dawn of conscious erotic desire appears" (Rofes, 1995: 82).

It is possible to modify the impact of the accusation by reacting appropriately or to exacerbate the situation by reacting poorly:

> . . . it was a bit like . . . a sort of test. If you knew what to say or
> you stood up then you'd be okay, but if you were targeted and
> did the wrong thing or said the wrong thing or . . . broke down
> then you'd be further targeted. (U21)

The alternative to the physical defense of a boy's honor when confronted with homophobia is to dismiss the accusation in the hope it would disperse as quickly as possible.

Homophobic impact depends on how vulnerable the person is and what sort of supports he has. Accusations have special significance for a boy who is starting to feel he might be gay, and when his confidence is low, accusations are much more hurtful. In the following example, two boys who both ended up being labeled as "poofters" in early high school provided mutual support for each other, even though their association with each other exacerbated the accusations. This is a "catch-22" because homophobic labels can be severely isolating for boys and isolation can exacerbate homophobia. Support from other boys is often not available because homophobic pressures encourage the avoidance of stigmatized boys or they risk being stigmatized too. Homophobia causes difficulties even with the support of others who were also labeled. In the following extract, a young Aboriginal participant describes how his non-Aboriginal school friend managed when he was labeled:

> It depended . . . sometimes he wouldn't feel very confident so
> like it wouldn't be you know, he'd sort of get upset and start
> crying and stuff like that and . . . sort of go to his mother. . . . But
> he had a real brave front too, like I think we all did. (DD30)

Participants also described how practices were modified by school-ground geography. The highest risk of homophobia was away from the classroom during breaks, particularly away from teachers and school buildings, and the risk was higher in the boy's areas, such as on the football oval or in the toilets, concealed by sheds or behind trees. There are also safety zones such as corridors, close to staff rooms, near buildings, in the classroom, and in girls' areas. Some participants described how they had to plan their way around the school ground or plan their way home fairly carefully to avoid harassment:

> I was always getting kicked out of the girls' weather shed . . . because I liked to spend my time with the girls. I felt safer there . . . or in the hallways, where you weren't supposed to be, away from everybody else. (B2)

Apart from physical avoidance, boys described two common methods used in an attempt to manage homophobic harassment. These are concealment of the "authentic" self and social withdrawal. Both have a cost for the individual's welfare and integrity. Numerous examples were identified where subjects recalled trying to conceal the "offending" characteristic (even boys not destined to be gay), and this urge to conceal often carries over into adult life. In the following discussion, a subject, age thirty-two, who was married for a number of years before he accepted he was gay, reflects on how his school experiences influenced how he sought to hide his sexuality:

> I don't know whether I felt ashamed for doing what I did. Maybe I feel like a bit of a hypocrite in some ways, 'cause I knew back then that I probably [was gay] . . . this is where my life should have been [gay] and I hid it for a long time. That's why I'm so overcritical of people nowadays that can't make up their minds. . . . You just didn't survive in those areas unless you could either hide it or you gonna get out of there as quick as you can. (B2)

But school is compulsory to the age of fifteen, and getting out is not a solution if you need an education. In the previous example, B2 left school as soon as he turned fifteen because of the harassment and worked as "unskilled" labor in light industry until he recently moved into management.

"Detumescence" Homophobic

In addition to evidence that homophobic pressures crescendo to a peak during school years, there is extensive evidence that explicit homophobia subsequently eases:

> Perhaps it [homophobia] looked like a more serious thing when I was a kid. Or perhaps as I got older . . . just the

composition of kids or something changed, and it wasn't as bad a thing to be a poofter, and . . . I distinctly remember it happening when I got to year eleven and twelve. . . . It was a complete turnaround by the time I got to year eleven. I didn't want to leave after the end of year eleven. (N14)

The reduction in homophobia starts to be noticeable in late secondary school, and these findings accord with a general decline in bullying in later school years (Olweus, 1991; Olweus, 1993; Rigby and Slee, 1991; Whitney and Smith, 1993). However, as might be anticipated, there was evidence that the effects of intense homophobia during the middle school years were not entirely reversible. One participant describes when he observed homophobia starting to diminish, but that some people persisted in being homophobic:

> . . . from year ten onwards the "faggot" name-calling thing just seemed to disperse. Except with one or two people. (L12)

Similar evidence was provided by BB28, who indicates that some boys remained noticeably homophobic, at least until the end of secondary school:

> There was an intense . . . racism mixed in with homophobia at [school name] which in some people doesn't go away. Even year twelve. (BB28)

Similarly, this easing continued into early adulthood, but some people continued to be noticeably homophobic:

> Some of them aren't accepting but . . . most of them are pretty cool about it. I mean even now I'll be walking down [town], you know, and people that had beat me up when I was in school, they come up and "Oh, how are you doing?" (DD30)

Evidence for at least partial reversal of homophobic feelings in young male adulthood also comes from descriptions of how subjects would react if propositioned by a homosexual. These accounts provide useful insights into the depth of feeling associated with such a scenario and also how much this can change as they age:

It's probably one of those gut things that goes very deep down but I'm not quite sure why . . . about six months ago and was approached by [another male] and I just sort of brushed it off, but that wouldn't have been my reaction when I was younger . . . in the past I think my action, my reaction was more one of blind panic. (W23)

Z26 also recounted how his reaction moderated in adulthood, and in the following extract, he relates what his previous reaction would have been:

I would have absolutely shat myself. . . . I'd be terribly scared. . . . If it was just me and him, I would have just got out of there real quick . . . if it was in a group, I would have probably given him a mouthful of cheek and even tried to punch him or something, just to show your friends that you're with, that you, you know, this is what happened. (Z26)

Notice how Z26's reaction is linked to demonstrating his credentials to his friends. A similar transition from an extremely intense reaction, potentially violent, was provided by F6:

S: . . . I'd cope well . . . I'm sensitive and mature enough to deal with it; if you asked me that question ten years ago . . .
D: What would you have said?
S: Ah, probably hit him [laughs]. (F6)

A reduction in homophobic pressures in early adulthood allows young men to be more demonstrative toward other males. Although this was possible during early childhood, it was out of the question in the middle school years because of homophobia:

. . . with my [male] friends now I don't have a problem if I'm not going to see them for a while, [I] give them a hug. I mean that happens now. I don't think it happened in school though. (BB28)

U21 helps to develop this point further when he says that his homophobic feelings have "faded" to the point that he can now "permit" the idea of everyone having homoerotic experiences:

> That sort of thing [discomfort with homosexuality] is, you know, has faded. And I guess that's why I can . . . I can now permit the possibility of. . . everyone potentially having a homosexual experience. (U21)

There are a number of reasons why homophobia might undergo a decrescendo in early adulthood. Consolidating an adult sexual identity, experiencing heterosexuality, and overcoming the uncertainties of adolescence are probably involved. Z26 associates his reduced homophobia with becoming more mature:

> . . . till a certain stage, to me it was a lot of "poofter," you know "filthy mongrel bastards" sort of thing. Until you're sort of mature enough to realize that each person has their own sexuality and sexual preference. (Z26)

Personal contact with gay men and replacing negative stereotypes and their associated feelings with actual experiences, also seems to contribute to reduced homophobic anxieties. This has been identified as a factor by other researchers (for example, see Herek, 1994: 209).

> . . . but never basically knew of them [gay men] or talked to them personally face to face and when I did, I suppose my homophobic tendencies started to dwindle down. (F6)

With further contact, F6 and his fiancée were invited to a "gay wedding," which he was initially hesitant about, but this helped to displace earlier stereotypes:

> . . . this [gay] wedding just virtually showed that the love was there and the other couples there, it wasn't dirty. It wasn't sickening, like people made out it was. (F6)

The net effect of these experiences was that F6 felt much more secure about his contact with homosexuals:

> . . . when I learned that, gays tend to stick to their own, they don't, they don't basically tread where they're not wanted, I felt more secure. (F6)

Homosexuals were no longer in the realm of the "virtual homosexual/poofter" that haunts adolescence.

The changes in peer dynamics that occur in late secondary school also contribute to the relative dissipation of homophobia:

> I guess once I'd started making friends with people in a group I became quite close to a number of them. That meant that the group . . . mentality was broken down, especially towards the end of school. . . . The pack mentality died down. (P16)

The opportunity arises for boys who are not academic to leave school, and academic success is increasingly important for those who remain. Once school is completed, the school-based peer groups assume less importance and new social structures intervene. However, homophobia is at its most intense in the mid–school years and this is an important, high-pressure developmental experience, the impact of which is unlikely to disappear entirely. The accounts in this chapter indicate a reduction in homophobia for a range of young men; however, it is still possible to identify a range of homophobic constructs in the interviews with these men and various negative attitudes in the ATLG (attitudes toward lesbians and gay men scale) responses (see Appendixes). The impact of childhood homophobic experiences is sustained, and further evidence for this will be reviewed in Chapter 4.

HOMOPHOBIA AND "OTHERNESS"

The observations in this chapter strongly support the conclusions from Chapter 1 and add further detail. There is a richness and striking similarity between independent accounts in this study. Homophobia appears to be frequent, intense, and highly patterned, and this research has identified a complex series of events referred to by the shorthand term "onion skinning." These include (1) a time when words such as poofter move into the vocabulary of young people —usually primary school; (2) sources of these words and their associated meanings—predominantly older peers; (3) groups of precursor words such as weak, wuss, pansy, sissy, and sook, which have their functions subsumed by "poofter" when it is adopted;

(4) the absence of homosexual connotations for poofter during a significant period, during which "poofter" nevertheless has rich meanings and complex conventions governing its use; (5) a coherent, progressive and cumulative layering of negative meaning into words such as poofter, eventually including (homo)sexual references (onion skinning); (6) the retention of previous meanings even after "poofter" gains explicitly homosexual meaning; (7) a crescendo in the frequency of use and intensity of feeling associated with words such as poofter, roughly centering on school year eight; and (8) a subsequent relative easing of homophobic references after that time.

In contrast, prohomosexual sentiment in childhood experiences, particularly on the school ground, is virtually nonexistent. Taking a more "philanthropic" position appears to be a luxury of adulthood and "multiple masculinities." Even intimate childhood "mucking around," sometimes romantically called "innocent childhood sexuality," becomes shrouded in shame and risk. This is what A1 attempts to articulate as he describes his experience of childhood homoeroticism, which he sees as "beautiful," but which he feels is violated at a later age when a cultural association is learned between homoeroticism and "hatred" and "atrocities":

> . . . to me it was beautiful and I'm sure that it was beautiful for those people. Though maybe not . . . as I said, there's . . . the opposite of the way I feel about it . . . the total opposite of it is hatred as far as . . . committing atrocities against gay people. Out of that simple instant, it's not the instant itself—it's the way that they've been cultured. (A1)

A Key Repository for Unacceptable Male "Difference"

A common theme running through all of the homophobic meanings identified in this research is that *"poofter" is a cumulative repository for everything a growing boy should not be:* (1) A growing boy should not be a baby. On the school ground, poofter is used to signify the boy who acts like a baby, who cries, is a sook, is vulnerable, and is a "mommy's boy." (2) A boy should not share characteristics with girls. Numerous studies have documented that boys and girls increasingly segregate themselves on the school ground starting from early primary school (Thorne, 1993; Clark, 1987, Jordan, 1995). "Poofter" is used to signify boys who don't respect boys' segregation from girls, who are effeminate, girlish, sissy, pale, blond, have curly hair, or who wear pink. (3) A boy should not separate from boys' groups or be a loner. There are strong pressures for boys to express allegiance with peer groups (Mac an Ghaill, 1994; Messerschmidt, 1994; Thorne, 1993; Clark, 1987). Poofter signifies boys who are not part of the peer group, who betray group standards, who do not play team sports, who are loners, who conform to adult authority in preference to peers, or who seek the company or safety of girls' groups. (4) A boy should not be weak or cowardly. There are expectations that boys will become increasingly physically competent and mature (Mac an Ghaill, 1994; Messner, 1992). "Poofter" signifies boys who do not succeed in sports, do not fight, are academic and nonphysical, who lose contests, are weak, or who are late to develop physically. (5) A young man should not be sexually "deviant." There are strong expectations of "compulsory heterosexuality" for young men after puberty (Connell, 1995; first coined for women by Rich, 1980). Poofter takes the additional meaning of being sexually lacking or deviant, and, of course, eventually homosexuals are poofters too. Young men who do not objectify girls, who do not boast of heterosexual exploits, who are not in a heterosexual relationship, or who do not get a girl pregnant are suspected of being a poofter. Compulsory heterosexuality implies fatherhood, and fathers have socially defined roles, expectations, and responsibilities. In contrast, as we saw in Chapter 1, the stigmatization of poofters can include attributions such as being failed fathers, against "the family," child molesters, sexually "out of control," antisocial, evil, sinful, criminal, unnatural, subhuman, animalistic, monstrous, defective, and sick.

These findings imply that homophobic "onion skinning" is more than simply a matter of gender (if gender is ever simple). Homophobic processes are not only about differentiating "real boys" from feminine boys or from girls (example (2) in this section). It is also about the differentiation of adults, and it is more generally about distinguishing and marking undesirable otherness (being alien).

Example (1) concerns the role that homophobia plays in differentiating boys from babies. While all babies (male and female) are encouraged to grow up, only boys risk being called a poofter if they act like a baby later. Example (3) concerns how homophobia regulates peer group allegiances. Example (4) is about separating the men from the boys and dominance from immaturity and physical incompetence. Finally, example (5) shows how homophobia differentiates "successful" men from "antisocial" men, sexual conformists from the nonconformists, and "real men" from less differentiated forms of unacceptable male "otherness." In every example, homophobia is (by definition) an attribution of the quality of being undesirable, and implied in all of these cases is its role in differentiating "good" from "bad":

> . . . the whole premise of acknowledging that this is a gay person starts from a negative premise of this is somebody who's deranged and not part of acceptable community or religion. (Q17)

In the next quote, the bonds between homosexuality, otherness, negativity, and the logical links with violence start to become visible:

> In high school, it [being homosexual] was, well there was a lot of shame attached to it. It was seen as a shameful thing. It was seen as here's something that should be hidden and probably destroyed or muffled or subdued as much as possible. (CC29)

The previous five categories of difference illustrate increasing differentiation of the developing identity and between the new identity and "otherness," and these appear to be forced apart by homophobia. Although this roughly parallels chronological development, this discussion intentionally stops short of a formularized, unvarying, rigidly staged model. There is no claim that the five classes of difference are complete, and the section on "modifying factors" is intended to introduce space for considering the role agency, resistance, and social change to what are very dynamic and powerful processes. These categories do not constitute independent steps; they are linked by common factors that inject continuity. These continuous factors include the following: the processes are about being male; they concern what is unacceptable for males; and they relate this to an unacceptable entity known as a "poofter" who is richly described and instantly recognized by boys (even though they have never knowingly met a homosexual and know nothing about a poofter's sex life). Homophobia is not simply a reaction to homosexuality and cross-gender behavior. For young men, homophobia is what distinguishes "the other" from collectively authorized views of the acceptable "self":

> It was just a label marking the other . . . people. (U21)

The "poofter" is *the* principal repository for unacceptable male "otherness" and homophobia is a cluster of powerful processes that orchestrates this.

Other Otherness

As well as "poofters," there are other forms of otherness, and homophobia interacts with them too (Ficarotto, 1990). For example, racism and male homophobia are not mutually exclusive. Here is a conversation that attempts to clarify the experience of one (gay) Australian Aboriginal participant who had just remarked that his sexuality, rather than his Aboriginality, was his overriding problem at school:

> **D:** . . . But you never experienced hassling because of race at school?
> **S:** No, no.
> **D:** So it was all about sexuality?
> **S:** Yeah, definitely. (DD30)

In addition, he also provides evidence of the power of homophobia between himself and other Aboriginal boys:

> **D:** Did you ever get hassled by other Aboriginal guys about sexual issues?
> **S:** Yeah, mainly the [town name] boys. (DD30)

To add some balance to this picture, however, DD30 also felt that the local Aboriginal communities were less homophobic than local non-Aboriginal people were. A similar scenario was observed by Parker, who found that "intragroup cohesion" based on "shared masculine values" appeared to override ethnic loyalties (Parker, 1996).

However, the relationship between racism and homophobia is not clear-cut. There is considerable ambivalence about other forms of difference and key modifying factors elevated or deemphasized the importance of race in relation to homophobia. In addition, the different forms of otherness can be mutually reinforcing rather than mutually exclusive (Ficarotto, 1990). In Australia, it is not uncommon for people who originate from Mediterranean countries to be referred to as "wogs." Here is the opinion of one participant who came from a Mediterranean background:

> . . . "wog" dug in deeper because there was sort of a truth to it. Like a knife . . . whereas the nancy one, well I knew I wasn't. (M13)

This is an interesting example because M13's identity seems to draw some authenticity from his Mediterranean background: "there was sort of a truth to it." In contrast, although he reported a number of sexual experiences with a male cousin, some of which he initiated, he did not associate himself with the "nancy" label. In his interview, he consistently presented himself as believably heterosexual, he scored himself as exclusively heterosexual on the post-interview questionnaire, and although he provided good evidence for the powerful role of homophobia at school, he did not conceal his frequent homoerotic experiences with his older cousin. In contrast, he reported that the term "wog" was not as hurtful for people who were not of Mediterranean origin:

> . . . [for them] wog wasn't too bad; nancy was worse. (M13)

The same view was shared by Y25 who, despite his eastern European background, was not identified as a "wog." In this case, Y25 started being labeled a poofter in primary school and he suffered from severe homophobic harassment that led to protracted truancy. In his experience, racial and homophobic otherness are not mutually exclusive:

> **D:** . . . so if you were to call a Mediterranean kid a wog or a poofter, which one would he be more angry about? Or would it have been the same? . . .

S: Probably the wog.

D: Wog, okay. So, poofter was okay for them?

S: Oh, it wouldn't have been okay, I don't think. But if you called them a poofter-wog! Bad, yeah. (Y25)

X24, however, seems to find them roughly equivalent:

> . . . you know, poofter, fag, something like that, or a wog, I found the most deeply insulting. (X24)

In fact, it is perhaps not surprising that although there are different forms of otherness, they seem to occupy overlapping fields, and this probably contributes to the ambivalence detected in the interviews about any differences. The following statement illustrates the conceptual interface between homophobia and racism:

> I associate the term [fag] with homosexuals . . . taking homosexuals and putting them into a completely separate human race category is what a lot of people seem to have the tendency to do. (K11)

Physical difference, especially disability, is another key class of otherness and this, too, has significant overlap as well as significant differences from homophobic otherness. A well-defined theme in the data relates "being a poofter" with physical incompetence. In homophobia, the emphasis on male physicality equates the poofter with the one who is weak, fragile, timid, can't fight, and can't play sports. Other authors have also noticed this association on the school ground, describing "discourses of naturalization, in which homosexuality was constructed as a form of disability" (Mac an Ghaill, 1994: 94). Chapter 1 also includes statements by public figures that draw an analogy between homosexuality and disability.

In Australian settings, people with disabilities are sometimes referred to as "spazzo." In this extract, CC29 compares the significance of "spazzo" with "poofter":

> **S:** Yeah, never heard wog. Spazzo, yeah. And that was . . . another grade five, six, seven thing . . . it wasn't that bad really. I would have said it.

> **D:** Okay, now tell me, on the scale of things, which would have been the one that would have been worst, or which one would have been the one that would be most provocative to the school toughs, or which one would have been one that the kids wouldn't have liked used against them the most? Or did it vary?
> **S:** No, I think it was poof. Yeah. (CC29)

In contrast, J10 did actually use the word "spazzo" when he was a child and became severely embarrassed when he later discovered that he said it to someone whose brother had cerebral palsy. "Spazzo" had a special significance for him that was not apparent in any of the other interviews.

So homophobia is about unacceptable male difference that is not specifically explained by other forms of difference, such as being female, disabled, or racially different. Nevertheless, people's concepts of these categories of difference do seem to overlap. This depends at least partly on personal sensitivities and experiences. Furthermore, there is a sense in which different races and sexes occupy "legitimate" positions of otherness (such as "wife" and "original inhabitant"), even if they are subordinated positions, whereas that is arguably not the case for "poofters" (Bersani, 1988, 204).

One category of male "otherness" has been conspicuously absent from the discussion until now: what about the "bad" heterosexual male? This was recently the subject of an edited book titled *Just Boys Doing Business? Men, Masculinities and Crime* (Newburn and Stanko, 1994). A key theme in this book is that heterosexual men carrying out crime are in fact conforming with and enacting expectations of normative heterosexual masculinity, that is, by taking risks, being tough, and defying authority. Messerschmidt points out that there "is a strong relationship between youth group activities and youth crime" (Messerschmidt, 1994: 81). He also observes that the youth group is "unmistakably the domain of masculine dominance" and "normative heterosexuality is a decisive "measuring rod" for group participation" (p. 83). These findings are consistent with the peer dynamics found in the present research. Messerschmidt goes on to note that for some of his subjects, "public masculinity is constructed through hostility to, and rejection of, all aspects of groups that may be considered inferior in a racist and heterosexist society" (p. 94). The implication of these findings is that, although crime is undesirable in the eyes of some, at least in the (more important) judgment of peers, it is an affirmation of masculine identity and peer group allegiance and is not viewed as a manifestation of "otherness." It does not take a leap of logic to see how "poofter bashing," risk taking, and "lifestyle" diseases of heterosexual males might arise from pressure to conform to, and affirm the demanding standards of, the normative heterosexual identity and to escape the risk of homophobic labeling associated with taking an "easier" path.

Other Than What?

The catalog of homophobic references contains the clues needed to answer this question. This time the examination focuses on what is unacceptable in order to identify the complementary dominant expectations of boys. This raises a related question: acceptable according to whose expectations? Earlier it was observed how most homophobic activity occurs on the school ground, away from adult authority. It was also seen how N14 got into trouble for using homophobic references at school and how Z26 was not allowed to refer to "poofters" at home. The idea that homophobia becomes less intense toward the end of secondary schooling was also introduced. These observations point to peers in the school-ground culture as a principal focus of homophobic pressures. This possibility of the overriding importance of peers in propagating and enforcing homophobia is strongly confirmed in the interview data, and this will be examined in detail in subsequent chapters. The data reveal that a characteristic of the homophobia complex is that it can operate in "boys' culture" virtually independently of adults. One informant (K11) encapsulated this process in the term "rolling peer pressure": when school-ground culture can be passed continuously from one school generation to the next without needing to pass the scrutiny or intervention of adult culture (although individual boys might be disciplined). As K11 put it:

> I think that there's a lot of . . . "rolling peer pressure." . . . What
> I mean is that kids who have older brothers and sisters . . . get

taught something—"Oh, you just don't do this at school."As it
goes up, it gets taught and reinforced. And so the kids drop off
the top, but teach a new version of kids and it just keeps rolling
out. (K11)

This continuity in children's culture is documented in *The Lore
and Language of Schoolchildren,* originally published in 1959 by
Iona and Peter Opie (Opie and Opie, 1977). The importance of this
continuity is apparent even in the first paragraph of their preface,
where they state, "More than 200 years ago Queen Anne's physician John Arbuthnot, friend of Swift and Pope, observed that nowhere was tradition preserved pure and incorrupt 'but amongst
Schoolboys, whose games and plays are delivered down invariably
from one generation to another'" (Opie and Opie, 1977: 5).

Having identified peers as the principal arbiters of homophobic
expectations of boys, attention is now turned to what those expectations are. In fact, we have already defined some of the complementary expectations of a boy's peers in the discussion of "onion skinning." A growing boy should not be a baby; he should observe clear
differentiation from girls; he should express affinity with groups of
other boys; he should become increasingly physically competent
and mature; and he should observe "compulsory heterosexuality."
These requirements expose the yardstick of "normative" or "hegemonic masculinity" that underwrites the processes of homophobia.
In fact, in a very real sense, masculinity is "boys' stuff" and the
standards of hegemonic masculinity are negotiated and set on the
school ground. Perhaps it is more appropriate for Bob Connell's
well-known term "hegemonic masculinity" (1987: 183) to be called
"hegemonic boyhood." The comments by W23 expose the yardstick being used:

. . . I think when most of those kids are poking fun at people
who are gay, it's not the thought of the act of homosexual sex.
It's a set of characteristics that are different, that are, as I said,
maybe more effeminate than the very masculine characteristics that we particularly in Australia and New Zealand apply to
what it is to be a man. (W23)

U21 reminds us that homophobia has a profound effect on shaping the *heterosexual* male identity:

> If you're called a poofter enough times, you'd be extremely careful not to do anything which was poofterly. (U21)

In his book *Gender and Power*, Connell complements his notion of "hegemonic masculinity" with the term "emphasized femininity," which he uses as a counterpoint (Connell, 1987: 183). In this research, another key counterpoint used by growing boys is "the poofter," which, as we have seen, does not equate neatly with femininity—both signify "otherness" to masculinity. What the data reveal is an elaborate and rich progressive development among young boys of what a poofter is. This notion preoccupies boys' interactions, particularly for that period when there is considerable segregation from girls. Boys are able instantly to identify and target "poofters" and things that are "poofterly," and the targeting is powerful, intense, and decisive. At this stage, most children have never knowingly met a "homosexual," do not know details of the sex life of their targets, and the term poofter for a time does not have a sexual dimension. All of the layers that "poofter" has seem to have arrived there by a process of shedding them from ideas of "self." (This shedding is reflected in behavioral transitions that are described in Chapter 4.) Poofter therefore seems to be an important device in boys' identity formation and concepts of "self." The "poofter" they construct is easily recognized by them and almost palpably real. For this reason, the "virtual poofter/homosexual" should be added to "hegemonic masculinity" and "emphasized femininity." For a time at least, the "virtual homosexual" is not another form of masculinity that parades alongside the very topical "multiple masculinities" that are such a luxury for adults. Perhaps it is not until the poofter "has sex" that he is embodied and comes to life. Until then, for the earlier formative years, the virtual homosexual is not even real: it is a powerful symbol of masculine otherness. In Erving Goffman's words, "the general identity-values of a society may be fully entrenched nowhere, and yet they can cast some kind of shadow on the encounters encountered everywhere in daily living" (Goffman, 1963: 129).

CONCLUSIONS

At the end of Chapter 1, it was observed that two major antihomosexual themes in recent public debates on homosexuality portray homosexuals as the "other" and equate homosexuality with the end of "order." In this chapter, by tracing how young people come to comprehend and articulate notions of homosexuality, it has been possible to demonstrate the (homophobic) construction of "the virtual homosexual" and to hypothesize that this serves as a key repository for male otherness during the differentiation (ordering) of heterosexual masculine identity. These findings accord with the conclusion reached in Chapter 1: an important means of comprehending homosexuality is through understandings of "otherness." Furthermore, by linking homophobia with the development of heterosexual self-identity, it is possible to advance at least a partial explanation of why homosexuality is regularly associated with fears of a "breakdown of order" in homophobic discourse. The fears of disrupting the "order of things" reviewed in Chapter 1, were voiced in the context of calls for greater equality for homosexuals. Clearly, if true equality were to be obtained, then homosexuality would no longer be available to symbolize otherness. As a result, the masculine identities based on these differences would be challenged by the possibility that the boundary between self and other might dissolve and otherness could infiltrate notions of self. This blurring of the boundaries between self and otherness would also offer an explanation for the recurring fears of pollution and contagion.

Chapter 3

Separating the Men from the Boys

Homophobia is not confined to the private and personal biases of individuals who act alone. As Bronwyn Davies says, "Individuals cannot float free from social structure. They can choose to act on and transform social structures, but structures must always be recognized as constraining individual and social action" (Davies, 1989: 12). Earlier chapters have already highlighted the important role that social processes play in homophobia. Young men become homophobic between infancy and adulthood—conveniently called the "school years." The "landscape" of these years, according to Thorne, includes three major sites—families, neighborhoods, and schools (Thorne, 1993: 29). Additionally, this study has identified the central influence of peer groups and the mass media, and their prominence warrants their formal inclusion as elements of the "landscape." A feature of the present study is the important distinction between the classroom and the school ground, and these will be analyzed separately. Thus, the key contexts of homophobia in childhood include the school ground, the classroom, peers, family, and the media.

SCHOOL

Schools, and activities associated with schooling, are central to shaping homophobic experiences. While the details vary for each person interviewed, homophobia is reported by all subjects and the same general homophobic processes are described regardless of whether the subjects attended Catholic, Protestant, or government schools in urban or rural areas. It is not possible to determine whether the relative intensity (frequency, power, and effect) of homophobic events varies among the different school systems. However, it is possible to identify factors that influence intensity: age, the type of involvement in homophobic processes, the degree of exposure to older peers, how sports are organized, and school-ground arrangements.

There was no evidence that coeducational schools are less homophobic than single-sex schools. If anything, the dynamics are at least as intense in mixed-sex schools. Subject C3 illustrates the difficulty that mixed-sex schools posed for him when he describes why he dropped out of school rather than move from a boy's school to a co-educational school:

> I just didn't want to get back into a co-ed environment. . . . I think it would have been more pressure on me, to be totally down-the-line hetero. And I was already confused enough. (C3)

These findings are not surprising. The pressures to conform to compulsory heterosexuality would be more immediate in mixed-sex schools, and the nonconformist would be more obvious or more easily exposed. Also, girls do not have a universally moderating effect on homophobic dynamics; indeed they contribute to these processes too. At times, coeducational schools function similar to two single-sex schools that share the same campus. As Barrie Thorne notes, "there is ample evidence of extensive separation between girls and boys within contemporary coeducational schools . . . sociometric studies that go beyond 'best friendships' to ask about and map broader self-reported patterns of affiliation and avoidance have also documented a deep division by gender" (Thorne, 1993: 46-47). Australian writers have described this separation too: the "consequences of this dynamic is that boys and girls barely know each other and see each other as almost different species" (Clark, 1987: 57).

A dramatic difference was found between homophobia in the classroom and on the school ground. Although the classroom is not immune to homophobia and some teachers contribute to it, homophobia is generally at its most intense in peer groups when remote from adult authority. There is also evidence that group dynamics

and crowded conditions intensify homophobia and this can be exacerbated depending on how school life is structured: "collective regulation—or 'batch processing'—has a leveling effect; teachers and
aides cope with the large numbers of students by treating them as
members of groups" (Thorne, 1993: 31). An important example is
how sports are organized (see Chapter 5). Another example of the
importance of group dynamics to homophobia is described by
DD30:

> . . . they [homophobic bullies] were always in a group. They
> were only ever big and strong when they were in a group and
> never, ever one-on-one . . . and whenever they were on their
> own they'd always stay well clear of me. (DD30)

In contrast, subject M13, who describes powerful but seemingly
less dramatic homophobic experiences than other subjects, attributes this moderation to being at a new school where school-ground
culture was not handed down and enforced by older students:

> We were privileged in that we were the first year through and
> we never had years above us to sort us out. We were very
> unique. Always our own bosses in a way. (M13)

This supports the observations about the importance of "rolling
peer pressure" in the previous chapter: the pressure is less powerful
when there are no students in previous years. Other studies have
also found that students are bullied less as they progress through
their later school years, probably because there are fewer bigger and
stronger boys at higher levels (Rigby and Slee, 1991).

Chapter 2 illustrates the sequential nature of homophobia. While
boys are increasingly exposed to, and involved in, homophobia as
they move through school, they are also simultaneously exposed to
older children on the school ground who have already experienced
later stages. This is the essence of "rolling peer pressure." The role
of social context in learning about gender is summarized in comments by Bronwyn Davies, and a similar argument applies to learning homophobia. "As children learn the discursive practices of their
society, they learn to position themselves correctly as male or female, since that is what is required for them to have a recognizable

identity within the existing social order" (Davies, 1989: 13). Margaret Clark encapsulates the structural effects of school life when she states, "the primary school is a key 'site' or setting where 'regimes' of gender-specific behavior are produced through specific-habitual beliefs and practices" (Clark, 1987: 28).

THE DIVIDED SCHOOL GROUND

It is well-recognized that school grounds become increasingly segregated along gender lines as primary school children age (see, for example, Yee and Brown, 1994; Galambos, Almeida, and Petersen, 1990; Thorne, 1993; West and Zimmerman, 1987). This study confirmed these observations and also identified a similar phenomenon that occurs *between* boys. In contrast to the boy-girl (intergender) division, the latter division is an intragender one that becomes pronounced in primary school soon after the boy-girl division solidifies. Homophobic dynamics are a principal force that mediates intragender cleavage. Because the data from this research reveal similarities in how each of these (intra- and intergender) divisions arise, as well as identify relationships between them, the characteristics of both divisions will be recounted at different schooling levels.

Intergender Segregation

Although subjects reportedly developed a sense of their own gender at an early age—prior to commencing school (Connell, 1983; Yee and Brown, 1994)—sharp polarization of school-ground groups along gender lines was not prominent in accounts of kindergarten and the early school years. However, studies have demonstrated that not acting like the opposite sex becomes increasingly important until year nine for boys (Galambos, Almeida, and Petersen, 1990). These observations are consistent with other studies: "in the younger grades . . . girls and boys more often play together" (Thorne, 1993: 125). The following illustrates this point and uses the playground as the reference point for this observation:

> . . . in early kindergarten when recess or lunch came around . . . boys and the girls would play together . . . indiscriminately . . . it

didn't really matter. . . . I can remember even up until year three or four playing with a number of other boys, with the girls playing a girl's game. . . . (BB28)

. . . at kindergarten there was less demarcation. We were all just sort of thrown in there . . . the middle, sort of earlier-middle years of primary school were pretty split apart. (P16)

By early to mid-primary school, an important transformation has occurred and intergender divisions are pronounced (Yee and Brown, 1994). Girls' and boys' groups occupy distinctly different positions in relation to each other on the school-ground. "As children grow older, they tend to separate more and more by gender, with the amount of gender separation peaking in early adolescence" (Thorne, 1993: 52). Individual gender identity now appears to provide the basis for gender group identification, which also results in differentiation and separation from groups of the "other":

S: Girls were very strange creatures . . . there's always this dichotomy [between] boys and girls. Boys *and* girls. Girls were to be treated differently. You weren't allowed to hit girls . . . girls were supposed to be nice.
D: Does that mean you were allowed to hit boys?
S: Rough play amongst boys was not put under any sort of restraint. Well, I mean, it wouldn't be, amongst the student population, without the teachers being involved. (P16)

Notice how in the previous quotation, teachers moderate rough play.

By primary school, socially determined differences in boys' and girls' appearances have acquired considerable significance and these differences are exaggerated by the way adults organize childhood. One example is the dress codes for boys and girls. As Bronwyn Davies puts it, "each child's body takes on the knowledge of maleness or femaleness through its practices. The most obvious, and apparently superficial, form of bodily practice that distinguishes male from female is dress and hairstyle" (Davies, 1989: 14).

But, the way we were brought up, the girls only ever wore dresses, they never wore shorts, they never wore pants or jeans. To me it was sort of cut-and-dried basically. (Z26)

> . . . by the time we hit first grade all the girls were in their little
> fawny colored uniforms, the guys were in their grey shorts and
> their shirts, and the girls had all their hair in pigtails and some
> had actually taken a bit of care getting clean because they
> weren't going to be playing in the mud or the sandpit . . . and I
> suppose that uniform segregation made it very easy to pick
> from a distance who was boy and who was a girl. (K11)

The sharp division between boys and girls on the school ground
cannot be understood simply as a code that is imposed by the adult
world. Children actively impose their own divisions and they en-
force them when they are outside adult supervision (Jordan, 1995).
The following participant illustrates how the view of gender mixing
changes to be viewed as transgressive:

> . . . some of my best friends were female friends, whereas by
> third grade I can remember definitely there were boys' things
> and boys' games and there were girls' things and girls' games.
> And you were much more segregated and if you . . . hung out
> with the girls . . . that was a real sort of social downcast. But not
> so much in infants . . . it became daggy to hang round with
> girls, you know. People always used to say "Girls' germs,
> girls' germs, no returns" and vice versa boys. . . . Whereas
> girls' games were more things like skipping . . . it wasn't a
> boy's thing at all you know. Boys seen with a skipping rope
> would be dead, and hula hoops were girls' things as well. Boys
> didn't mess around with hula hoops! (W23)

This is a similar process and expressed in similar language to the
enforcement of homophobia (described in the previous chapter) in
which boys who mixed with girls at this stage risked being called
poofters by their peers.

Peer groups are very important in the gender differentiation process (Jordan, 1995). For example, in the previous quote, a boy who
was "seen" to have transgressed would be "dead." The scrutiny and
enforcement of intergender divisions by peers are described in ways
that reveal their significance. Importantly, from the child's perspective, intergender "differentiation" is repeatedly characterized by
metaphors of contamination (boys' germs/girls' germs). This asso-

ciation between the "clean" differentiation of identity and the risk of contamination has already been noted in relation to the differentiation of boys from "poofters":

> Girls were horrible . . . occasionally, you'd get a girl that comes and kisses you, probably an outgoing, forward sort of a girl, I guess. . . and all the boys go "Oh yuk!" "You've got girls' germs." (Z26)

> . . . we just weren't mixing together . . . we didn't even think about it at the time. It just happened. . . . I don't really know what brought that on . . . and then around that time the second, third grade . . . girls have the "germs," the "girl germs" you know. . . . And they become something you wanna avoid. . . . (BB28)

By mid- to late primary school, boys' and girls' social worlds are differentiated and highly polarized, but segregation is not permanent. In high school, the consolidation of boys and girls as "opposites" becomes the basis of resuming contact and for constructing new forms of relationships that are not dependent on boys identifying with girls. For boys, a pattern of increasing interest in girls emerges. Initially this manifests as forays by boys into girls' territory that closely resemble harassment. Notice the role of peer pressure in setting up this dynamic:

> It was only ever like pulling up dresses and things of the girls. It was nothing really involved and I mean it probably came from dares and things, you know? Or kissing. They were dares, "catch and kiss." And I think "catch and kiss" sort of, I don't really know where that game comes from, but it's in between the "girls are horrible" years and "girls are nice" years. (Z26)

However, by high school, this in-between stage, during which contact with girls looks more like playground harassment, is replaced by more lasting contact that becomes increasingly intimate. Instead of rejecting girls, "compulsory heterosexuality" now becomes the norm of "hegemonic boyhood." The following subject talks about how dancing with girls shifts from being undesirable to desirable:

> . . . we used to hate doing dancing when we were younger because there was this boy-girl thing. You don't do girl things. You don't touch girls [or] you get girls' germs. When you get in about sixth class, prior to puberty, you start thinking about girls and boys. Talking about [girls] and some of the boys tried to make out, or they might have been true stories, I don't know . . . the sort of things you talk about and what you want to do with girls. (Z26)

The public nature of compulsory heterosexuality, of talking about "what you want to do with girls" is clear in this statement, and there is also the implication that it could just be talk. The idea that talk was more important than action recurs in a number of accounts and confirms the importance of peer accountability for behavior.

A feature of this contact is that it is often very public and subject to intense peer scrutiny. "A defining characteristic of their [student] social identity was the projection of a publicly confident heterosexual masculinity" (Mac an Ghaill, 1994: 52). This public heterosexuality is a marker of status:

> . . . I'd say as it went on it got more polarized. Toward grade six and seven . . . things merged more, there was more contact. And I know at the end of grade seven there was more boyfriend/girlfriend coupling, really pretty heavy pashing . . . going on . . . not during the school lunch hour, but any sort of school function or sports thing or whatever. . . . So there was more contact, because they had to have contact to negotiate all those sort of "who's dropping who" and "who's doing what." So there was more of that in grade seven, but I'd say the maximum polarization was grade six. (CC29)

The importance of appearances and of measuring up to other boys' standards is clear in the next statement:

> . . . and was one of those sort of . . . first girlfriends where it wasn't someone that I particularly liked or anything like that.

> It was just . . . having a girlfriend . . . it was the most important
> thing to get things to start and to not be the last one to have a
> girlfriend. . . . It was obviously meant to be an aim, according
> to the standard measures around. You were meant to aim to
> have a girlfriend and . . . you didn't want to fail at that. (U21)

As Nancy Netting observes, sexuality has a central place in youth culture, and one of the reasons for this is that sexuality is "far more than a biological need, it is also a key marker of adulthood" (Netting, 1992: 974).

Intragender Segregation

Intragender segregation is a complex process that interrelates with the intergender differentiation just described. At the same time that separation of male and female school-ground social worlds develops, the division widens between boys who successfully conform to peer expectations and those who don't. The deepening gender divide intensifies the split between boys and "other boys" (poofters):

> . . . these things come out more as you get older I suppose. And
> people split off more into males and females. And that's when
> I really . . . I hated football. I hated all those contact sports that
> people used to play at lunchtimes. So I was more at home
> doing skipping or something like that, but of course that means
> that you're . . . a target for ridicule. (O15)

The concurrent processes of intergender and intragender differentiation witness some dramatic shifts in the positioning of boys and girls, and boys and poofters, and these events highlight how fluidly "the poofter" symbolizes otherness. In mid-primary school, dominant notions of boyhood identity are based on rejecting contact with girls (Jordan, 1995). Boys who mix with girls during this time are vulnerable to being labeled "poofters":

> . . . But at that age we wouldn't have had much respect for the
> girls at all. You didn't play with them; girls were girls and if
> you played with the girls, you were a pansy or a poof. (Z26)

Paradoxically, a couple of years later, this has reversed and boys are expected to show intense interest in girls while those who don't are now vulnerable to being called "poofters."

Peer Groups

Segregation of the school ground is more complex than simple divisions between boys and girls and between boys and "other boys." At around the same time they differentiate from girls and from "poofs," boys subdivide into character groups that reflect shared "subidentities" (Kinney, 1993; Willis, 1977; Connell, 1989). "Character groups" will be used here to refer to peer groups in which certain characteristics are integral to how boys identify the groups and the role the groups take in the school-ground subcultures, for example bullies, sportos, "footy-heads," brainiacs, and nerds. Names given to the resulting groups and their characteristics vary from one account to another, and this reflects differences in school-ground culture and the age of the participant. However, there are key similarities, and shared underlying dynamics can be identified in all of the accounts. "It was 'your [male] mates' who were the significant others in relation to evaluating what school is 'really about' and 'where you are going in the future.' Their vocabulary of masculinity stressed the physical ('sticking up for yourselves'), solidarity ('sticking together') and territorial control ('teachers think they own this place')" (Mac an Ghaill, 1994: 56). Máirtín Mac an Ghaill's observation indicates how important the scrutiny and approval of peer groups is for young men, a prominent feature of the present study.

Character groups are constructed around physical prowess, technical competencies, studiousness, and groups are positioned in opposition to loners and boys who seem unacceptably different (Kinney, 1993):

> . . . all the "techos" were the smart kids. They all hung together. They played chess or Dungeons and Dragons or whatever it is that smart people do. And I wasn't in that league by a long shot . . . the footballers were out on the oval and kicked round a bit of leather . . . other kids sort of fell into different groups and they went to different ovals or they did different things

during lunchtime. I had my own kind of group of nerdy friends, I guess. (R18)

Not all boys' groups have equal status on the school ground. There is a hierarchy of power and prestige that is based primarily on physical prowess and toughness (Kinney, 1993). At the top of the school-ground pecking order are the sporting and tough groups:

> They formed groups, and once in groups they were unaccepting of people for individual qualities . . . physical achievements were very big. It didn't matter if you had a brain. (R18)

In contrast, being smart and being nonphysical or weak are not valued highly (Kinney, 1993):

> . . . the smokers were always pretty tough sort of people, you know, they were tough because they smoked. . . . Then you'd have your dags and your brainy people would definitely be on the bottom. And as it turns out, these days, they're always on the top [laughs]. But, purely because they just, sort of, didn't fit in with other people. They'd like to sit in the playground and read a book. . . . But, or they might have dressed a bit differently, you know, a bit smarter or something like that and that's basically why they got paid out on. (Z26)

In addition to the hierarchy among groups, there are also different roles for members within groups. Group membership is provisional and unstable and this contributes to the power of groups, but it also makes groups susceptible to the agency of members. There is evidence that even though students move through a school, as they move from class to class, similar groups outlive particular members and recur in different schools. Groups reflect childhood culture and the school ground belongs to that culture. The cultural dimension passed through generations of school groups ("rolling peer pressure") gives character groups a "life of their own" that is reflected in groups being associated with particular qualities and territories rather than depending on individual membership.

The allegiances that develop on the school ground are described as an important part of school-ground politics:

> . . . associating with . . . and maintaining allegiance . . . with a
> range of people, and certainly the . . . sporty types and the
> opinion leaders . . . was quite important. (V22)

Instead of groups being portrayed as a virtue of school-ground
culture and as sources of social fulfillment, they are often described
as a means of providing security and safety:

> **S:** . . . Actually I think the whole idea, the whole goal for that
> time was not to stand out. You wanted to be happy. If you were
> . . . part of that group, or a group, you were happy. And . . . that
> was your aim.
> **D:** Okay, so if you're part of a group, you're happy. If you
> stood out what happened?
> **S:** . . . well then you're teased and rejected. (BB28)

This is confirmed by C3:

> If you don't have a group you don't have the protection . . .
> you've gotta be in a gang or you're [laughs] a target for any-
> thing. And that covers everyone I think. (C3)

Both of these accounts attest to the influence that groups have on
school dynamics and they imply that the school ground is a potentially dangerous place, particularly for loners (Whitney and Smith,
1993):

> I think schools are bit of a dog-eat-dog sort of world . . . kids
> can be pretty cruel. (X24)

This is contrary to the "romantic" view of childhood in which the
playground is a haven.

The "downside" of school groups is a theme that recurs in all of
the accounts. One explanation of the difference between the roman-
ticized view and what was found in this research is that the account
depends on the status and perspective of the speaker:

> . . . Schools can either be a really pleasant thing, but if you are
> not perfectly heterosexual and [a] perfect size eight, ten [or]

whatever, then you're fucked. All that stress does catch up with you. It does. People give themselves ulcers and shit, just worrying about it. (AA27)

Because groups are always in flux and membership is provisional, and because the standards of "hegemonic boyhood" are demanding and narrow, it is not surprising that no accounts saw school group dynamics as entirely unproblematic.

A further testimony to the power of peer-group culture is the capacity of groups to influence people's personality and individuality:

> . . . The boys weren't nice when they got together on the football field. . . . When they're by themselves they're a bit better. . . . When they're in a big group they're oppressive. (R18)

In the following extract, the increasing importance of groups and the homophobic standards set by groups are explained. C3 suggests that becoming a group member is necessary for protection, but the price of membership is to sacrifice a person's individuality in order to conform to the standards set by the group:

> So all of a sudden everyone started acting really "macho." Okay. So you had this fear, that if anyone acted a little bit softer at all they'd just get the shit beat out of them all the time . . . all the friends that I went to school with all of a sudden, they wanted to hang out with a tough group. For protection I suppose you'd call it . . . everyone all of a sudden just lost their identity, put it that way. Where I felt comfortable with myself, all of a sudden I couldn't feel comfortable being that person anymore. I had to change, [so] I started hanging out with the tough guys of the school. And I ended [up] brainwashing myself into believing that I was this super-macho human dude; I was the one that ended up beating the shit out of softer-looking kids. (C3)

Here again, the standard for group membership is toughness and homophobia, which is in opposition to softness, friendship, and being "true" to one's self. The quotation is especially significant because at the time of the interview, C3 was engaged in an extremely difficult (unresolved) struggle with his own homosexual desires.

The idea that group behavior did not reflect the personality of the individual occurred in other accounts as well:

> I'm pretty sure that it was somebody else's anger, not their own. They were just doing it because they were in a group and in order to be . . . in good with that group they had to abide by the rules. . . . If you stay in this group you've got to go and beat up on these fairies. (DD30)

But group hierarchies don't comfortably accommodate boys who are different, who don't belong to groups. The criteria used to recognize unacceptable difference include those identified in Chapter 2, that designate "otherness." Mac an Ghaill documents how valued forms of heterosexual masculinity vary among groups with different social backgrounds, but demonstrates similar dynamics underpinning the various group forms. In particular, most groups (publicly) share similar assumptions about acceptable masculinity. "Alongside the heterosexual male students' practices of compulsory heterosexuality and misogyny, many of them displayed virulent modes of public homophobia" (Mac an Ghaill, 1994: 94). Holland, Ramazanoglu, and Scott make a similar observation and anchor this more clearly in group dynamics: "what the group does seem to support, is a particular concept of hegemonic heterosexual masculinity, and separation of effeminacy, or homosexuality" (Holland, Ramazanoglu, and Scott, 1993: 12). In the present study, "poofs" were viewed as outsiders, not as a group that reflected an alternative form of masculinity: "poofs" are generally positioned as the lone archetypes of unmasculinity on the school ground. And while being a member of a prestigious group is viewed as a sign of success, being a member of any group was viewed as important, and being an outsider, as abnormal:

> That whole male culture thing was just too up front . . . it was . . . do-or-die basically. That whole pecking order was no longer, you know, like there's these people on the top and everyone else would just be in the middle, and it doesn't really fucking matter. Like, you had to be somewhere I think, and if you weren't somewhere, then there was something wrong with you. (A1)

Not being a group member was clearly linked with risk (Boulton, 1995):

> . . . once you get a pack culture going, I think it's like a lot of these male groups, to not join in is a big risk. And you get caught up . . . with the adrenalin of it all. (P16)

Belonging to the tough group or the sports group was protection against homophobia:

> I copped it [homophobia] although the person who said it to me quite a bit, called most other people, (except . . . the people who weren't always dressed in black and smoking and being "booners" [the tough group] . . . or a big sporto jock that was just fantastic) . . . they were normally the "faggots" or "the poofters." (L12)

The following excerpt is a reminder of the saturation of school life with homophobia, as described in Chapter 2, but it also indicates the role of groups in modulating homophobia:

> . . . It [homosexuality/homophobia] would be sort of the topic of conversation, wherever you went. . . . Even in the classroom. It would be out in the playground. It would be in the library. It would just be every spare minute. . . . And it did seem more prevalent among that group: the sportos, the footy-heads. (T20)

Accounts of school groups of young gay males were not prominent in the interviews, and these groups existed only in limited forms. Most common were pairs of boys who became allied because they were targets of homophobia and obtained mutual support from each other:

> . . . we started to get a lot of abuse. . . . I started to get really rebellious about it. He got really rebellious about it. We had great ways of throwing back their stuff. I didn't even know at the time that I was throwing it back at them. But we had this great way of throwing stuff back at them, you know. They'd

> come over and say, "Oh you bloody poof," and I was well
> known in the school as [homo Thomo] and whaddaya get if
> you take the [T out of Thomo]? It's just all of that stuff. And it
> was really full on, and we were really good comfort for each
> other. We were always laughing and I think that that really
> helped. That really really helped me out. (DD30)

However, this affiliation is at the cost of increased visibility and
intensified the homophobic targeting, and there are also accounts of
boys avoiding other boys to escape further labeling.

In the one firsthand example from the interviews of a grouping of
"poofs" at school, the grouping was loose and the labeling was
"vague":

> Well, as I said, there was this group that was probably about
> five [coughs] which I was an occasional member of which was
> vaguely referred to as "those poofs." (V22)

Furthermore, the group is united in their sense of being different
from other boys and it is this "difference" (not sexual orientation)
that attracts the homophobia:

> . . . what characterized . . . the group of poofs was . . . differ-
> ence, I guess. (V22)

Significantly, sexual orientation was not articulated as the reason
for the "group of poofs" forming, and even in this group, homosexuality was handled in isolation. It was not until *after* the end of
schooling that some members revealed their homosexuality to each
other.

Groups and Agency

Group processes are susceptible to the agency of members, and
the alternative to being marginalized from groups is to participate in
them and use them (Kinney, 1993). This is a two-way process
because participants also have to yield to group standards to maintain their involvement. Several informants who are now gay gave
accounts of how they managed their involvement with group pro-

cesses to their advantage, although there is a clear sense in these accounts that the informants were hiding and being "untrue" to themselves. P16 describes how, despite experiencing a deep sense of difference and marginalization earlier in his school career, on arriving at boarding school, he was faced with a choice:

> . . . I started playing football because [it] was "you either played sport or you had to do chores." So it made the choice easier, but I found that there was a hell of a lot more camaraderie and sort of brotherly love and team spirit when you were involved with the sports. You were part of the boys now. And so I took to that. (P16)

P16's management of peer groups was skillful and he became school captain in his senior year. But he also describes a growing severe tension between his public self and his private feelings that reached a peak at that time:

> And I felt as though I had to compensate [laughs] for other areas of my life, like being gay. I thought that's it, you dip out there, but you can make up for it in other areas. (P16)

The "success" of this strategy depended on concealing his homosexuality. P16 does not believe that he would have become school captain if it were known he was gay.

Similarly, N14 worked "successfully" at group dynamics and became a prefect in senior school. His approach was carefully planned so that he would not become a victim of group processes. N14 also had a girlfriend at that stage and he felt that this provided additional protection for him:

> . . . I tended to float between groups. That was another way of maintaining my popularity. I had a couple of best friends, one who has since "come out" . . . who I hung around with a lot of the time, but then I'd go from group to group, about three or four groups, and I would tend to spend a bit of time in those groups with people. I don't know whether it was because I was asserting my place in the school, or watching my back in case I fell out of one group and had another group to go to. (N14)

In addition, N14 describes his strategy of dealing with powerful groups. He recognizes and exploits the increased risk associated with groups and uses his social skills to forge alliances outside the group, which modify group dynamics. In effect, N14 compromises key group members by forming an association with them when they are not in a group context:

> . . . I recall cornering them all, often trying to get those who were in groups during the day on their own, in the library or something and talk to them. And I developed friendships that way. 'Cause I used to often get phone numbers, and exchange numbers with boys, never with girls. Yet during the day, in the public eye, I'd often play with the girls or hang around with . . . . If they [boys] were in a group I found them threatening . . . . I think as a group they posed a threat because they would travel 'round in a pack. That sort of boys do in the playground. (N14)

In the next example, CC29 describes how he relied on "bluff" and how he always surrounded himself with allies so that it was unlikely his bluff would be put to the test:

> . . . just made it clear that I was big enough and strong enough and ready to fight, even though I wasn't. So I bluffed a bit and I also had a hell of a lot of friends and I never got too far away from friends. And I had friends, because of my sisters I knew heaps of people in the years above, through church I knew heaps of people in years below. I knew all the teachers; I was really good friends with all the teachers. It was pretty hard to get me in a spot where I wasn't surrounded by friends. And that was a big tactic, I think. (CC29)

I9 describes how he purchased the services of "bodyguards" who were also "different," but whose difference was explained by race, so that questions of sexuality did not undermine their authority:

> . . . at the school in some respects I felt more protected because I had a couple of really large Samoan guys that I could help out with their academic work and [they] were far bigger than

anyone else at the school, and they certainly put a few bullies into line. It was, I suppose a sort of symbiotic partnership in a way. We each had a quality that the other didn't have, but together we could sort of deal with anything. (I9)

In contrast, C3 found protection and power by gaining membership in the most homophobic group in the school:

Once I got into the so-called "cool gang" I was set. I more or less had control of the school. And as long as I was seen as being tough at school, I was fine. [I] got on well and never got beat up any more. I only ever got flushed once. . . . Oh, they stick your head down the toilet. Whereas that was a regular occurrence for most of the other kids. (C3)

An important consideration is that strategies for securing safety by forging alliances with other people and with school groups are only available to boys who are not highly marginalized. Boulton has described how bullies tended to be in larger groups than other children while "victims" spent significantly more time alone (Boulton, 1995). Those who are isolated and who do not have access to protective social resources often seek protection by exploiting characteristics of the school landscape (see the section in this chapter titled Territories).

Girls' Groups

From a boy's point of view, the solidarity and group loyalties demanded by boys' groups seem more rigid and cohesive than in girls' groups:

I don't remember them [girls] being grouped into groups as there were for the boys. Boys tended to be mates, and band together and pick on other . . . pick on girl groups (N14)

Also, although the "rules of engagement" between boys and girls vary at different stages of schooling, the rules are not as ambiguous as the protocols that govern the relationships between girls and "poofs." In some situations, girl groups provide refuge, safety, support, and friendship for boys who do not fit comfortably into dominant boys' school-ground culture. Paradoxically, boys who seek safety with girls risk further homophobic targeting and marginalization because they appear to have an unacceptable affinity with girls. Once a boy is marginalized, "rehabilitation" back into boys' culture is difficult and the marginalization is self-perpetuating. Other boys can't afford to be associated with outcasts, as BB28 explains:

> . . . once you move, you go out of your group to somebody who was a loner, then it becomes difficult to go back . . . because the other people identify you with that person. (BB28)

In Bronwyn Davies' words, "the failure to be correctly gendered is perceived as a moral blot on one's identity" (Davies, 1989: 20), and in the context of this research, this could be expanded to read, the failure of one's associates to be correctly gendered (according to current peer-group expectations) is perceived as a moral blot on one's identity.

Once again, this research concurs with Barrie Thorne, who found that "heavy social pressures were applied to those who didn't act in 'natural' ways especially boys who liked girls' forms of play" (Thorne, 1993: 1). In this study, the so-called "heavy social pressure" referred to by Thorne is revealed to be homophobia:

> Well, like one of the guys sitting there with the girls or if he had feminine gestures and things, you know? He was known to the so-called "boys' boys" [chuckle] as a poof. You know, because he associates with the girls and we don't because we are tough boys [chuckle]. (Z26)

Despite the "heavy social pressures" it is a reflection of the arbitrary division between boys' and girls' domains that the same activity can sometimes be classified as boys' activity and sometimes as girls', and therefore unacceptable for boys. Playing cards is a girls' game in the following description, and a boys' game at other times (see Chapter 5):

> I knew that there was a game of football going on down on the bitumen area . . . and I sat down and played cards with the girls

and . . . I just asked them what they were playing and they said "Here, have some cards," and I sat down and played. And I remember guys walking past and calling out something, you know, about playing with the girls. But, I just kept playing. . . . Oh, it was hard to keep doing it. Hard not to throw the cards down and walk away. But I remember thinking it was the right thing to do. I thought it was a good game and I thought there was nothing wrong with it. (CC29)

Seeking refuge isn't the only reason for marginalized boys to mix with girls. In this example, the association with girls is depicted as "the right thing to do." The belief that it is wrong for the sexes to be rigidly segregated, and for boys who are different to be marginalized, featured in several interviews. Cases in which boys steadfastly adhere to their difference will be examined further in Chapter 4.

Girls do not always simply provide safety and friendship, and the relationship between "poofters" and girls is not always a comfortable one. Some girls resent the intrusion of (marginalized) boys into their domain:

. . . it's complicated 'cause I played with girls and felt more comfortable with girls . . . not that the girls necessarily wanted me to be around them. (Q17)

Sometimes boys can be locked out of mainstream girls' and boys' groups, and the isolation that comes with being different can be extreme:

I used to be quite interested in being friends with girls. And we'd get on quite well, but there was always a problem with being too friendly because they had such a rigid structure to their, social groups that wouldn't allow me to get in. (P16)

Furthermore, most schoolgirls subscribe to the gender conventions of the school ground and can also be heterosexist and homophobic. In the first example from early primary school, a girl's arbitration on gender boundaries has an enduring impact on L12. Here he recalls an episode in which he clipped his hair out of his face while he was in art class:

Mum had bobby pins, 'cause she had long hair at that stage. I remember seeing them . . . [and] I knew she wore them in there and I stuck it in my hair to keep it out of my face. . . . Plus, you know, it was something Mummy did so I thought it'd be something nice to do, and I remember getting bagged out real bad by a girl, for having them. 'Cause she said "That's what girls have." (L12)

In the next case, O15 recalls that both boys and girls were involved in persistent homophobic taunting during his childhood:

. . . and it was a daily sort of . . . hassling, all the time. . . . It wasn't just the boys; there were girls who used to . . . you know, rough girls, who sometimes I think can be far more terrifying, but generally more terrifying to the other girls. (O15)

Territories

Segregation of the school ground into girls, boys, character groups, and "poofs" is reflected in school-ground social geography. In addition to boys' areas and girls' areas, there are also intermediate areas:

. . . But definite areas in [and] outside the classroom in primary school. And the girls' [areas] were all grassed or flat areas under the awnings, so they were in the shade. And, there was football, which was just for boys, on the oval or on this gravel slope and then there was areas in the middle, where predominantly boys, but anybody could play. (Y25)

The interviews convey a clear sense of the school ground being a quarantined cultural space belonging to student groups. However, for boys who do not find a place in boys' groups or girls' groups, it is the intermediate zones outside groups and between allocated areas that have special importance:

. . . there were certain spots in the playground where there'd be boys' territory, like the back of the oval. The girls would have the arbor, for their little domain. I was never in either. I could never feel comfortable in full-on boy's territory or full-on girl's territory, so I'd spend a lot of time wandering sort of in the never, in the DMD [sic] zone between the two . . . demilitarized zone [laughs]. (P16)

For children who find themselves marginalized and the target of homophobia, the school ground is conceptualized in terms of danger zones and safety zones. P16 describes the proximity of his "demilitarized zones" in relation to sites associated with adult authority. Safety zones are almost always located adjacent to or within school buildings and close to adult authority, whereas sites that are considered most risky are in the center of boys' sporting areas or at some distance from or hidden from adult supervision—places where peer culture is the least restrained (Olweus, 1991; Olweus 1993; Whitney and Smith, 1993, Boulton, 1995). Whitney and Smith (1993) have found that schools with high rates of bullying are more likely to have pupils who dislike recesses and spend the time alone.

In schools where the buildings are open to students during breaks, spaces such as hallways and libraries provide escapes from school-ground politics (Whitney and Smith, 1993):

> . . . my first two years of high school. . . . I tended to find sanctuary within the walls. . . . I just didn't relate to the psyche of the people outside the school, that you know, the students and . . . invariably for one reason or another I either didn't feel comfortable about dealing with them, or they didn't want to deal with me. . . . I suppose the corridors became a whole new space that I could explore and veg out . . . there were distinctive places where I knew I could be and no one would hassle me. (A1)

In schools where buildings are "out of bounds" during breaks, safety is more tenuous and has to be continually negotiated by boys who are heavily targeted (Olweus, 1991; Whitney and Smith, 1993). In the following extract, B2 outlines his attempts at finding safety, which arose from continual and severe homophobic harassment by peers:

> **S:** I was always getting kicked out of the girls' weather shed and all this sort of thing, because I liked to spend my time with the girls. I felt safer there.
> **D:** Safer there.
> **S:** Yeah. Or in the hallways where you weren't supposed to be, away from everybody else.
> **D:** You often took refuge in the hallways?
> **S:** Yeah. Just didn't want to go amongst all the rest because I didn't feel safe.
> **D:** So one place you went to was the girls' sheds, another place was the hallways. Anywhere else that you found you could?
> **S:** As often as I could forge a note and get down the street. [laughs].
> **D:** Down the street.
> **S:** Yeah. Away from it all. (B2)

Boys who were vulnerable had to be strategic about negotiating group areas and transiting the school ground:

> . . . there were places at high school where . . . you could go, like you could walk within a meter of this really tough group who all hated you, but only if you were heading to the oval or only if you were heading to the tuck shop. You had to have a reason for walking past. If you just stood there and hung around, it wouldn't take long . . . but I never did that. (CC29)

It is also important to avoid isolated and hidden places, and this put constraints on the use of basic facilities such as toilets and change rooms because of the limited adult supervision there. Ironically, too much interest in these facilities by adults exposes them to the risk of homophobic accusations too:

> I can remember things like. . . . I certainly would try and avoid going to the toilets. And I would do that either during class time or wait till I was at home. Certainly not in breaks . . . because it was an out-of-view area . . . and I was really sort of threatened, I wouldn't. . . . (O15)

Another situation having increased risk for vulnerable students is going to and from school (Whitney and Smith, 1993). This is a transitional time between the supervision of parents and teachers, and it is a time when peer groups are assembling or before they disperse for the day. A number of gay participants describe how going to and from school is like "running the gauntlet":

> . . . I recall lots of people throwing stones at me on the way home from school. (Q17)

Safety considerations require some boys to be strategic. For example, being forced to modify their route home or the time they leave for home to avoid any risks:

> . . . and I even used to hate the walk home sometimes 'cause you were frightened you'd meet up with some of these idiots. See, you'd sort of have to pick your time and you'd have to be out of there really quickly or you'd hang back and go later so that they'd be all gone. You picked your time. (B2)

Some boys become extremely isolated and fearful and they avoid school altogether. Not surprisingly, several reports of truancy were obtained from gay participants, particularly those who were severely targeted.

THE CLASSROOM

Homophobia is much less prominent in classroom accounts. Nevertheless, classroom structures and interactions with teachers are important. As Margaret Clark says, "gender appears to be a primary category through which teachers make sense of experience and reflect on their pupils," and she adds that structures of discipline and control "have a very strong influence on the shaping of gender" (Clark, 1987: 26 and 28). Mac an Ghaill extends this analysis so that links with homophobia start to emerge: "a number of teachers and the students positioned the 'academic achievers' as 'effeminate'" (Mac an Ghaill, 1994: 61). So although homophobia appears to be more restrained in the classroom, subjects reported overt and covert homophobia by teachers, which has a special significance because of the teachers' status.

Homophobia can silence teachers, and teachers can respond with silence. The result is that there is often no counterbalance to intense school-ground homophobia and there is a chance (sometimes intentional) of tacitly endorsing homophobia. Positive role models are rare for boys who are subject to school-ground homophobia. They do not know which teachers they can confide in and their isolation is intensified. The influence of homophobia over teachers restrains them from addressing issues and isolates them too. As O'Conor notes, "unlike other minority teachers who can serve as role models to minority youth, gay and lesbian teachers nearly always hide," and furthermore, "silence on the part of teachers and administrators also makes schools unsafe" (O'Conor, 1995: 99). The possibility that silence lends tacit approval to homophobia and compromises school safety was also articulated in the present study (e.g., comments by G7 in the previous chapter).

It is a reflection of the power of homophobia that students can use it to undermine and control teachers. X24 has already described how overt homophobia between boys was moderated because his class was always the most senior class in a new school. Despite this, there was still ample opportunity to express homophobia and to witness its impact:

> . . . even though there was no poofter bashing or anything like that at the school, you really could see how taboo it was to "come out" by the way gay teachers would be castigated . . . it's more acceptable amongst lesbians but with males it's . . . there's a taboo about touching . . . for some reason with guys it seems like it's a hell of a lot closer to the bone . . . it's a real touchy issue for a lot of men I think. Very few feel comfortable about it . . . and I think for this gay teacher in the music department that it really undermined . . . his authority . . . and I think he just didn't feel comfortable there at all . . . and left. (X24)

C3 describes another scenario in which a teacher was assaulted:

> We had one teacher that was beat up pretty bad . . . he was a music teacher. They never found out who did that and he had a real bad lisp. . . . He used to just dress like something you see in a gay bar [laughs]. So he was a target. He was a pretty good

target and he got beat up pretty bad one day at school and we
never saw him again. . . . The fourth formers or year ten or
whatever you call it—they beat him up and we never saw him
again, and there was never any questions asked. (C3)

Support for homophobia by teachers can be hidden or overt.
"Homophobic comments are typically unchallenged, and sometimes even perpetrated by teachers" (O'Conor, 1995: 99). Support
can be implied by how teachers approach the most homophobic
groups on the school ground:

So if I got in with the tough gang, even though they had really
low marks, the teachers still liked them, cause they were real
men [laughs]. . . . The main reason why I got into the tough
gang was for protection. And to deny who I was [homosexual
orientation]. So I started to learn all the crap that the brothers
were teaching. (C3)

Participants also gave accounts of frank homophobia by teachers,
which was not confined to male staff. In the following example,
homophobia and criticism for gender transgression are overtly articulated by a female teacher:

. . . but I can think of another, he was pretty much a loner and
he used to like skipping, you know, not with ropes but skipping and he used to skip to school, and one day I remember the
[female] teacher ridiculed him for doing that. (O15)

In contrast, rare occasions when teachers are supportive can be
important for gay students who are otherwise isolated (although
few subjects reported positive experiences). In the following case,
the student was already privately grappling with his homosexuality
and received the only positive portrayal of homosexuality in his
school career:

. . . she was sort of talking about the fact that . . . not all of you
here are going to be straight and . . . some of you are probably
. . . you already know the fact that you're attracted to other
males . . . or something like that. I can't remember word for

word what she said, but it was one of the few times where I really listened to what she said and I just thought "Shit! This really applies to me" [laughs]. And it was something I really thought long and hard about after she said it. I really paid very close attention to what [my] English teacher, who was a lesbian, things that she said. I think because at the time, I really didn't have anyone that I could talk to about it and just getting kernels of information or opinions that they had that I thought sounded okay to me. And that sort of fitted into my experiences. (X24)

Sex education was highly problematic. Rather than addressing the issues of concern for students, some participants reported no formal sex education, while others reported that the usual approach was to nest sex education in biology, sports, or religious studies. The accounts of school sex education portray it as clumsy, biased, and not addressing the needs most pressing for students grappling with difficult issues:

D: . . . Okay. So what sort of sex education did you get at school?
S: Bugger all! We did! No! That wasn't actually being advised [both S and D laugh]. . . . It was an abominable evening . . . the whole of year eight was taught at the same time with one parent there in this huge theater, auditorium.
D: Was homosexuality mentioned?
S: Oh, God no! (R18)

Sometimes sex education was a part of religious instruction:

I can remember year eight there was . . . some sex education, not much though. And it was in a religion class. . . . I mean, I can remember thinking, "This is really ironic; this has really sinister undertones," you know, "We're being taught this in a religion class" . . . and then there's the compulsory reproduction thing in year nine . . . science/biology. There was a bit in PE and health . . . but it wasn't very extensive and it . . . was very hidden. (BB28)

Also, instead of sex education being an opportunity to help students, it can be used as a site for unequivocal homophobia:

> I remember . . . in year eight, having the most appalling attempt at sex education . . . with a pretty awful teacher . . . who at length . . . described how unacceptable and immoral homosexuality was. *At length* . . . and I remember . . . openly challenging him on that . . . and, interestingly enough . . . only being targeted by my schoolmates fairly softly for it. (V22)

> . . . one teacher who'd stand up in front of assembly preaching that you're gonna burn in hell for even thinking queer thoughts. (C3)

The combination of biological accounts of reproduction and religious accounts of "love" against a foreground of intense schoolyard homophobia and misogyny results in a highly biased schooling that compounds the difficulties students face while negotiating adolescence. Mac an Ghaill also notes this problem: "in contrast to the processes of desexualisation found within the official curriculum, sex and sexuality were compulsively and competitively discussed and played out between and within male and female student peer groups" (Mac an Ghaill, 1994: 90). Often the playground is identified as the principal site for sex education. The next quote locates the importance of obtaining information on sex from peers in the schoolyard, but this comes through the filter of peer approval, competition, and bravado:

> . . . if my brother and my cousin were sort of talking about things or trying to impress each other, I'd try and impress them as well . . . you know, it [sex education] all came from the schoolyard. (Z26)

It is not difficult to see how young people reach the end of their school years ill-equipped to protect themselves against unwanted pregnancy and HIV while simultaneously under enormous pressures to be sexually "successful."

HOME

The interviews indicate a general easing of homophobic pressures away from school. Getting away from peers is a relief for boys who are targets of homophobia largely because they can escape the intense school-ground peer-group scrutiny. This accords with Thorne's observation that there are "several basic features of schools that distinguish them from neighbourhoods—their formal age-grading, their crowded and public nature, and the continual presence of power and evaluation—enter into the dynamics of gender separation and integration" (Thorne, 1993: 51). However, depending on the approach of parents, siblings, and neighborhood peers, relief is not guaranteed but, at best, is an improvement relative to the school ground. The dilemma is encapsulated by O'Conor, who finds that "unlike teenagers from other oppressed minority groups, gay teenagers find little or no support or understanding at home for their societal difference. Most often family members are the most difficult to reveal sexual orientation to" (O'Conor, 1995: 98).

There were several accounts of frank homophobia by parents—both mothers and fathers. In the first example, J10 is "shocked" that his mother should exhibit behavior that he believed was confined to school, and his anxiety about his own homosexuality is deepened by his abrupt realization that his mother may harbor similar attitudes against him:

> . . . the time I can remember it being used and being shocked was when my mother said it of [an Australian politician] . . . "Poof." I can remember that . . . it really shocked me that she would use a word which I'd only ever heard being used by boys in the schoolyard. . . . [It] shocked me that . . . she'd use that word . . . 'cause I realized that that was what I was like, and that she might use that same tone with me. (J10)

Descriptions include very graphic examples of homophobia by parents that have a special significance for the child, for example, AA27, who is trying to deal with his emerging homosexuality:

> Mum used to go on about those "Fuckin' arse fuckers who give each other AIDS and give innocent people AIDS." (AA27)

Attitudes such as these contribute to the child concealing his homo-sexuality and fearing disclosure:

> I thought my dad would just have a hernia [if he found out that his son was gay] because he has said to me numerous times that he hates poofters. (Y25)

Homophobia may not be expressed equally by both parents, but all of the family can be homophobic (including siblings, some of whom would eventually be gay), as X24 (now gay) describes:

> . . . my brother went through a very homophobic stage. And I sort of went through a similar thing. It's a bit of a self-denial phase, and Mum and Dad. Not so much my father, my father's very indifferent toward it. But my Mum's very homophobic I find. (X24)

Although, in some cases, brothers and sisters are a source of support and an older sibling protects a vulnerable child, siblings can also function as an intrusion of the peer group into the home and homophobia can be exploited for the purposes of sibling rivalry. Harassment and isolation is exacerbated when siblings bring teasing home—and when sibling confidences are relayed back to the school ground:

> . . . probably the parent's influence wasn't quite so relevant. But, the brothers and sisters that perhaps were older at school, who were bringing it home. Calling them poofters. And they'd run—they in turn would come back to school and call their peers poofters. (T20)

This illustrates another component of "rolling peer pressure."

The school-ground tactics of older peers using homophobia to target younger boys for not observing the standards of "hegemonic boyhood" also arises in the data concerning siblings:

> As I became older, they [older brothers] always thought I was piss weak, I wouldn't grow up to be a bikie or what they were. I was a pansy, poofter, all that sort of thing. There was no issue of me being gay, it was just name-calling. (Q17)

Homophobic targeting by siblings is sometimes as severe as it is at school, and there are a number of reports of violence:

> . . . it was a pretty solid door. It's not solid wood, but it was pretty thick, two slabs of door, whatever. And he [brother] just put his fist through it, and the whole time screaming, "You fuckin faggot," bang! Because I think I kicked him instead of punching him, and that just wasn't on. (AA27)

Descriptions of homophobic violence between siblings included physical assault:

> **D:** Okay. Ever aware of any poofter bashing going on?
> **S:** Only towards [friend's name]. [He] got a fair amount of it. They'd really hassle him and beat him up. Even his own brother beat him up. (DD30)

There is also evidence of sibling homophobia causing the boy being harassed to assaul the homophobic sibling:

> . . . Constantly calling me a faggot, constantly calling me little poofter. . . . Picking on me so I couldn't live with him. I had a really bad temper too, so I chucked these tantrums. Major tantrums that would end up always in a fight and my mother would end up frantic and in tears and stuff because we'd be fighting. And I took to him with a knife one day and she saw and she chucked an absolute spastic and I ended up having to stay over [at] a friend's place because I couldn't come home, because of [brother]. (L12)

Silence and Concealment

Silence can be highly meaningful and ambiguous. Previously, Z26 described punishment for using the word "poofter" at home because it was considered unmentionable. Parents often differ in how they handle homophobia; for example, one parent may be overtly homophobic while the other responds with silence (Cramer and Roach, 1988). This loosely follows a gender pattern, with fathers being notable for holding back. However, being "reserved" can be interpreted as disapproval, as AA27 illustrates:

> From pretty much the beginning of the AIDS epidemic. She [Mum] was like, right through, hate 'em. Faggots were just little poofters and pansies. Dad never said much. He was a bit more reserved. Dad's very reserved. But, he didn't like it really. Somehow you just know it's like, "Don't mention that to Dad. Just no, don't." (AA27)

There were indications that a wish to silence homosexuality conforms to shared cultural images. A common code word used in the interviews when talking about people's reactions to homophobia was to "flaunt" homosexuality. Although "flaunt" is a relatively innocuous word, in this context it is highly loaded and conveys distaste.

Even silence that signifies indifference can be interpreted as homophobia because silence or indifference does nothing to counter the external lore of pervasive homophobia. In the face of silence and apparent "neutrality" school-ground homophobia is definitive. For example, D4 is the subject with the most negative views on homosexuality, based on Herek's "ATLG scale" (see Appendixes; Herek, 1994: 206), yet he denies being exposed to homophobia at home:

> I was living with my grandparents and they didn't get into calling anyone a poofter or things like that. (D4)

Presumably, he learned to be homophobic from peers and this was not challenged at home.

In addition to silent hostility and indifference, there are also numerous examples of a wish to conceal homosexuality. Often this was linked to a fear of being exposed to public scrutiny, much the same as the fear of peer scrutiny learned on the school ground:

> I think they [parents] feel they've gone wrong. My mother didn't handle it at all. Could not cope . . . and I can still remember one of her arguments was what if someone finds out? What if somebody found out and what if you get AIDS? And I said . . . "How are they going to find out unless you tell them?" And I said, "Is that going to be your main problem? You're worried about if I get something, but what's the neighbor going to think?" I said, "Fuck the neighbor." (B2)

Sometimes, knowledge of homosexuality was considered a danger-ous knowledge, that had the power to kill, and this was used to justify censoring it:

> . . . as far as my Dad was concerned, I think . . . it didn't make much difference to him other than he was really worried that his father might find out and have a heart attack. (S19)

Parental Expectations

An important part of the context of growing up with homophobia is the relationship between homophobia and the pressures placed on boys by parental expectations:

> . . . ultimately you want the stamp of approval from your family. You can probably cope with rejection from people you know, in society, but ultimately it is family approval that means the most 'cause they're the people that are closest to you, and to have that sort of rejection would be the ultimate form of humiliation that you could suffer. (I9)

Parental expectations invariably assume that the child is hetero-sexual. Because of this, casual comments can unwittingly take on special significance for boys who find they are gay and put consid-erable pressure on them:

> "We stopped having kids when we had you, because now we had someone to carry on the family name." I heard that defi-nitely a couple of times. And that put a lot of pressure on me and I felt like I really had to be straight and try and have a family and that sort of thing and I didn't really want to have a family myself. It wasn't something I remember wanting to have: children. So I definitely felt from Mum and Dad's point of view that they wanted me to grow up and marry and have kids. So it came from there and it came from the fact that being a poof was a bad thing generally in society. I mean, obviously, through all primary school I picked that up along the way. (CC29)

A prominent theme was the importance of reproducing, of continuing the family line, and of providing grandchildren. Such pressure may ease when a sibling has a child:

> . . . when he [brother] had it [first child], the pressure went off me a lot. . . . 'Cause Mum was desperate for grandchildren. Now she's had three so she's quite happy. But wants more. (J10)

Invariably, heterosexual expectations by parents come at a difficult time for the boy who is silently facing his own homosexuality. Pressures can be enormous, and there is a real risk that the young gay man will marry inappropriately in response to homophobic and heterosexist pressures. Although not always a disaster, the results can be unhappy:

> **S:** I tried to avoid the issue [of being gay] as not being a possibility, although I knew I had sex with boys and that I had quite enjoyed that, but it just wasn't a possibility because of my life circumstances, because of my family, because of the expectations. At that stage . . . the expectations were being instilled into my life, about what my family expected of me.
> **D:** Like what?
> **S:** To get married. To settle, to join the family business, and to do well, and to succeed and all that sort of stuff. (N14)

After starting to come to terms with a homosexual orientation, the most difficult decision for young gay men and women is to reveal to parents "they will not be fulfilling the heterosexual dreams" that parents hold for them (Savin-Williams, 1989).

Estrangement

Homophobia distances and estranges family members and disrupts family life in a variety of ways. Subjects describe becoming aware of events that interfere with family interactions as early as the age of eight. The subjects retrospectively interpreted these events as having a homophobic basis. For example, some young men recounted how they became aware of increasing distance from their father as they got older. This was retrospectively "read" as the father being unwittingly influenced by homophobic societal expectations:

> Mum would always kiss us goodnight, but Dad started to—I
> can't remember when he stopped, probably about [the] end of
> primary school, but whenever he did, it was always a really
> reluctant sort of peck. It was not really anything he felt com-
> fortable doing, whereas Mum would say, "Well, give us a kiss
> goodnight then," and often we'd demand it. You know, if we
> went or were sent to bed we'd say, "Oh, you will come down
> and give us a kiss goodnight won't you, and Dad too?" . . . Dad
> would sort of like quickly whip in, it would be peck "Good-
> night," and out again. So there was definitely less open affec-
> tion. I'm not saying that he didn't love us, but again, he prob-
> ably just felt uncomfortable. A man kissing small boys or
> something. (I9)

Notably, the distance is not primarily from "little boys," for whom
affection is demonstrated easily, but arises in later childhood closer
to sexual maturity, at which time intimacy ceases to feel appropriate. A similar implication is being made in the following description
by P16:

> . . . he adored his kids. He was very tactile at that stage, when
> we were kids. And I've seen it since in my brother, at similar
> ages he would be quite affectionate, but that came to a definite
> halt, you know, like prompted a certain age. . . . Oh, it would
> have been seven or eight or so. He was quite affectionate up
> until then. (P16)

In addition to reaching a point at which they feel that affection
for their children needs to be curtailed, fathers can also distance
themselves from sons who don't pursue conventional boys' interests or when their interests are unconventional:

> I don't think he . . . accepted me completely because I didn't
> know how to kick a football. . . . He enjoyed teaching me that
> and I don't know if I tried hard enough or whatever but . . . I
> couldn't do it. I didn't like doing it. (R18)

Furthermore, the child in the process of discovering his homosexuality finds himself estranged from family members even when (or because) they are unaware of the difficulties he is facing. Initially, this involves all family members and is usually accompanied by a fear of discovery and disclosure. Later, if they are accepting, he can become closer to some members after he selectively discloses to them.

The dilemma for the child and for family life is that homophobia can have adverse effects no matter whether the child discloses his homosexuality ("comes out") or not (Cramer and Roach, 1988). Coming out to the family may alter the type of distance rather than eliminate it. Prior to coming out, alienation is due to concealment and the family not really knowing their son; afterward, family members may be unable to get close to a child who is homosexual. A young gay man who has not yet revealed his sexuality to his parents articulates this dilemma. In this case, distance is already present because he expects his parents to react unfavorably:

> I just can't really tell her [Mum] that, and I can't really have a frank discussion with her about what's going on. Mind you, even if I told her, I'm not really sure that she'd feel comfortable about it because it would probably make her feel uncomfortable, and you still wouldn't be able to talk about it. (X24)

In the following examples, the dilemma becomes reality for P16. We have seen (earlier) that P16's father became more distant as P16 got older, as a subtle effect of homophobia. After P16 revealed his homosexuality to his father, their relationship continued to be unsatisfactory for different reasons:

> . . . if pushed, he'll still do it now, he'll give you a hug, although that's become problematic in the last five or six years. He certainly has that capacity, but he has certain cultural and social barriers that get in his way. . . . I think that our relationship has changed a lot since I came out to him as a gay man. . . . I was about twenty or twenty-one. About five years ago. And our relationship has changed completely. (P16)

The change P16 is referring to is an increase in distance between his father and himself. Here P16 describes his relationship with his father after he revealed his homosexuality:

> . . . one of the rationales of me coming out to my father especially wa, my relationship is very superficial, how could it get any worse? Reality of it is, it's still just as superficial. He knows something, but he chooses to ignore . . . so it's very superficial still. It was beforehand. (P16)

In extreme cases, homophobia can disrupt a family and the child can be rejected and become homeless (see Chapter 4; Savin-Williams, 1994; Martin, 1982).

Attempts at Control

Although estrangement from the family is one possibility for the boy who is different, sometimes family members react to become more controlling. What constitutes "difference" in the eyes of parents generally conforms to the catalog of unacceptable difference documented for peers (see Chapter 2). This is not too surprising because presumably they also experienced some form of rolling peer pressure when they were in school. In the first example, O15 describes how both of his parents disapproved when he played around with a bra and some oranges:

> **S:** I happened, one day, to see a bra and, you know, like you watch Benny Hill or . . . Dick Emery shove oranges down a bra. I must have been about ten when I did it, and I was in a lot of trouble for doing that sort of thing.
> **D:** From whom?
> **S:** My parents. (O15)

The next example shows the subtleties of masculine behavior and how significant they can be for parent-child relationships:

> **S:**. . . in the senior year I was putting on sun cream, I think it was sun cream on my face, and he [father] got violently angry and took it from my hand and threw it in the corner and it was

because instead of squirting it on and squirting it onto my hand, and I was putting it on like that. [demonstrates].
D: Dabbing it on?
S: Yeah . . . so he got furious about that . . . which I interpret as being a girlie, effeminate way of putting sun cream on. (J10)

J10 felt that this apparently minor transgression could be explained more easily if it were seen as the culmination of a series of transgressions. There are similarities between this episode and the role that social credit plays on the school ground:

> . . . first of all, the dislike of playing football, secondly, I wasn't, I was more I guess introspective and read a lot, and I think also I had very strong friendships with one or two other boys rather than just generally liked everyone . . . also I was really friendly with girls. And I had lots of girlfriends. (J10)

Whereas men's reactions were more often described as "reserved" and they were often prompted to react in a decisive manner only after a series of transgressions, women often take an active role in controlling unacceptable difference in boys. In the final example, L12's mother sees it as her role to attempt to control the "transgressive" behaviors of the boys in the family:

> . . . I always remember my mother also saying "Don't do that!" and it was the way I walked or the way I acted or something, and she does the same thing with my nephew; he's really camp and he's about ten. He's a lot camper than I ever was at that age, 'cause I was always quite frightened. And he's got a different type of personality. . . . He's a dancer and he doesn't want to play football and stuff, and he's going to be a professional dancer and all these sort of things. (N14)

Family Support

Not all family reactions are negative:

> . . . in year seven . . . I recall watching the parade, something on television about homosexuality and gays. And I recall hav-

ing a very open and honest discussion with my parents about homosexuality, about what caused it, or what were these, what or how could they be interested. . . . (K11)

Even in an "open and honest discussion," implicit negative bias can be identified. His positioning of homosexuals as "they," his concern about "cause," and his puzzlement about how they could "be interested" all reveal his position as heterosexual and in opposition to homosexuality, which is alien and, unlike heterosexuality, has a cause.

Some boys who were subjected to heavy homophobic teasing were also able to get comfort from parents. O15 describes how finding Mum at home was a relief after a difficult school day:

. . . it wasn't fun, because I know I used to come home and be quite upset and often, sometimes, I would be in tears. I don't know if it was often or sometimes, although less as I got older, and my father's response was just, "Why you just hit them." Intelligent! And my mother . . . she was good about it. I always liked the fact that she was home when I got home, so I could talk to her. But she was more a listener without offering any advice which was probably as good. It was nice to come home and have her there, but . . . I dunno. It was really dreary. (O15)

His mother's presence is comforting even though he doesn't recall her saying very much. This makes sense considering she is unaware of O15's sexual orientation (he is gay). The special significance that the teasing had for O15 and his accompanying anxieties about being homosexual could not be raised. In the face of extreme teasing, homophobia can limit people's ability to seek support and others' ability to give it.

In contrast, his parents discovered CC29's homosexuality, and they made a genuine attempt to be supportive and to help him adjust. However, this gesture of support by his parents was only recognized by CC29 in retrospect because at the time he was not comfortable with his sexuality, nor was he in a position to entertain the possibility that his parents might be supportive:

. . . there was an incident where Mum and Dad found out about me having sex at a beat [place where men meet for sex] and they wanted to talk about it and they said, "We want to sort this out." . . . They were very understanding, more understanding than I realized, in fact, now that I look back on it; they were actually hinting that, trying to get me to say I wasn't, you know, I wanted to be that way, and I was comfortable with it. And they didn't put those words in my mouth, and I probably wasn't comfortable with it at that stage. So I said "I'd like to do something about it, and I'd like to be straight. I'd like to try and sort out why I've made this terrible mistake." And they said, "OK, go along and see the psychologist." (CC29)

Whether parents know of their son's sexuality or not, in most cases, their support is quite limited. This dilemma is outlined by P16, who earlier related how his relationship with his father was superficial before he revealed his sexual identity and how it didn't improve after. This time he is speaking about his mother. She, too, has difficulty offering support and P16 believes this is partly because of her religious beliefs:

I get the impression she's trying to remain on a high moral ground. I'm sure she doesn't like it [his homosexuality] and I'm sure she thinks to herself that if she . . . gives a bit and sort of accepts it, then that's gonna demote her in the eyes of what she believes. And she withholds . . . in the four years since I've told her, she has not once said, you know, "How are you?" "How you going?" . . . Only at a very superficial level. She doesn't want to know about when a two-year relationship broke up . . . she said to me, "There's something wrong. You've broken up with [name]?" And I said, "Yeah?" and she said, "What are you gonna do about the house." That's all she said. (P16)

This example also illustrates how relationships between men are not acknowledged to be as legitimate as heterosexual relationships and so parental support is not forthcoming if they end.

Cases were also identified in which families failed to provide support and participants sought alternative family arrangements (Martin, 1982). In one instance, AA27 was given the choice of not being gay or leaving home. As a result, at the beginning of his

Higher School Certificate year (year twelve), he found himself homeless. He was subsequently "adopted" by a philanthropic gay couple whom he had never met before. They gave him sufficient support to complete his studies successfully. In another case, DD30 describes how he had to leave the care of one (homophobic) sister because of her homophobia and live with a (lesbian) sister:

> I couldn't be out of there fast enough. So when I moved in with [lesbian sister] I got a lot of support from her, and she talked to me about stuff . . . and it was really good because she was a dyke; she was in an openly gay relationship and it was great . . . whatever I did was fine. She got me videos, she got me stuff, she talked me through stuff, you know, and everything was cool. And she was my savior. I moved in with her when I was thirteen. . . . It was perfect. It was perfect timing because I really had to get out of . . . [homophobic sister's] way. 'Cause she was just driving me up the wall. But see, once Dad was out of the picture, I didn't have that support anymore so I needed some other support. (DD30)

DD30 ended up in the care of other members of his family when his father was sentenced to prison for pedophilic offenses. Significantly, DD30 found the homophobia of his sister much more intolerable than his father's sexual assaults on him (from whom he found some security against the homophobia he was experiencing at school and from his sister)!

THE MEDIA

The media, particularly television, play an important role in providing information and images concerning homosexuality and homophobia. The media reinforce taboos and provide role models, often simultaneously. Role models are almost universally heterosexual stereotypes, and this contributes to the pressures on adolescents to conceal their differences:

> . . . I suppose I was interested in having sex with them [girls], but it's more of a case that I used to. . . see on TV . . . beautiful

women, and some of the more popular guys at school at that stage had girlfriends as well. And I'd think, "Oh, I want to be like them," and I'd want a girlfriend. . . TV shows always showed males and females together. (M13)

Subjects described growing up with few role models for boys who felt they were different:

. . . television is always boy/girl. Boy meets girl and all this sort of shit and so forth. All the love stories of boy meets girl and all these sorts of things. That's what's accepted as normal and it's boy/boy or girl/girl that [is] classed as the unnatural and not normal situation. (B2)

There is evidence that peer groups are more influential than the media are. Subject Z26 grew up in a conservative family without television or radio and he was strictly prohibited from watching television or movies elsewhere. Yet his account reveals exposure to homophobia at a very early age through brothers, sisters, and peers, and he reported experiences of homophobia similar to those of other participants.

The media and significant others can interact in complicated ways, and the outcome of issues raised by television often depends on how the subjects are handled in the home or by peers:

I remember staying at a great Auntie's house. It must have been primary school. And they had . . . Don Dunstan [the South Australian Premier responsible for Australia's first homosexual law reforms] on the TV, talking about homosexuals, and I just asked her, "What's a homosexual?" And she just lost it! "You don't ever want to know, blah, blah, blah." She never explained to me what it was. But I think it was the first time I remember even registering the word, or asking a question about it. (P16)

And I remember seeing a show once where they were talking about relationships and there were various married relationships and things like that. And what they did, which was really interesting, they had two gay men, who'd been together for a very long time . . . and my Mum was horrified by this. (X24)

Although show business is stereotyped as a safe industry for homosexuals, more often than not, television reinforces stereotypes that are prevalent on the school ground. DD30 contrasts the stereotypes available on television with the diversity of gay life as he now knows it.

> . . . there was a lot of effeminate men on TV. And they [the media] really played on that, basically. But [in real life] there were a lot of men that weren't effeminate and they were gay, right? (DD30)

However, because they were often stereotypical, many images presented in the media were difficult for young people to relate to:

> . . . my basic experience [was] of watching television and seeing gay guys in leather outfits with mustaches or wimpy queens wearing women's clothing. . . . I wasn't into women's clothing. (Q17)

Despite these reservations, many young men describe an affinity with homosexual portrayals in the media, and it is common for young gay men to take notice of even the briefest references, to seek out and record programs, to save articles, and to use the information to comprehend their own identity and to relieve their sense of isolation:

> You just sort of "thought-identified" with what's going on here. And it was so strong . . . you had to read it . . . if there was something on TV about it or whatever, you know, I'd tape it. Or if it was the Gay Mardi Gras, I'd tape it. . . . (X24)

Early exposures to homosexual themes in the media have special importance, and details of portrayals from twenty or more years ago retain their significance:

> **S:** Poofters are two men that have sex together. [I] still didn't really understand in earlier stages what that "sex" was. In the teenage years . . . television also helps to play a little bit of

role, in that, back then, you'd get the occasional little skerrick*
of homosexuality through television. You know, like *Number
Ninety Six* [television soapie] [laughs].
D: So, did you remember that particularly?
S: Dudley Butterfield and Don Finlayson [gay characters].
D: Did you take particular interest in them?
S: Yeah. I did. (B2)

The isolation that young gay men experience as they deal with
their emerging identity is usually extreme, and for many young gay
men, exposure to homosexual images in the media is profoundly
significant and ultimately leads to their "liberation":

> . . . So I went up there and I turned on the TV and there was a
> gay movie on SBS. And I thought . . . I was totally, totally
> taken, swept away by this movie, and I thought, "That's it
> [P16]. You've got to do something about it. This is you. You
> don't fit in. If you fit in anywhere right, it'd be here." Saw the
> two men dancing together and I thought, "Why can I relate to
> that so closely?" And anyway, not long after that I was listen-
> ing to "Triple J" [radio station], and . . . they [had a] gay youth
> worker on, and they were talking about it. And they gave a
> number out to call. And so . . . I rang the number but [laughs]
> up until, that year . . . I was trying to find a node that I could
> latch on to. I'd do things like secretly go to a gay photo
> exhibition. I'd make sure that no one knew where I was going.
> So I'd wander down there, or as a group, if we were all out on
> Saturday night we'd walk past [name of bar] or something. I'd
> think "Oh. There's a gay bar" . . . I'd staked it out. I was doing
> my homework at this stage. I was constructing a new base
> from which to take off. (P16)

CONCLUSIONS

Processes whereby young people become homophobic are focused in peer-group networks and in school-ground culture. In addi-

---

*Skerrick is a colloquialism for a hint or a small fragment or scrap.

tion, this chapter illustrates how those events take place in a context of wider social arrangements that reinforce homophobia. Finding homophobic events outside peer structures is a reminder of the special importance of peer-based dynamics in enforcing and propagating homophobia: school has a sustained influence and everyone has been there. With notable exceptions, the presence of teachers generally has a moderating influence on school-ground homophobia and the most intense events occur at places remote from adult authority. This is consistent with other studies that have identified bullying in schools as "essentially a secret activity" that takes place out of the view of adults (Mooney, Creeser, and Blatchford, 1991; Olweus, 1993), and teachers have been found to underestimate the amount of bullying in schools (Rigby and Slee, 1991). The background homophobia against which development occurs and the way that school life is structured provide an arena for the enforcement and perpetuation of homophobia by peer culture.

This chapter confirms findings from other studies on intergender segregation, and it extends the analysis to intragender segregation between "hegemonic peer culture" and "poofters." The coherence of findings reported here with those from other studies suggests that the events described in this thesis are not confined to the sample being studied and that these processes are found in other settings around the world.

Antihomosexual bias is expressed in four basic modes: explicit homophobia, implicit homophobia, silence, and heterosexist expectations. Explicit homophobia is articulated unambiguously. Implicit homophobia occurs when other components of the "homophobia complex" are exploited such as "sissy," "crybaby," "wuss," "soft," and so on, and antihomosexual connotations are not articulated, but the associations are generally understood. Silence extends from indifference through to signifying that homosexuality is so bad that it is unmentionable. However, silence is never truly neutral because it fails to counterbalance the potent, prevalent homophobia in peer culture and leaves vulnerable boys to fend for themselves (often in the face of considerable hostility). Heterosexist expectations of children are pervasive, and there is little opportunity to consider alternatives, which appear subordinate and illegitimate in comparison.

In the home, a boy's growing sense of "difference" and the homophobia that gravitates to a "different" boy can lead to estrangement from family members and to attempts at controlling a child's "difference." There is evidence that estrangement from a "different" child and attempts to control him have a gendered dimension. Homophobia is a powerful regulator of distance between males, which interferes with a father's affection for a son, particularly one who shows signs of being a "poofter." Homophobia does not regulate distance between males and females in the same way, and mothers can be prompted to "correct" a son's "transgressive" behaviors in an attempt to conceal his difference or to rescue him from a difficult situation. These observations raise an important question: is there some substance to earlier claims by psychiatrists (Biber, 1962) that homosexual sons have "absent fathers" and "controlling mothers"? The present research offers a new interpretation for these findings. Instead of absent fathers and controlling mothers being responsible for causing homosexuality, this research suggests that by marginalizing a child, estranging a father and prompting a mother to attempt to control a child's differences, homophobia generates the distant father/controlling mother pattern.

Perhaps the normalization of homophobia has concealed this alternative explanation and made the distant father/close mother theory more attractive to a biased society because it offers a "pathological cause" for homosexuality; that is, parents are to blame. As Ronald Bayer writes in *Homosexuality and American Psychiatry*, when discussing the influence of sexuality research on psychiatry, "newly found facts did little to frame the understanding of homosexuality; rather, it was the perspective on homosexuality that determined the meaning on those facts" (Bayer, 1987: 21). This work describes how homophobia is a pervasive perspective through which homosexuality is conceptualized and constituted. If adults are to "blame" for anything, it is for not being more understanding of childhood difference, for not challenging a context in which homophobia can flourish and be perpetuated, for not providing sufficient protection for children who are victimized, and for not stating explicitly that homophobia is destructive and bad.

Chapter 4

Fashioning the Male "Self"

Homophobia exerts heavy pressures on men and shapes their behavior. These pressures affect how men interact with others: their relationships, how close they get, how demonstrative they are, and with whom they have sex. Homophobia also affects a man's concept of himself, the masculine image he seeks to project, and what aspects of "self" he conceals. The impact of homophobia on males varies with age and sexual identity. Prior to adulthood, the "poofter" is principally an important mythical construct (a virtual poofter) that is used as a yardstick for what boys shouldn't do or be. During this time, homophobia exerts its influence on behaviors and appearances and any boy is a potential target. Later, sexual maturity heralds the formation of adult sexual identities, and when this happens, homophobic constructs become embodied in homosexuals. In adulthood, individual men can be targeted by virtue of their sexual identity as well as because of certain surrogate characteristics, while others are preoccupied with homophobic labeling and with avoiding homosexual associations. This chapter focuses on the influence of homophobia on "self" and how males fashion their behaviors and their selves in response.

HOMOPHOBIA PRIOR TO ADULT SEXUAL IDENTITY: PRESSURES THAT SHAPE BOYS' BEHAVIOR

Prior to consolidating adult sexual identity, homophobic rhetoric is used frequently and with meaning, even when there is little or no concept of what a homosexual is and a definitive target in the peer group is lacking. Although the negative connotations are constant, homophobic meanings continually shift and are frequently non-sexual. It is these shifting meanings that mark out the "other" and designate targets, and in preadult times, sexual identity shifts, too, as it progressively forms. Prior to adulthood, instead of targeting rigid sexual identities, homophobia targets unpopular traits (behaviors and appearances), particularly those which transgress male peer-group expectations. Furthermore, because these characteristics are not welded to individuals with stable identities (all boys express these behaviors at certain stages), any boy is a potential target.

This section documents a series of transitions in which behaviors cease to be acceptable and stop being expressed. Although these transitions are diverse, they share important characteristics. Change coincides with realizing that certain behaviors are no longer acceptable, and peer pressure appears to be highly influential in most of these shifts. While the transitions are seen as normal parts of growing up, the forces that contribute to suppressing behaviors and bringing transitions about, and the penalties for not completing a transition, illustrate a dimension that is relevant to this project: boys who resist transitions, or who transgress later, attract homophobia.

Boys Don't Cry

Crying is one of the first identifiable behavioral transitions that can be isolated and analyzed. Crying is of special importance because patterns of crying unequivocally change as boys grow; we have already seen in Chapter 2, attitudes to persistent crying are linked to homophobia. Notably, boys don't lose the ability to cry as they grow older; rather, they radically modify where and when crying occurs.

Most subjects were able to identify a period when their patterns of crying changed. For W23, crying is not what boys do; it is not in accord with social expectations:

> . . . when you're about seven and eight, you start to get a real perception that . . . girls cry and boys aren't meant to cry. That's not a boy's thing to do: cry. (W23)

In the next account, BB28 identifies a transition in crying behavior and links it to reaching a stage at which he would deliberately try to control his crying:

> . . . you'd fall over and hurt yourself and that would be allright to cry . . . up until there was a point where you didn't, you tried as hard as you could not to [cry] . . . when would that have been? . . . Probably when we went from the transition from infants . . . to primary . . . up to . . . third grade. That was probably . . . when it changed markedly. (BB28)

U21 describes how he feels he learned that crying had become unacceptable:

> . . . firstly, you get to see other kids crying more I think, and . . . you work out that from someone else's perspective it's sort of, not an attractive or good thing to do. And you also see other kids' responses to what you're doing and what they're doing and you just work it out, that it's not the done thing. (U21)

U21 uses the same framework in his explanation for learning about homophobia: observation, deduction, and by experiencing homophobic responses directly.

The underlying rationale for modifying patterns of crying is because it is not "tough," that it is unmasculine and therefore unacceptable for growing boys to continue:

> . . . you had to be a male, had to be . . . tough. Yeah, all of that butch stuff. You know, boys just didn't cry. (DD30)

The pressures to resist crying were described in powerful terms and as an important means of differentiating strong boys from the weak:

> I didn't really cry a great deal at all . . . in my mind it was very strong [the pressure not to cry]. And if I ever saw anyone break down and cry, I just saw that as being a real sign of weakness. That someone would, you know, just do that in front of others. (X24)

Crying also differentiates boys from girls. The previous example and the following example indicate that peer scrutiny is an important source of pressure to resist crying:

> I don't think it's the same for boys and girls, because girls through school, and even still, seem to show their emotions a lot more than the boys. Where to me it must have been another "male thing," that you didn't cry. If you did you had to try and hold it in. . . . I mean if you got punched in the mouth there was nothing worse than to cry. As much as it might have been hurting like hell, it was just not accepted to cry in front of other boys. (Z26)

The open-ended statement that "boys don't do that" creates dilemmas for boys. One response might be: If I am a boy and I cry, then the statement is wrong and the authority of the statement is suspect. Alternatively, if the truth of the statement is accepted, then the statement invites different responses: If boys don't cry, then who (or what) does? If I am crying, then who (or what) am I? It is in some of the implicit answers to these questions that we can locate the sanctions against crying, the power behind pressures not to cry, and associations with homophobia. The link (as the questions suggest) is with otherness. In the next example, otherness to being a boy is being a baby:

> . . . if you are a boy and you cry in the playground, other boys will call you a crybaby. You don't want to be humiliated, so you realize that this is not an acceptable thing to do. (I9)

While this finding seems to repeat what was already found in Chapter 2, the additional point here is that these dynamics do influence behavior.

In the next example, crying is linked to being a "sissy":

> My father always said that to me. . . . "Stop being such a sissy." And my brother [name] always said stop being such a bloody sissy. Yeah, crying was a big thing. . . . I think it was about third class that I actually stopped crying. I basically cried a lot if I got hurt or anything, but by the time I was in

about third class. . . . I don't think it was because . . . people were telling me it was bad. I think it was a lot . . . of like appearancewise . . . if somebody was giving me a real hard time I'd stand very defiant and say, "Well no. You're not going to get a tear out of me, you know" . . . and even if I did falter and I would cry, I'd feel really guilty about it. I'd feel really full-on guilty about it. (DD30)

And while the previous examples start to unearth the links between crying and being unmasculine, the next example consolidates the association with homophobia:

. . . if it was just because you were teasing someone, and they burst into tears, that sort of . . . points out the fact that you know they're wimps or poofters. (Y25)

Crying links into homophobic dynamics through the identification of male crying with otherness, and boys' crying patterns undergo a transition in early primary school that has demonstrable links with homophobic peer-based scrutiny. Further, although crying is inhibited in the presence of peers, boys retain the capacity to cry in situations that are quarantined from peer scrutiny. When asked if he remembered crying much during early school years, K11 replied that he cried "privately" and that it started to become a solitary practice:

. . . when I started going to school, boys weren't meant to cry. (K11)

In another instance, the usual peer-based sanctions against crying are lifted and members have given themselves special dispensation to cry. This example comes from the end of secondary schooling when homophobic pressures are starting to ease and the peer group is about to fragment:

. . . all the really butch guys who were the ones who . . . for all those years had picked on and hassled and chastised, all these guys in the school [the "poofs"], ended up huddled together in the middle of this dance floor, left the girlfriends, left all the women behind, they were crying because they all knew that they won't be seeing each other again. (N14)

The final example provides insight into the extent to which sanctions against crying might be internalized and how these can be lifted only when conscious control is surrendered:

> **S:** I don't cry now.
> **D:** What happened to that?
> **S:** I don't know. I'd like to be able to cry. I haven't been able to cry for a very long time.
> **D:** When was the last time?
> **S:** A few years, probably five years ago. No, maybe three years ago in a dream, but it wasn't. It was a dream that made me cry. (R18)

Dress Codes

The practices governing the appearance of boys and young men are complex and highly codified. Similar pressures to those which apply to crying can be discerned for boys' dress codes, and homophobic dynamics can be identified as playing a crucial role in shaping dress conventions and influencing behavior. This similarity is not surprising given that the governance of crying largely appears concerned with socially acceptable appearances and the presentation of "self" to peers.

It is possible to map how an undifferentiated "polymorphous" interest in color and form becomes increasingly constrained, particularly by peer-enforced dress standards. After a time, a previously undifferentiated interest in colorful and interesting clothing is reinterpreted as transgression. However, transgression really only becomes possible after boundaries have been internalized, prior to which the same practices are better thought of as uninhibited. This retrospective attribution of significance should be borne in mind when interpreting the data.

An undifferentiated or uninhibited approach to clothing is evident in (heterosexual) U21's response to his discovery of his mother's wardrobe when he was a child:

> . . . the colors and the different materials. . . . Just things that I hadn't seen before. It's like . . . discovering a new toy box. (U21)

In the next example, H8 (also heterosexual) recalls his childhood play with adult clothing. Notice how he clarifies and differentiates his ungendered interest in clothing from a "transgressive" interest in cross-dressing:

> . . . probably earlier, playing dress ups and sort of, stomping around in Mum's high heels. . . . That wasn't necessarily dressing up as a woman. It was a case of, here's a bundle of clothes to play with and some of them were clothes that Mum wears and some were clothes that Dad wears. (H8)

Instead of signifying transgression and being cross-gendered, clothing can have other significance for children: colorful, interesting, fun, "grown up," and stupid:

> Nan's furs and things . . . that was fun because my cousins and I were being grown-ups. We were . . . being stupid as well. (T20)

Some dress codes were entirely orchestrated by adults and occurred prior to the conscious memory of the participant:

> . . . in those days, the babies used to wear dresses and stuff anyway, male or female. Which I can't remember. . . . But, ever since I can remember, we were dressed very boyish. (Z26)

It was possible for subjects to remember and locate the approximate timing of transitions in dress behaviors. Often these were confined to significant items of clothing and appearance (such as hairstyles, shoes, cosmetic products, colors, and fabrics) rather than complete outfits:

> . . . I walked around in high heels for a while, but I never got into a dress . . . that probably stopped around . . . probably four or five. (BB28)

As boys got older, they became increasingly aware of the significance of appearance for gender. At times, this was tinged with a sense of being restricted and resenting the restraints that gender was placing on them:

> I knew in preschool about their [girls'] interests and ribbons and girls' clothes and . . . preening and all these trinkets and stuff. And guys never did that; I suppose that was something I noticed, that they [boys] looked boring to me. As in clothes, dresswise . . . they were just plain, they just seemed boring. (L12)

Although boys may initially resent the sacrifices of growing up, the pressure to conform to codes of appearance is unrelenting. In the following extract, T20 acknowledges the common and uninhibited nature of childhood dress ups as well as the inevitability of having to stop:

> . . . from mixing with other boys . . . to find out you know they weren't dressing up anymore. Like everyone's done it I think . . . everyone had . . . raided Mum's wardrobe every now and again and played silly buggers with it. But then there comes a time when you just stop doing that. (T20)

T20 also gives an indication as to whyboys must be more restrained in their use of clothing when he uses the term "drag"—a view from the other side of the transition when transgression is meaningful:

> Nine- or ten-year-olds just aren't running around in "drag" [both chuckle] at that age are they? . . . It's just not the done thing. And probably the parents are sort of thinking, you know, this is not the norm. (T20)

The significance attached to transgression is nicely illustrated in the following extract, in which the father is described as "horrified" and the subject reports embarrassment:

> S: . . . I remember my grandmother telling me that I used to get into the makeup and stuff like that. My father was horrified at that, but I don't remember. . . . But I sort of look at that in an innocent sort of way. I don't think there was anything terribly serious, but . . . I think they bring things up like that more to embarrass you than anything else.

D: But does it embarrass you?
S: Yeah, it does. (X24)

Although it has been demonstrated that undifferentiated dress practices become increasingly codified and restricted as boys grow older, it remains to link these processes with homophobia. In the next quote, M13 associates transgression with being a "nancy" or a "girl":

> I can't remember other boys wearing dresses . . . and if someone did . . . I'm pretty sure that they would have got the "nancy" tag or the "you're a girl" tag. (M13)

Z26 ties the loose ends together when he links "difference" with being targeted, transgressing dress codes, and being a "poof."

> . . . anybody that's slightly different from everybody else immediately cops criticism. Which is why we would have treated our cousin like that. You know, because he liked to come out in his Mum's dress or shoes or whatever. Straightaway we'd call him a poof, without even knowing what a poof was. [chuckle] (Z26)

The previous extract refers to a young age (early primary school) and being a "poof" is associated with male difference, but not yet with being homosexual. Finally, N14 gives this response when asked how he became worried about the clothes he would wear to school:

> . . . because the pressures about being a "poofter" at school, which was very big at our school, because there were some quite effeminate boys at our school . . . who were often hassled. (N14)

Gender Play

It is well accepted that toys differ along gender lines; this section will focus on how this differentiation is governed and the role homophobic dynamics play in it. The reason that T20 gives for adhering to gender rules once again attributes responsibility to the influence of adverse (peer) scrutiny:

> Girls would bring in dolls [to school]. Boys would bring remote control cars . . . it would seem very strange for a boy to bring in a Barbie. And a girl wouldn't bring in a truck. . . . Because no one else would. And you don't want to stand out. And particularly because I was very shy, I wouldn't have done that. (T20)

Similarly, BB28 identifies the fear of being humiliated as the reason why he avoided transgressing during play:

> . . . if you went to play with the girls' toys then . . . there was that feeling that you were very scared of humiliation. (BB28)

But do BB28's fears reflect genuine concern or does his explanation gloss over an inherent indifference to, or rejection of, girls' things? BB28 (who is heterosexual) clarifies this when he describes a genuine interest that he felt obliged to curtail:

> . . . in kindergarten at school there was . . . a doll house and the dolls in the corner of the kindergarten. And I can remember being really curious about it . . . and wanting to go over and see what it was all about, 'cause . . . there was the little stove with the pots and everything as well. And . . . they looked like they were having fun. But then I didn't go over because . . . I just didn't go over. Maybe because I was aware that I shouldn't go over and . . . that was one of the first times that I can remember where I'd sort of made that decision not to, even though I wanted to. (BB28)

DD30 provides a clear description of how he modified his behavior after he learned the disapproval boys attract if their play transgresses gender standards. Here again, there is a pattern of undifferentiated interest, followed by learning about transgression, followed by changed practices:

> I used to play with dolls. I used to go up to my grandmother's and all of the girls, they'd be playing with dolls and I used to

like playing with dolls . . . one stage I had to do it secretly because if any of the aunties or uncles had cottoned onto what I was doing, then I'd get a really hard time about it. (DD30)

The final account in this section develops the theme fully by graphically illustrating the links between transgressive play and homophobia, and how a dramatic and highly symbolic gesture is used to resolve the conflict:

> . . . it all started when I was younger. . . . I had a handmade doll that I'd made myself that I kept . . . right up until year seven . . . . See it all sort of happened in a big bunch, and that's when I burned it. I just felt I didn't want it anymore, so I burned it . . . it was like this puppet doll thing. And he [brother] was constantly calling me "faggot" and "girl." (L12)

Impact on Schooling

Gender standards are internalized at an early age and are very important at school. The following example provides an elegant demonstration of an early, acute, and enduring memory of when these standards were transgressed:

> . . . this stands out because I was really really embarrassed about it. But my earliest memories from kindergarten . . . I might have just turned five or I was still four. . . . We had . . . a thing called a "sentence maker." . . . And I wrote "Am I a girl?" question mark, "Yes," and full stop . . . after that, every time I went back to give them my book to write another sentence in, I'd want to make sure that they didn't see it . . . 'cause I was really embarrassed about this sentence that I'd written . . . . I did my best to keep that away from people. I really did . . . . All I can remember about it is my intense embarrassment about writing *that* sentence. (BB28)

It is important for boys not to be too different from their peers, and getting good marks at school can be risky. In Chapter 2, it was shown that being academically inclined was sufficient to invite homophobic criticism. The types of subjects and the way that boys approach them are also influenced by homophobia. How boys position themselves with respect to schoolwork, how they present themselves in that context, and ultimately how they fashion their lives and careers are comprehensively affected. The following example illustrates how boys feel pressured to respond in stylized ways (in this case with indifference) in classroom settings:

> . . . there was no room to be sensitive . . . you weren't allowed to like . . . things that sissies or girls would like . . . you weren't allowed to show your feelings about anything . . . you weren't allowed to give sensible answers or anything. . . . If one of the teachers said to you, "What do you think of a black person not being allowed to vote or something like that?" If you said, "Oh, it made you angry," you would be laughed at. If you gave a serious answer to that, you'd be laughed out of your seat. . . . If you said something sort of nonchalant as though you didn't care, either way . . . then that would be acceptable. . . Being an individual was not the way to go. (R18)

The effect of homophobic dynamics can best be demonstrated in accounts of how boys approached subjects that were viewed as artistic. In the following quote, the choice of subject is suspect and the way it is approached is fashioned in response:

> **S:** If you were a drama type you might have got hassled a bit.
> **D:** So you had drama classes, and if boys did drama, that was not a status thing?
> **S:** Oh, no, you could do it. It was quite fun to do, I never did a drama class, but . . . you couldn't get too feminine about it, I don't think. (M13)

Being interested in dancing also attracts homophobia because it involves getting close to girls at an age when this is not accepted among peers. The effect is that young boys develop an aversion to dancing (which is reversed later). T20 describes how his interest in aerobics at secondary school was associated with dancing and this was linked to homophobia:

> There was a teacher at our school, actually, who was a dance teacher, and he was a "poofter," . . . he was . . . a "known

poofter." And he used to . . . cop all sorts of shit for, being a dance teacher . . . that's when it really stuck; I was sort of branded a poof from then on. (T20)

O15 provided a similar observation of a classmate who was talented at playing the piano:

He was treated really badly because . . . he was actually very good at playing the piano, and he was an artistic sort of person. (O15)

Q17 describes the same reaction to singing:

. . . I used to sing, and I think that might have been . . . fourth, fifth, sixth class. . . . And that was also something that was wussy or pansy, poofter. And I used to really like singing. And so, I was annoyed because everyone else used to persecute me because of it. (Q17)

While the last three examples illustrate how different school activities can attract homophobic criticism, in each of these cases, the students persisted with their activities in defiance of the criticism they received (a response that will be examined later). However, P16 shows that pressures not to pursue artistic activities can lead to them being relinquished:

. . . we had a very enthusiastic brother who was a music teacher. Very talented one at that . . . he worked so hard to get us little shits to play in his band [laughs] and we did. And we disappointed him. . . . We played for about a year and we were getting good, and then we all just thought "Oh we're just gonna buggerize around and play sport." And it broke his heart I'm sure, because it wasn't the thing to do. The culture to do other things was too strong. It was too artistic. (P16)

HOMOPHOBIC PRESSURES FROM A NONHOMOSEXUAL PERSPECTIVE

The analysis now moves to examining homophobic events largely after adult sexual identity formation. This is a relatively arbitrary division because forming an identity is complex and consists of many transitions. Nevertheless, the perspective is informative because it offers alternative vantage points for examining homophobia (specifically the relationships between homophobia, nonhomosexual adult identities, and adult identities that include homosexual elements). Similar to the preceding analysis of homophobia prior to adulthood, the relationship between homophobia and a nonhomosexual adult identity concerns relationships between "self" and that which is not accepted as "self." In that sense, preadult and nonhomosexual adult identities form a continuum and many issues are shared. However, while homosexuality comes to be positioned as "otherness," homosexual identities also arise out of and form a continuum with preadult dynamics. In other words, both homosexual and heterosexual identities emerge from a common context. Furthermore, it will be argued that homophobia is internalized during childhood, becomes "sexualized" around puberty, and the resulting homophobic prohibitions and boundaries force undifferentiated erotic interests apart to form the hetero/homosexual dichotomy. Homophobia is the wedge that splits modern male sexuality along the lines of "otherness," and in that sense, (early, presexual) homophobia precedes and underwrites homosexuality and heterosexuality. This will be pursued in the final chapter.

Since homophobia is consistently characterized as a powerful rejection of boyhood otherness, it might be anticipated that homophobia will lead males to avoid any associations with homosexuality, and to restrict the circumstances in which such an association might arise. As Greg Herek puts it, "Because of the stigma attached to homosexuality, many heterosexuals restrict their own behavior in order to avoid being labeled gay" (Herek, 1991: 75). This dynamic should be distinguished from homophobia because it is actually an aversion to being associated and labeled: a fear of homophobia, or homophobia phobia! Boys fear being different and attracting homophobia rather than fearing homosexuality per se, and it is only later when homosexuality is incorporated into concepts of otherness that boys become averse to it too.

Restricting Emotion

Stereotypical associations between being "emotional" and being unmasculine are well recognized, and the evidence from this project reaffirms the importance attached to these stereotypes. There are also substantial similarities between data on "emotions" in this section and earlier data concerning crying: taboos against showing emotions reflect analogous processes to those which regulate crying. Emotional expression is described as being restrained rather than being absent. The implication is that social scrutiny contributes to the regulation of emotional behaviors, particularly their expression:

> . . . there certainly were things that I wouldn't have done because of peer pressure at school, and you certainly did try to avoid being sensitive. (H8)

Restriction of emotional expression is reiterated in the next quote. This time it is associated with a metaphor that suggests the importance of being seen to be solid, unmovable, "stony," and detached:

> . . . you just don't show emotion. You've got to be this Rock of Gibraltar. (B2)

The constraints on being visibly emotional were portrayed by subjects as cross-generational. Descriptions of restrained emotional expression by fathers revealed parallels with the subject's experiences:

> . . . my father doesn't show a lot of emotion, and to me, that was the way things were, and as it turns out, that's the way I am too. I won't show a lot of outward emotion. (Z26)

Respondents described stereotypical links between being "emotional" and being homosexual, as the following quote by a heterosexual male indicates:

> . . . often gay men are, say, for instance, better at expressing emotion, better at dealing with emotion, and are more interested in a lot of the things women are often interested in. You know, that more artistic, creative style. I think often gay men are better at dealing with women than straight men are. (W23)

In addition to the association of homosexuality with being emotional, the failure to restrain emotions sufficiently can attract homophobia, as this heterosexual subject reports:

> . . . the inferred weakness of . . . "poofter" probably was a bit
> harder to wash off. And especially seeing as . . . I was probably
> a bit more sensitive than, I would show my emotions a bit
> more than . . . that harder element of the school ground. (H8)

While the restrictions on emotion were described in generic
terms—as if all emotion was similar—certain forms of emotional
expression by males do not appear to be restrained and some are
encouraged. For example, although the "habit" of not expressing
emotions is restated, there are some emotions that appear to escape
control:

> But my father never showed his emotions. It was incredible . . .
> and . . . as I got older, I just got into this habit where I really
> didn't either . . . . I mean if he gets the shits he does . . . if he's
> happy he does. But if something really gets to him, he won't
> show it. (X24)

The emotions that are not restrained are anger and happiness, and
both of these are permissible probably because they indicate
strength and therefore don't undermine masculine status. In a more
cynical vein, R18 also makes the distinction between acceptable
and unacceptable expression:

> . . . I suppose if you beat someone up on the [sports] field then
> I suppose that was a bit of an expression. (R18)

The data reveal how emotions can be divided into those associated
with weakness and those with strength, and how displaying emotions that reflect "weakness" are subject to (homophobic) scrutiny
and constraint.

Being Tough and Affirming Aggression

The pressure on boys to avoid occupying a social position vulnerable to homophobic scrutiny promotes tougher posturing and
more aggressive roles (Mason, 1993). P16 refers to these dynamics:

> It was sort of cool to give people bruises. It was cool to bash
> people up. It was cool to taunt people and . . . it was cool to

make fun of people. And it was cool to gang up on people and, you know, I saw it happen a lot. (P16)

He goes on to describe how he avoided being publicly associated with the victims because he feared being "branded." In a similar vein, this was the response of F6 when asked whether he had any homoerotic experiences ("exploratory experiences with other boys") as a child:

> . . . as much as I had a soft side at school, I always tried to portray the more macho image, and whether it came into it, I dunno if that conflicts with the macho image or not. (F6)

Notice how he reads the question about homoeroticism as having a "soft side" and how he justifies not having any experiences that he could recall by saying that he expressed a more macho image at school. You might recall that C3 also used his association with toughness for protection when he joined the "tough gang" at school.

The association between homophobia and violence is similar to that between homophobia and toughness. In the next example, homophobic violence is valorized by school peers:

> . . . [there] was a group from the public schools that used to go round bashin' up poofs . . . in the city. So that was like a pretty cool thing to do. (D4)

The justification for this is that

> . . . you were always brought up to think that that wasn't the right thing to do, so it . . . was okay for poofs to get bashed. (D4)

Notice how D4 implies that antigay violence has social approval. A similar theme is articulated by B2:

> [male-to-male sex] was probably the worst thing you could do . . . if you went out and bashed somebody you'd be almost considered a hero back then. You know, you had to be really tough to fit in. (B2)

In addition to male homosexuality deserving violence (or for that matter anything that attracts homophobia), there were also several

examples where homophobia could be used to legitimize and mitigate against violent behavior, even though there was no suggestion
that the victim was "gay." The following example illustrates how
boys used homophobic accusations to justify their attack:

> . . . the guy wasn't gay but it was great leverage. He was
> basically a policeman's son and . . . he was worse than worst. . . .
> We basically [laughs] punched the living shit out of him . . . all
> in the name of calling him a "homo". . . but that wasn't the
> issue. The issue was that he was a spoiled little rich kid, and
> that's it. (A1)

The description of the aftermath of that attack illustrates how the
homophobic content appears to have indemnified the attackers. The
victim was humiliated by homophobia again at the hands of the
adults in charge, and although the aggressors went unpunished,
action was taken against him:

> **D:** So the cover story was that he was gay, that he was a
> faggot?
> **S:** Faggot. Uh huh.
> **D:** Because that made it acceptable?
> **S:** [Affirmative response] Yeah. Totally acceptable. . . . It
> actually prevented us [from] getting into trouble.
> **D:** Why? What happened?
> **S:** He was moved within two days to another place . . . the only
> thing that happened was he was brought out of the office. . . .
> With all of us standing there, this poor guy had to say why we
> bashed him up, and it was his word against ours. He said
> because they kept calling him faggot, you know. And that was
> it, that was the end of it. (A1)

Intolerance

Respondents described a range of reactions to being confronted
with scenarios involving homosexuality. Generally these concerns
did not relate to overt sexual acts but to public expressions that in
some way were taken to indicate sexual orientation (San Miguel
and Millham, 1976; Gray, Russell, and Blockley, 1991). These in-

clude public declarations of sexual orientation, public behaviors from which sexual orientation is inferred (such as certain mannerisms), public expressions of cultural forms identified with gay culture (such as certain styles of dress), and male-to-male affection (Gray, Russell, and Blockley, 1991).

F6 describes how his brother reacted after leaving the football stadium to find a meal:

> He [brother] said, "This is a faggot restaurant." I said, "So?" He goes, "I'm not eating in a faggot restaurant." And my sister-in-law said, "Look. Wake up to yourself. They're not going to hurt ya." And so we got the menu and we looked at the menus and . . . we couldn't understand any of the food that was described on the menu. And he goes, "That's it, I'm gettin' up," and he just got up and walked out. And I felt insulted; I felt bad for the people there, 'cause we said we were going to eat, and then he just bluntly said, "I'm not eating here," and got up and walked out. And, I said, "They're not gonna hurt you." He said, "I don't care; I don't care." I couldn't talk to him. (F6)

It seems that the world they had entered belonged to the "other," where even the language and the food were indecipherable.

A phrase that frequently arose in the context of publicly visible homosexuality is "flaunting it," which, along with "parading it," inevitably had unsavory connotations:

> . . . [father] can't stand seeing men showing affection to each other. He can't stand seeing men walking around arm in arm. . . . And even since I've come out to him and he said, "It's fine, I don't care, but one thing I can't stand is when people flaunt it. So don't flaunt it." (O15)

The curious implication of O15's description is how being homosexual is not as troublesome as making it public is. A similar difficulty is articulated by BB28 when he uses the term "parading it":

> I mean, it's only homosexuals that do that. You don't see heterosexuals parading their sexuality . . . or bisexual people, they don't parade their sexuality. (BB28)

It is significant that homosexuals are singled out and that the speaker fails to reconcile his statements with the public prominence of heterosexuality in modern cultures and with his descriptions of compulsory heterosexuality at school (he completed secondary school only weeks before the interview).

Scenarios with homosexual associations appear to pose difficulties when they become public. This is reminiscent of the school ground where it is very important not to publicly do anything that was "poofterly." Reactions rarely concern overt sexual behavior, but a range of surrogate markers, all of which share a capacity to trigger homophobia. That is not to say that people aren't concerned about men being intimate; they are. In the next quote, the complaint focuses on being confronted rather than men simply showing affection:

> . . . the only thing I don't like about homosexuality is when it's pushed into your face. Like when you see gay men kissing each other, fondling each other, purposely in front of people. (Z26)

Shared homophobic codes permit male affection to be depicted as a deliberately defiant act rather than being primarily affection. This view is also encapsulated in the next quote, which describes U21's reaction to seeing affection between men:

> . . . in the past it was like watching something wrong or watching some crime being committed. (U21)

The intuitive links between male-male intimacy and criminal behavior have a long history. In this case, the "criminal" associations preceded more accepting attitudes, and this adds to the case that by adulthood, homophobic attitudes have become status quo and that being less homophobic involves unlearning:

> I still have residual . . . homophobia has been you know, bred . . . or put into me . . . from a very young age through school and stuff like that so . . . watching two men making love is still to me a bit . . . difficult, I think. (U21)

Nevertheless, U21 is indicating that he is becoming less homophobic.

D4 had the most "homophobic" of Herek's (1994) scores measuring attitudes toward gay men (see ATLG scores in the Appendixes). In the following extract, he tries to define his feelings toward homosexuals and suggests that the problem with public intimacy arises when it impinges on him:

> . . . as long as they're not really pushin' into my space . . . well if I have to look at a couple of poofs kissin' each other then I suppose that's my space. (D4)

His homophobia is not absolute: in the next quote he differentiates between homosexuality that confronts him and homosexuality in private:

> **D:** Can you imagine one day that Australia might have a gay Prime Minister?
> **S:** I don't really mind that either. As long as he's not sucking face with a husband on TV. (D4)

D4 explains this difference in a reference to "flaunting," which he uses to indicate an important distinction between public and private behavior. Once again, significance is attached to social scrutiny as a controlling agent, but in this case, it is the failure of that scrutiny to contain the behavior that D4 finds disturbing:

> **S:** Well no one else is watching. They're not doin' it in public; they're not flaunting it. Not flaunting being a homosexual.
> **D:** So you don't have a problem with homosexuality per se, it's when it's public, when people see it?
> **S:** Yeah. I suppose it's when they're not feeling guilty for being that way as well, then they should be punished for it. (D4)

For D4, therefore, the significance of his concern about publicly visible homosexual behaviors is that the men involved seem to be escaping the usual social restraints of scrutiny and guilt.

Special Dispensation: The Limits of Intolerance

In addition to the public/private boundary, there are three other notable examples of boundaries beyond which homophobia moderates and tolerance of homosexuality changes: these exceptions are situational homosexuality, narcissism, and female homosexuality. The latter will be examined here.

The very different positions that subjects take with respect to female homosexuality shows that homophobia is neither rigid nor absolute. While discomfort and some visceral reaction was described when discussing male homosexuality, strikingly different reactions emerged when discussing homosexuality among women. All twelve subjects who rated their sexual orientation as heterosexual reported feeling erotically aroused by the idea of women making love. Not one was repelled by female homosexuality:

> . . . a lot of men find two women very erotic and two men's just off-putting. I don't know why that works, but you know, to me two women together is fine [chuckle] . . . if I could find two women to make love at the same time . . . it wouldn't worry me if I couldn't be part of it, I'd just like to watch it [chuckle]. I don't know, it's a bit of fantasy, I guess. (Z26)

For Z26, it is not simply an opportunity to be involved, and by that involvement resolve the scenario into a heterosexual one. Z26 clearly states that he'd be happy just watching and that it wouldn't worry him if he weren't involved. In this case, he doesn't find the explicit homosexual element disturbing.

D4 provides another illustration of this differential homophobia, clearly contrasting his different attitudes toward male and female homosexuality:

> **D:** Do you find the idea of sex with lesbians sort of exciting?
> **S:** Yeah.
> **D:** Why? What's the . . .
> **S:** I dunno [laughs]. It's good.
> **D:** Yeah? What would you achieve?
> **S:** 'Cause when you were havin' a bit of a breather they could still be goin'.
> **D:** And you'd enjoy watching?
> **S:** Yep. (D4)

Notice how he would enjoy watching explicit female homoeroticism. Yet he scored as one of the most homophobic of the interview subjects. Now contrast this with his reaction to two males in the same situation:

> **D:** But if two guys were doing it?
> **S:** That's disgusting!
> **D:** Disgusting? Okay. That's very interesting. It's still homo-sexuality.
> **S:** But it's not the same sex as what I am.
> **D:** So it's got something to do with what you are?
> **S:** Mmm [affirmative response]. Oh yeah. Two females is a lot better than two males being together. (D4)

He constructs the acceptability of the scenario in relation to himself. So if it is not explicit homosexuality per se that men find disturbing, then what is it about male homosexual scenarios that triggers responses such as "that's disgusting," and what does this tell us about homophobia?

> . . . I'm not disgusted by the idea of two women together as compared to two men, there's a feminine sort of thing to it and they're enjoying it, whereas man on man polarize each other, and shouldn't match. (M13)

So while the homosexual element is not uniformly taboo, it does seem that there is a strong reaction when men transgress the bounds of socially acceptable intimacy. The data provide several possible explanations, all of which appear to be influential. The first concerns the relationship between the people in the act. From its earliest (presexual) appearance, boys' homophobia did not primarily target girls. It was a powerful issue between boys and focused on boys. It is therefore not surprising that a male homosexual scenario provokes a stronger reaction. A second possibility is that homophobia is put aside for a scenario involving two women because heterosexual males find women attractive. A third possibility concerns the relationship between the sexual scenario and the observing "self": to observe male homosexual acts implies an interest in male homosexuality that is not implied when observing females.

Avoiding "Guilt By Association": Fearing Homophobia

A key effect of homophobia on males with nonhomosexual identities is a wish to avoid being associated with homosexuality (Herek, 1984; Wells, 1991; Mason, 1993; Connell, 1995). Connell writes, "the classic barrier to friendships among heterosexual men is homophobia . . . a standard part of hegemonic heterosexuality in Australian culture is antagonism to gay men and fear of being called homosexual" (Connell, 1995: 133). Here again, adult practice echoes the experiences of the school ground. A number of tactics to avoid that association were described. For example, F6 describes the dilemma posed by his sympathy for victimized classmates:

> I never liked seeing someone being stirred. I felt sorry for people who didn't look right. . . . I hated people making fun of other people that had disabilities . . . and still to this day. I must admit when I was young, to fit in, I probably made fun of other people. I probably called other people poofter to fit in and to take the onus off myself. (F6)

Another example of the risk of associating with the victim of bullying comes from C3, who maneuvered to join the tough group (who would "terrorize so-called poofters") for protection and to "deny who he was." Once in that position, he was unable to moderate bullying practices because of the risk of arousing suspicions about himself:

> I couldn't. There was a few times where I did say "I think he's had enough," you know, "Leave him alone." Then they'd come look at you as if to say, "What's the matter?" "How come you want to stop?" So, that's it, you'd just let someone else decide when they'd had enough. (C3)

It is understandable how "poofter bashing" might culminate in extreme consequences if homophobic dynamics are sufficiently intimidating to prevent group members from acting as "circuit breakers" and moderating the outcome.

The pressure to avoid association with homosexually identified people and events involves more subtle behaviors as well. In this context, the gaze becomes a significant factor because looking can imply interest. I9 describes how the act of looking at two men being publicly affectionate places him in an awkward position:

> If I was observing I'd probably still feel a bit uncomfortable. But if other people were around, because if I was observing it and I was watching it, people might think, "Oh, he's watching them kissing. Maybe he's interested, maybe that's because he is like them too." (I9)

Of course, looking wouldn't matter without homophobia. We will return to the importance of the gaze in the next chapter.

A similar dilemma of association arises if boys ask questions about homosexuality without qualifying their curiosity with homophobic undertones. I9 relates this dilemma, which is probably more acute for him since he rated his sexual orientation at 5 (bisexual):

> . . . the fact that it's "not normal" [homosexuality] makes me feel uncomfortable because I feel like I have a sense of curiosity about it, but I'm afraid to discuss it or question it because I'm afraid that I'll be labeled something that I'm possibly not, and it's a sense of rejection. I guess, maybe it's because it calls me into account. (I9)

The way homophobia restricts curiosity and isolates men is reflected by A1 when talking about men's capacity to be intimate:

> . . . there's another reason why the male culture works so well against itself; it is designed fundamentally to stop that [men confiding in each other] from happening. Males have to be an island unto themselves. (A1)

This echoes an earlier part of the chapter when the expectation that men should be like an emotional "Rock of Gibraltar" was discussed. It also raises the significant division between private and public because the implication is that homosexuality should be confined to the private domain, not that it can be eradicated (similar to the "Don't ask, don't tell" dictum of the U.S. military).

Guilt by association also extends to a heterosexual male who is propositioned:

> I'd feel insecure myself if I was "hit on" by a guy. I'd think there was something about me that makes me look gay if someone hit on me. Like, why did that person hit on me? He must see something in me that looks gay. Or I must be portraying something that is gay. (F6)

Guilt by association also seems to influence how men react to the possibility of having a gay son. D4 (the most "homophobic" of the subjects) had considerable difficulty in coming to terms with the idea:

> **S:** Well, if I was gonna have a kid and I knew that it was going to turn out to be a homosexual, then I'd [abort] if that was possible. That'd be excellent. Fix it.
> **D:** Is that fair on the kid?
> **S:** I dunno. It'd be more fair on us.
> **D:** All right. Why would it be unfair for you to have had a homosexual kid?
> **S:** I reckon it'd be unfair to the kid too, 'cause I just wouldn't treat him the same as what I would. . . .
> **D:** Why not? He's your kid?
> **S:** Yeah. But he turned out wrong. . . . Well, I'd be lookin' to have an abortion. (D4)

By way of comparison, some of the heterosexual subjects in this study had low "homophobia scores" on Herek's (1994) ATLG scales, yet they still found questioning toward the end of the interview about having a gay son challenging. K11 tries to explain:

> . . . I've got too many good friends who are homosexuals and I haven't shunned any of them. But the son being homosexual, again I don't think it would feel . . . maybe it is the fear of being homosexual. . . . There's definitely a residual . . . phobia. (K11)

Having a gay son was a novel idea for K11, as it was for the others. He found himself unprepared for it and struggling to understand his own response. In the previous statement, he frames his reaction in terms of a "residual phobia." He confirms that he was previously more homophobic and that he has gone through a process of diminishing homophobia. He also distinguishes between his intellectual reaction and his emotional reaction: while he sees homophobia as unreasonable, he still has homophobic feelings (Ernulf and Innala, 1987):

> . . . Because it has nothing to do with the intellectual level, it has to do with the emotional. The emotional level of me says "Okay. I will be uncomfortable . . . if I was personally involved in a homosexual act, or with a homosexual . . . with homosexual offspring." (K11)

Similar arguments were made by U21. Notice in the next quote how he says he'd "still struggle," implying once again that he was previously more homophobic, and how he relates this to "programming." Also notice how he feels that, given sufficient time, he could come to terms with it and how he views his reaction as a struggle with his "gut reaction":

> I think I'd still struggle to see him [his son] kissing another man . . . there's still something in there that is programmed to say, "This is not quite right." But I know that I'd overcome that and that I wouldn't cause him any problems for being gay. . . . I could deal with it . . . it wouldn't be ideal . . . my gut reaction would be a little bit off . . . but you know, in a few years, maybe I'll be fully, you know, [it] wouldn't bother me at all. (U21)

These findings suggest that homophobia at some distance can be subdued more easily than when it confronts subjects in novel ways and more proximally.

The interviews reveal an explanation for the strength of the reactions to having a gay son: it reflects on the father. Social scrutiny recurs as an important factor and while the parents can moderate their own homophobia, they have no control over the homophobia of others. F6 describes having a homosexual son as implicit failure:

> It would have, [the] implication. . . . I was not a proper parent; I've let the child down. . . . I didn't teach her/him properly. . . . I suppose I would have failed as a parent. (F6)

H8 takes this further when he expresses his concern that having a gay son would stigmatize the father as a "poof in the school sense":

> . . . society as it stands at the moment may, or some elements of it may, think that it means I was a weak father . . . and that I was a bit of a "poof" in the school sense . . . that I was weak, I wasn't being blokey enough with him. (H8)

BB28 also expresses concerns about a "failure" of fathering, and this seems reasonable to him because of his assumption that everyone is born heterosexual and it is events after birth that alter that:

> I'd start to wonder if the way I brought him up had contributed to his being homosexual. And if so, what aspects of his up-bringing, also . . . I think I'd look back and think. And then, once again you'd redefine everything the child had done to try and fit it into this new mold. Because I think when a boy is born and when a girl is born he's born heterosexual. It's only when he's older that he turns homosexual. (BB28)

Finally, D4 is the most blunt:

> 'Cause it's too close to home . . . if I had a child and he turned out to be homosexual. . . . I'd feel like it's my fault . . . he's a product of me not doin' things 100 percent myself properly. Like . . . I've got something wrong with me 'cause I've pro-duced a defective child. (D4)

Limiting Opportunities

Homophobic targeting and pressures to avoid homophobic label-ing polarizes peer-group dynamics and limits and skews the oppor-tunities young males can pursue (Willis, 1977). An important stan-dard of success for young males is physicality, whereas academic success can lead to homophobic labeling. On the school ground, physicality is embodied in the sporting and tough groups. Because they operate as groups and toughness is emphasized, tough groups have the means to disrupt and dominate areas of the school ground. These groups were most often described as the "top of the pecking order" at school, and even though they might also occupy a minority position, tough groups have legitimacy because they represent valued standards of masculinity, possibly "hypermasculinity." But although tough gangs can dominate the school ground, their dominance is short-lived and both the homophobes (Kurdek, 1988; Seltzer, 1992) and the boys who are subject to homophobic targeting appear to be severely disadvantaged by homophobic dynamics:

> **S:** . . . that's really funny to think that all of those that were on the top are now social outcasts, almost . . . in my class you know, I'd say that the top twenty-five are all unemployed.
> **D:** Is that top twenty-five academically or. . .
> **S:** No . . . powerful. They're all tattooed and they're all drug-fucked [laughs] But they're the ones that literally, "held the standard." They're the ones that controlled whatever people thought about male power. And now they're social outcasts. (A1)

Several other respondents offered similar observations. C3 provides an equally dramatic description:

> **D:** What about the other members of the tough gang?
> **S:** They haven't changed. Most of them are either in jail or dead.
> **D:** So, they might be successful at school, but after school?
> **S:** Oh, they fell to pieces. Yeah. That's right. I don't think any of them got a real job . . . they just became the shit kickers of life. Like they had a really big time at school, they controlled the schoolyard, but once you got out of school, once school was finished, that was it. They turned out to be big nothin's. (C3)

P16 contrasts the "quiet achievers" with boys whose success at school was derived from physical prowess:

> They haven't become influential in other areas, in fact, quite the opposite. The people who have made a real success of their careers have been the quiet achievers who were no good at sport. (P16)

Other authors report that former school bullies have almost a four-fold greater chance of multiple court convictions than nonbullies. (Smith, 1991)

HOMOPHOBIA AND BEING HOMOSEXUAL

Homophobic impact varies depending on a person's self-concept. If a self-concept includes being homosexual or elements identified with homosexuality, then homophobia impinges directly on "self" and identity. For men with an established or emerging gay identity, the sense of personal assault associated with homophobia is particularly acute. Young gay men are confronted with considerable reprobation against strongly held collective beliefs (Savin-Williams, 1994). Boys with emerging gay identities in the school system are placed in extremely difficult circumstances with few, if any, supports or safe havens.

This section traces some paths into young gay adulthood in order to examine the effects of homophobia. For almost all young gay men (and presumably lesbians) there is a difficult dilemma: hide and experience the consequences of not being yourself, or don't hide and risk being victimized (Savin-Williams, 1994). This dilemma is analogous to Goffman's transitions between the discreditable and the discredited states of stigma, depending on disclosure (Goffman, 1963). This section considers four aspects of homophobia and growing up gay: first, the direct impact of being targeted and the consequences for education, career, and family membership; second, the individual's responses to homophobia when "difference" is resisted/rejected; third, responses where "difference" is accepted and homophobia is rejected; and fourth, homophobia and identity formation. This chapter also directs attention to how the agency and resilience of targeted individuals can moderate the effects of homophobia, often with positive outcomes. In Foucault's famous words, "Where there is power, there is resistance" (Foucault, 1990: 95).

Direct Impact

Harassment, Threats, and Violence

One of the most frequent manifestations of homophobia is harassment, which can range from subtle to lethal. Andi O'Conor writes that in the United States (as in Australia), school is "a hostile and dangerous environment for most gay and lesbian teenagers" (O'Conor, 1995: 98). In a powerful personal testimony, Eric Rofes writes, "We will never forget that we were tortured and publicly humiliated because we refused to be 'real boys,' acted 'girlish,' or were simply different" (Rofes, 1995: 80). The present project yielded extensive evidence of homophobic harassment, and it is the intensity and impact of this harassment that the next few pages will attempt to convey:

> ... there's half a dozen people I can think of, just off the top of my head, who were mercilessly teased with being fags and wimps and poofters. (P16)

Z26 recollects how he behaved toward boys who were "poofters":

> Any boy like that [poofter] used to cop a bagging from the rest of the boys ... even ... when girls were accepted, if there was boys like that, they still copped a terrible bagging. I mean it's not until you get older that you realize how much of a bastard of a kid you really were. (Z26)

The next three quotes, from three young gay men who were on the receiving end of the harassment, also indicate considerable pressure:

> By some cruel twist of fate I was stuck in the same class as a couple of these people. ... It was a constant sort of torment ... at the time it just seems like that's *all there is to your life.* (O15)

O15 previously reported how harassment at school lasted for years, and DD30 uses "downright cruel" to describe his experiences:

> "Thomasina" you know, "Oh, that looks poncy" ... "You're such a sissy" ... "Stop being such a sissy" ... [sister] used to lay all that kind of stuff on me. And they used to joke about things ... it was just downright cruel ... there was no need for it. (DD30)

Harassment can be linked to associating with the wrong boy. Notice again how the intensity of the harassment is conveyed, this time by a sense of exasperation:

... he arrived from [name] High School. And he was an even bigger "poofter" than me, so you know, almost all of my harassment just stopped and then they just focused on him. So that's kind of a blessing actually. It was like, "Oh, whew!" [chuckle] "I can breathe easy for a while," and then slowly, in the first term of year eight, we actually became friends, and so you know, it was back on for [laughs] all [frustrated exhale]. (Y25)

Harassment included threats of violence, which were common talk among schoolboys, as K11 observes:

... if the number of people who actually bashed equalled the number of people that were claimed to be bashed. . . . I'm surprised that no one at the school got "done for" on assault. (K11)

Often quick thinking averted these threats, and boys were able to bluff their way out of awkward situations:

I don't even know what provoked it either; all I know is they said, "Oh," you know, "We're going to bash you. We're going to put you in hospital you faggot" . . . And I think I came out with "Okay. Oh, gee that'll make me rather rich . . . I'm going to sue. I'll have to take you to the cops and see if I can sue" . . . and "What a tough girl, listen to you!" (L12)

Notice in this example, how the homophobic dynamic is also used in defense.

Harassment was also physical. Y25 describes how harassment at school included being spat on for being a "poofter":

... all of a sudden, I was just in this big horrible building with these *horrible* people . . . and I suppose that's where the abuse really started happening. . . . I was the "poofter" of the school and got spat on and all that kind of stuff. (Y25)

Single punches, elbowing, and kicks also frequently accompanied homophobia:

... you'd walk past a group and there'd be an elbow and "poofter," and that sort of thing. But that was pretty much commonplace. (T20)

N14 also provides a range of examples of limited physical harassment:

> . . . they would often be alone in the playground or . . . would often be sick on sport days . . . you'd get one guy would go up to them, you'd see it happen, and sit next to them and do something to them. Whether it's mark them with a pen or pull their hair . . . and these guys would react in a very effeminate way, by hissing at them or getting up and storming off, or slapping them or something . . . that would cause a fight. . . . They'd cry and run off or something and then get chased . . . if they were in sport, they'd often get pushed over. (N14)

The impact of this sort of behavior should not be underestimated. In this example, the person being harassed ended up crying and having to move to safety, and as we have seen, harassment can be relentless:

> I think they just spent the whole school life being beat up . . . it was forward tackle them with their ties you know. That sort of stuff . . . mainly it was more like gang stuff. Like it was never more than one of them at a time that'd get attacked. So it was always at least five on one. (C3)

Notice the group nature of homophobic harassment and the singular status of the person being harassed.

School-ground harassment can be extreme and include humiliation, danger, and physical injury. N14 describes an example of homophobic "crucifixion." In this incident, a student was stripped naked, tied up, and labeled:

> I'll never forget one day, one kid was tied to a stake in the middle of the oval, stripped naked, and branded a poofter. . . . He was labeled a poofter, and he was staked up between a couple of trees without any clothes on, and a teacher . . . she went and rescued him. . . . She went up there and she'd had enough, and she went up and got him and put a jumper around him, and brought him back down to the school. (N14)

You will recall from a previous chapter, that the oval is frequently mentioned as a "danger zone" and the above act is tantamount to being held hostage in enemy territory. N14 also recalled a homophobic incident that posed considerable danger to the person being victimized:

> I also remember another "poofter" being hung over a balcony with his trousers down . . . he was a year ten kid who was being terrorized by a year-twelve group . . . a vindictive display. (N14)

Sometimes school-ground homophobic harassment can lead to physical injury, as J10 recalls:

> . . . he was very angelic and blond. He was [at] the top of the cement steps and someone called him a "poof" and tripped him and he fell down the steps and broke his leg. (J10)

The data also include descriptions of a number of incidents outside the school. The first of these illustrates a homophobic mob response to young people whose different appearance was presumably viewed as provocative:

> **S:** [friend] would make sure he'd look different, so he'd have a high Mohawk and rings and pink hair and that sort of thing. And one [Blue Light Disco] was actually at [suburb] High School, and basically two hundred people turned on us. It had finished, and we were all outside waiting for [girlfriend's] father to turn up and then these two hundred people came out and circled us because we were sitting on the ground. And [they began] abusing us and kicking us and slagging on us and that sort of thing. And their aggression was toward [male friend] mainly because he was the strangest out of all us. And so [male friend] actually got up and took off and this hoard of people, everyone went after him, like two hundred kids just went after him . . . what happened was [male friend] actually jumped in somebody's car on, this main drag in [suburb], whatever that is. And this person actually took him home.
> **D:** . . . what reasons did they give for turning?
> **S:** Oh, because we were "poofters" and "freaks" and "should die" and that sort of thing . . . he got in the car, this woman's

car, who was at this set of lights and they started beating up her car. (Y25)

Harassment can also focus on gay venues and meeting places, and while these venues are often assumed to be safe places, there is evidence that the risk of assault is higher in the vicinity:

First gay nightclub I've ever been to . . . we were seen coming out. They got out of the van and started laying into us . . . there were two girlfriends, scraggy and nasty bitches screaming from the panel van, "Kick the bastard!" (R18)

For younger gay men, often their first and only available place for meeting other gay men is in rest rooms—particularly when gay-friendly pubs and bars are ruled out because of age limits, cost; lack of a car, license, or transport, or lack of other venues. V22 describes how, as a schoolboy, his early sexual contacts were in the toilets at railway stations because he knew of no other venues. In the following example, he describes the danger associated with seeking sexual partners in unprotected areas:

. . . heading back toward the road when two other guys had come around the other way and cut me off . . . they basically punched and punched me and threw me to the ground, kicked me a few times and . . . two of them had PVC piping. [laughs] Good thing it wasn't lead piping and [they] were beating me about with that . . . they were certainly abusing me and calling me a "dirty filthy poofter" and those sorts of things while they were doing it. . . . I'd gone down and was covering my ribs with my arms and I copped one in the arm, which later I found out had broken my arm. (V22)

The final example describes even more severe injuries following homophobic assaults. In this extract, the subject, a health professional, mentions a "beat" (a meeting place for gay men):

S: . . . when I worked in Neurosurgery, we had two that came in . . . one from a nightclub and one from the park. And they both came in with dreadful head injuries.

D: And were they poofter bashings, do you know?

S: Yes. Because they were written up in the gay newspapers and it was right outside the gay nightclub and it was right in the heart of the biggest beat in [capital city] . . . you could see boot marks on their skin, dirty boot marks on their skin when they came in . . . bruised and broken ribs. . . . I can't remember about broken limbs, but they were certainly bruised all over, really kicked for a long time. And, just boot marks everywhere on their clothes . . . he had huge ICP [intracranial pressure] problems when he was admitted. . . . And a lot of tonal problems after it. He was the real neurological patient for a long time, but did really well, and got a full recovery, but he had incredibly bad tone and all sorts of trouble. The other one, I'm not sure if he was unconscious when he came in or not, but he was paralyzed and sedated because of his head injury, so he was quite bad. (CC29)

No Reliable Safe Havens

Being targeted by homophobia is an isolating experience and finding support, safety, and protection can be extremely difficult. For the child who is subjected to homophobia, descriptions of school life sound more like imprisonment, than safe places for children to grow and develop:

> Looking back, I think it's [school] one of the cruellest places. The way people, well the way I was, and the way kids can be, I reckon school is a really cruel place. (Z26)

If anything, schools appear to provide a haven for behaviors that would be illegal elsewhere:

> . . . if I walked down the street and said some of the things to someone in the street that you'd say in the school, you'd be up for defamation and things like that for sure. (Z26)

Homophobia's capacity to silence parents and teachers prevents children who are being harassed from knowing who can be trusted and undermines the child's ability to seek help. A number of studies have documented boys' reluctance to seek help from teachers, particularly in secondary school (Smith and Levan, 1995) and the failure of teachers to recognize when bullying is a problem (Hazler, Hoover, and Oliver, 1993; Rigby and Slee, 1991). Homophobia also interferes with obtaining assistance from police and justice from the courts. A recent discussion paper from the New South Wales Attorney General's Department titled "Review of the 'Homosexual Advance Defence'" explored the difficulty of obtaining a fair trial when allegations of homosexual behavior are made (Working Party on the Review of the Homosexual Panic Defence, 1996). Similar concerns exist with police who have also fashioned their approach to law and order around powerful homophobic experiences at school.

C3 provides a description of how gay mens' trust in the police can be undermined:

> . . . like freak shows I think . . . parked me car and . . . started walkin' toward the club, all these coppers started laughin' at us. (C3)

V22 describes the reasons he felt compromised and mistrustful and decided not to report the attack described previously (see pp. 171-172):

> I felt fairly clear that I wouldn't be treated well by the police once they realized the situation. . . . I'd had interactions with the police at beats before and I knew that . . . they felt that it was particularly distasteful. And I guess there was the . . . added element that I didn't really want to tell people about it anyway. There was the shame. . . . (V22)

Notice how part of the reason why V22 decided not to contact the police was because of past experience—his concerns were not unfounded. Evidence of widespread difficulties with homophobia and law enforcement agencies was reported in Chapter 1.

Education and Career

The impact of homophobia on schooling is a recurring theme in the literature on young gays and lesbians (Savin-Williams, 1994).

Andi O'Conor encapsulates this in a paper in which one subject is quoted as saying, "I saw what happened to other kids who got called queer at school. I dropped out" (O'Conor, 1995: 97). Fears expressed about school life appear to be well-founded (Savin-Williams, 1994; Martin, 1982). Gay subjects in this study provided descriptions that linked homophobia to dislike of school, declining school performance, ceasing "unpopular" school activities, truancy, leaving school early, and altering career paths. Similar findings have been found in studies on bullying in schools (Hazler, Hoover, and Oliver, 1993).

Y25 experienced homophobic targeting from the beginning of high school, and it became a daily battle just to face going to school:

> I was different to this mob of five hundred odd people, knowing that I didn't want to be like these five hundred people. . . . I don't know if it's being afraid of being odd. . . . It was just a battle . . . every morning it would be, "It's time for school, it's time to," you know, "get tensed up." (Y25)

Y25 also explains how homophobic harassment he experienced at school impacted on his academic performance:

> I used to hate going to school and getting up and thinking, "Yuk, I just don't want to be there today among all the Neanderthals." . . . My schooling actually started to drop . . . my grades started to drop then. (Y25)

Eventually, Y25 stopped attending school regularly, which he attributed to the weight of homophobic harassment:

> . . . I actually started, probably in year eight, in "wagging" a lot. . . . Once every few weeks I would just take a day off school and not turn up and slowly that turned into three or four days out of every week that I just wouldn't go to school. (Y25)

After a protracted period of truancy, the school notified his parents, who decided to move him to another school. Given a fresh start in an "alternative" school, away from the entrenched patterns of homophobia at the previous school, Y25 successfully completed his secondary schooling.

Without a fresh start, homophobia can be responsible for truncating a child's education:

> **D:** So being picked on [for being a poofter] was a problem?
> **S:** Major.
> **D:** Major.
> **S:** That's the reason why I left school.
> **D:** At a young age.
> **S:** Yeah fifteen. God!
> **D:** If you hadn't been picked on would you have completed school?
> **S:** Yes. I would have struggled, but I would have done it. (B2)

Although N14 completed his schooling, he had to be strategic about how he fashioned and presented himself to his peers because he had already observed what happened to boys who didn't escape homophobia:

> . . . got quite traumatized and they'd end up leaving in year ten. (N14)

And instead of declining performance at school, the fear of homophobic labeling caused him to modify the types of activities he pursued when he was at school:

> I became aware of put-down of gays, socially and within the family. I stopped playing piano. I stopped ballroom dancing at a very young age, 'cause I was frightened of being labeled gay. (N14)

Career paths are also shaped by homophobia. AA27 describes what deterred him from becoming a teacher:

> I was going to be [a teacher], but I decided not to. . . . I thought if . . . somebody accused me of sexual abuse, if I was a "queen," then I would be more likely to . . . be considered guilty. (AA27)

DD30 describes leaving his job because of racism and homophobia. He later turned this around when he went back to continue his

secondary schooling. After he returned, he wasn't as troubled by
homophobia, probably because he was now older than the others in
his class.

Family Membership

Homophobia can be extremely disruptive of family arrangements
(Cramer and Roach, 1988), essentially because the nuclear family
has difficulties finding a legitimate place for homosexual members
(often homophobically reconstructed as homosexuals rejecting the
family). Frequently this means that the homosexual child ceases to
have a family as soon as he (or she) is openly homosexual. Strommen writes of "parents applying their negative conceptions of homosexual identity to their child. This creates for the parent a subjective perception that the child is suddenly a stranger" (Strommen,
1993: 250). Stommen goes on to conclude that "for the family, the
most significant aspect of negative social values concerning homosexuality is the perception that homosexuals are not family members at all" (Strommen, 1993: 260). Evidence for similar dynamics
can be found in P16's description of his parent's reaction when he
disclosed he was gay. This paragraph contains an extensive catalog
of homophobic constructs including the "loss of a son":

> . . . my father was saying things like "Oh this is worse than
> murder," you know, and "How many people know? This is the
> worst thing in the world. It's a crime against nature. You
> should go to jail and we're not going to support you financial-
> ly anymore. You can get out of our flat." . . . the whole works.
> Mum just cried the whole time. And she said "I feel like I've
> lost a son," blah, blah, blah, blah. And I sat there going "God.
> This is so difficult." I felt like I was having to just take on all
> their crap where really I would have liked to have just done the
> opposite. Like off-load onto them, but they wanted to off-load
> onto me! (P16)

The family of N14 acted out a similar scenario when they threatened to "cut him off" when he revealed that he was gay:

> And during that week I was talked to a lot and shown my place
> in the business and what I would lose if I decided on this

lifestyle choice [being gay]. And all the inheritance papers were taken out, all the wills and everything. I was shown I would be cut off. You know, so the end of that week, of course I packed up my car, much to their shock and horror, the family crying, and Mum and Dad crying. (N14)

Notice how words such as "choice" and "lifestyle" (similar to the word "flaunt" discussed earlier) fail to acknowledge the extremely difficult and hazardous personal struggle that precedes disclosure and the courage required to do so. Similarly the word "style" in lifestyle suggests superficial artifice rather than a core part of a person's identity. In a similar vein, AA27 was faced with an "ultimatum" of giving up his sexual orientation or becoming homeless:

I was a queen, he [father] was a big, butch, straight boy and no room on either side . . . there's still . . . a lot [of] anger now. I haven't spoken to Dad in years. . . . They [father and stepmother] didn't want to deal with it. It was just too much. Because if the neighbors found out, that would be just too much. . . . I was given an ultimatum, that if I went out on Friday night, I was never allowed back. So, I just went out Friday afternoon and never came back. (AA27)

It is a further testimony to the power of homophobia that disclosures of homosexual orientation can be so traumatic for parents (Cramer and Roach, 1988), but according to Robinson, this reaction can ease and eventually lead to acceptance (Robinson, Walters, and Skeen, 1989: 59).

The alternative for young (and not so young) gay men who value their families can be to try to relinquish or hide their sexual orientation. This also disrupts family life; as Greg Herek argues, "The need to pass is likely to disrupt longstanding family relationships and friendships as lesbians and gay men create distance from others in order to avoid revealing their sexual orientation" (Herek, 1991: 74). Here is an example from X24, who is describing his sense of alienation from his parents:

I can't really be frank and have really frank discussions with them. And in fact I haven't been able to do that for some time

> because. . . . I just to have to tell a lie. You know, "I'm really busy," or "No. There's no girlfriend on the horizon at the moment!" and shit like that. (X24)

In addition to being gay sons, homosexual (and bisexual) men can also be husbands. Once again, the conventional nuclear family has difficulties accommodating them (Strommen, 1993: 260). Many of the gay men interviewed for this study had previous heterosexual relationships, including two who subsequently divorced, one of whom later married a gay partner and is still good friends with his ex-wife.

In the section titled Avoiding "Guilt By Association" (see p. 160), the analysis included responses to the possibility that participants might have a gay son. A key concern was how having a gay son would reflect on the parent. A further recurring concern was for the welfare and safety of the child. The next quote illustrates a mix of the homophobic themes explored so far: abnormality of the son, associating this with "difference," and then fear for the child's safety and welfare:

> In practice I know I could accept it, but I think I would have to do a lot of thinking first. It would take some coming to terms with . . . "Why are you different to me?" "Why are you abnormal in that regard?" . . . I think a lot of that's because of . . . what has happened at school. I would have to overcome the difference. But I would also be extremely worried for him, at high school . . . his safety from the threat of physical violence . . . and his happiness because I mean if he is living like this, [school friend] of my sister's it would be very unhappy. He would be extremely unhappy. (H8)

It would be impossible to discern the significance of H8 slipping and referring to his gay son as "it"; however, in the context of abnormality and otherness, this looks suspicious. In addition to happiness and safety, subjects also voiced fears about homophobia endangering the child's opportunities. Gay subjects voiced similar concerns.

Discussions toward the end of the interview considered whether gays should be allowed to adopt children. Similar fears about homophobia emerged from these discussions. M13 acknowledges that heterosexuals can be poor parents and gays can be good parents, but that homophobia at school would be a problem:

> . . . there are a lot of kids that come from heterosexual parents who . . . should never have been allowed to have children. So in terms of supporting [adoption by gay couples], I can't give you a straight out answer, yes or no . . . they'd get a lot of love and support from their family I'd imagine, but on the other side of the coin, they'd be ostracized when they got to school. (M13)

Z26 implies his sense of the intensity of school-ground homophobia, while talking about gay adoption:

> . . . providing that the kid can cope with it. Because I wonder why some kids didn't go and knock themselves off? You know, like the amount of trouble that they would have had. And I guess that some of them ended up doing it. (Z26)

All of the fears documented here reinforce the emerging thesis that schools are a site for frequent homophobia, and this is implicitly confirmed, judging by the depth of concerns that potential fathers have of homophobia—fearing how it reflects on the parent and impacts on the child.

Trying to Conform to Homophobic Standards

Whereas the previous sections focused on the more immediate effects of homophobia, the next two sections examine the way young men respond to homophobic pressures. In broad terms, these responses form two main groups. The first (accepting homophobia/ rejecting difference) is when an identity, behavior, or particular characteristic targeted by homophobia is rejected. In accepting the standards implicit in homophobia, the person strives to conform to homophobic expectations of acceptable and unacceptable behavior. The alternative is to question the premise on which targeting is based and to reject homophobia/accept difference. Either way, homophobia can cause psychological distress, including guilt, unhappiness, and depression, and lead to isolation.

Psychological Distress

Guilt is a common response to homophobia. Sometimes guilt relates to being associated with people who are stigmatized. DD30 describes the impact of one homophobic sister (who had custody of him) concerning another sister (who is lesbian):

> . . . she'd [custodial sister] be laying all of this stuff on me, like real full-on homophobia stuff: "Don't have anything to do with her!" [lesbian sister]. So when I'd be walking down the street from school or something and she [lesbian sister] came across, you know, "Hi! How are you doing? . . . It's really good to see you" . . . I'd feel really guilty; I'd feel really guilty because I'd have to put on this front like . . . "I can't talk to you." But I loved her so much that I had to talk to her. And so there was always this guilt and I couldn't go home and talk to [custodial sister] about it. (DD30)

This guilt was intensified because of his own emerging homosexual feelings and his awareness of the social disapproval of homosexuality:

> I knew inside me what was going on and I was really paranoid . . . . I used to think if it's not legal yet, what are they gonna do? Are they gonna take me to prison or stuff like that? I was sleeping around when I was about fifteen . . . fooling around with other boys, experimenting and stuff. I was still really paranoid that I was going to get found out. (DD30)

AA27 felt so guilty after an early homosexual contact (for which he was paid) that he took fairly drastic measures to cleanse himself afterward:

> So then he offered me fifty bucks and [clap] in there. Right in there and give him a "good old going" and I can remember after that I went home and just had a shower, and got steel wool and whaww! I just felt really dirty. I was fourteen years old. (AA27)

AA27 had had other (unpaid) homosexual experiences prior to this.

Religion and the church feature in a number of descriptions of homophobic guilt. In the first description, even though the local church appears to be relatively benign, this stops short when it comes to attitudes about homosexuality:

> ... I don't think the kind of Catholicism I grew up with was particularly strict or dogmatic, I was ever conscious of ... a moral regime which set homosexuality apart ... and that there was an enormous amount of guilt. (V22)

This effect of homophobia is differential and does not extend to equivalent heterosexual behaviors:

> I never felt Catholic guilt ... with having sex with women because it was okay. 'Cause that's what I was supposed to be, supposed to do in some ways. But I've always had Catholic guilt about having sex with men. (N14)

Homophobia seems to occupy a special place in religious prejudice, and people who are not religious continue to use religion to justify their homophobia (even though the Bible has little to say about homosexuality, which, for example, is not mentioned in the Ten Commandments). X24 illustrates how his homophobic guilt endures even though he is no longer religious:

> ... you have these ideas that, just in case there is a God, you're really going to burn in hell for it. (X24)

While it has been argued that religion is central to homophobia, the data from this study suggest that the authority of religion is exploited to support a predominantly "secular" bias.

Subjects also reported being depressed about their homosexuality. While the formal criteria for depression were not collated, the descriptions relate subjects' distress to their unhappiness about being homosexual (whatever the formal diagnosis). In the first case, we return to Y25 who suffered considerable homophobic harassment from early high school. He became ostracized; the prospect of going to school each morning was distressing, and eventually, he became truant:

> . . . just depressed. I had this fear of . . . going back there [school]. It was more of a fear thing. Turning up there every day . . . just having to have to go through all the sheer plight of being hassled all the time and maybe beaten up. (Y25)

DD30 independently provides a similar report even though he attended a school in a different Australian state:

> . . . I still didn't feel really good about myself. All through high school . . . it was just being bombarded with it [homophobic harassment] every day. It was really getting me down. And because there was violence involved as well, that made me really depressed all the time. (DD30)

The descriptions of the impact of homophobic harassment for Q17 are also dramatic and reflect the considerable tensions that arise as a result. Notice in this extract how he (rather than the harassment) was identified as the problem kid:

> That period of my life was a nightmare in terms of being alone, not having friends, being the odd one out. Teachers going and approaching my Mum and saying "Look, we've got a problem with this kid 'cause he's the odd one out." (Q17)

An indication of the extent of the distress really becomes apparent when it momentarily abates:

> I remember at one of the practices for the musical. . . . I felt my face quivering trying to work out what was happening . . . I was actually smiling, so in year ten, for the first time in my life I was smiling and noticing that my jaw didn't quite know what to do with this smile that was on my face. So definitely the interaction I was having with these people made me very happy. (Q17)

C3 describes a crisis in his life that led to a self-destructive act after a gay friend died of AIDS. The crisis appears to be related to the way homophobia has interfered with his capacity to grieve for his friend:

S: My friend had died and I couldn't do anything about it. [Sigh] I didn't even have the courage to go to the funeral in case anyone saw me there.
D: Okay. Keep going.
S: [Nervous laugh] . . . my mind just cracked up and just went downhill from there. (C3)

Isolation and Withdrawal

Homophobia can cause young men to be severely isolated. According to Mac an Ghaill, "going through the school system as a gay person is a terrible ordeal, one full of loneliness, anxiety and isolation, and one suffered by a tenth of the population. The usual fears and worries of adolescence are magnified tenfold" (Mac an Ghaill, 1994: 161). Often, boys who are different and already marginalized find themselves targeted by homophobia. Once stigmatized, the (homophobic) penalties of being associated with them can make forming friendships, finding support, and securing safety difficult (O'Conor, 1995: 95; Martin, 1982; Savin-Williams, 1994). The nature of homophobia makes it unlikely that the boy will be able to find sympathetic support, let alone being able to talk about why he is being harassed. Homophobic stigma is also powerful at silencing the boy who is targeted:

> I just felt so completely isolated. I didn't imagine that there was anyone within my reach who would want to do what I wanted to do. So I just, I didn't take that risk of showing that, because . . . even my . . . existence or my presence was enough to incite such anger . . . that anything beyond that . . . in my mind would've incited much worse. (O15)

In an environment where it is risky to offer support to a boy who experiences homophobia and where people in a position to help remain silent, homophobia has few restraints and is unlikely to be challenged. And because peer culture is infused with homophobic references, silence is in no way "neutral." Isolation is intensified by attempting to hide sexual orientation or by withdrawing. Withdrawal can be a deliberate response to being targeted, and according to John Gonsiorek, "it is common for gay and lesbian teenagers to withdraw from typical adolescent social experiences" (Gonsiorek, 1993: 476). Distance can be deliberately maintained in relationships rather than risking homophobia by disclosing:

> Started getting called that [fag] and they all must have thought you were, and you'd get that sort of a tag and usually it'd stick to you. You'd cop it for the rest of your school years. . . . I got hit a few times. Nothing bad, but that's why I avoided any contact, 'cause I didn't want to be bashed. (B2)

The net result is that young gay men even become isolated from one another (Martin, 1982). In the next example, P16 describes the isolation of a gay man in his university residential college. Although P16 is gay, he did not make contact with the person in this description:

> . . . that was the first time I ever came in proximity with an openly gay man. And he was so ostracized that it wasn't funny. There was a college community that was so tight-knit, and there was one person, I can't even remember his name but he was gay, and all we used to talk about was "Oh, there's what's-his-face". And all eyes would be trained on him . . . if he walked into the dining room. And to make matters worse . . . everyone else lived in the same building . . . he had one room separate, which was part of the garage [ironic laugh]. So I mean, not only was he different . . . sexually, he was different geographically. And, you know, all those demarcations were there. (P16)

Even more extreme isolation is possible, and family disruption and homelessness because of homophobia have already been illustrated.

Concealment

Homophobia exerts considerable pressure to conceal stigmatized characteristics, including sexual orientation and identity (Martin, 1982). This can lead to forming what Goffman calls "virtual" and "actual" identities (Goffman, 1963: 19). For gay men and lesbians, concealment is a common response to homophobic stigma and is the counterpart of "avoiding association" for nonhomosexual identities. You may recall a previous quote by B2 that hiding is a matter of survival and the only alternative is to run away. For some gay men, stigma and the associated guilt is felt so deeply that hiding seems to be impossible, even in private. This is illustrated by X24, who refers to his guilt about masturbation, which he relates to his guilt about homosexuality later in the interview:

> . . . when my aunty died . . . I was so suspicious and paranoid that, you know how they talk about ghosts and things like that . . . whatever you do in private can be seen. . . . And I was bloody paranoid that . . . nothing I did was private. (X24)

Some young people engage in antigay violence in an attempt to hide their sexual orientation (O'Conor, 1995: 99). One participant described being a fairly "soft" child at primary school, but he found himself becoming increasingly aggressive in response to mounting pressure from peers:

> . . . becoming really aggressive myself . . . because I saw how these softer kids were getting beaten up all the time. I didn't want to get beaten up, so I used to all of a sudden, get in with a cool gang and then, it'd end up being that I had my own little group of people and we used to go 'round and terrorize so-called poofters. (C3)

He goes on to describe how he "weaseled" his way into the group and how he turned on someone with whom he now partly identifies with:

> . . . But somehow I . . . weaseled my way in I suppose by . . . there was this one kid in class . . . since then he's had a sex change and he's now a girl. . . . And the way I got him was he was out in the schoolyard and I was talking to these guys. The great big tough guys, and this kid comes prancing past, so I just tripped him over and just . . . beat the shit out of him. Straight-away . . . I got called in front of the school and punished. . . . So straightaway the tough gang respected me; it was more or less like an initiation I suppose. . . . Made me a hero. (C3)

Later in the interview, C3 makes it clear that he doesn't feel proud of activities such as the one described here.

The previous example raises questions about the common (homophobic) stereotype that the chief perpetrators of "poofter bashing" are closet homosexuals. However, this does not appear to be a tenable proposition. While there was evidence that some boys with emerging homosexual identities became entrapped in these powerful homophobic processes (as do young males with emerging heterosexual identities), it has already been shown that homophobia is a much more general social problem than this explanation would allow for.

The case of C3 is informative because rather than being a static description of how he was always tough, he provides a description of how he "refashioned" himself in response to the increasing weight of peer-based homophobia. Using a combination of the shift from primary school to boarding school and a careful use of social skills, P16 also reinvented himself. Although he described himself in terms of "otherness" at primary school, by the end of secondary school, he was school captain:

> . . . once I'd started making friends with people in a group, I became quite close to a number of them. That meant that the group mentality was broken down, especially toward the end of school. (P16)

Both of these cases represent "concealment" because the descriptions clearly outline how both subjects felt that they were not being their authentic selves in order to be successful. Thus, while in the eyes of their peers they ceased to be "other," they privately identified with their "otherness within." P16 provides an elegant indication of this process:

> I was just fascinated by finding kids who were able to say exactly the right thing at exactly the right time. . . . "You are the master of . . . creating an image for yourself. . . ." I used to think, "This must be so much effort for you to do this, because you do it from the moment you open your eyes" . . . I used to discuss it with my good friend in our little escapes. It never dawned on me that I was doing the same things. (P16)

Many gay men become quite adept at hiding their sexuality and presenting different "selves" depending on circumstances. In effect, the world becomes divided into "a large group to whom he tells nothing and a small group to whom he tells all" (Goffman, 1963: 95). R18 refers to "leaving yourself at home" but notice how he adds the proviso about home. This is a reference to the homophobia he has experienced there:

> It's not hard to fake it, you just have to leave yourself at home . . . . Well, that's if your home's a good environment to be in. (R18)

CC29 refers to his tactics of concealment and leading a double life when he draws a parallel between being homosexual and working in espionage. Even after "coming out," the use of camouflage is often a necessary or strategic way to manage situations in which heterosexuality is demanded and to avoid awkward "scenes." But the chameleon nature of growing up gay is perhaps most clear in the next statement:

> I never ever said anything about it . . . it's one thing that you do when you've got so many secrets you can be so many different people. And I learned that from a really young age, you can be whatever you wanna be. (DD30)

The underlying concern with all of these examples is the impact that "hiding" has on people's integrity and their capacity to form meaningful relationships.

The discussion of how boys reinvented themselves or fashioned their "selves" in response to homophobia leads to some examples of protective façades and dual lives (called a "false, heterosexual self" in O'Conor, 1995: 99; or "false persona" in Anderson, 1995: 24). BB28 alludes to the protective value of disguises in the following extract:

> . . . if they got themselves a girlfriend eh? . . . That certainly would quash any rumors. (BB28)

The pressure to create a façade is difficult to avoid. X24 reveals one of his responses to this pressure when he complains about

> . . . basically having to bullshit on about . . . aspirations to get married. (X24)

In comparison, C3 describes an elaborate scheme to maintain his "camouflage," which acts out the strategy suggested by BB28 that:

> I moved to [capital city], got meself a girlfriend, got meself a motorbike . . . grew me hair long, and grew a beard. And became this great big tough macho guy just like what my family wanted me to be. (C3)

Although DD30 didn't attempt to elaborate a false heterosexual identity for himself, he did find the need to protect himself by inventing a rebellious and tough façade (which he later shed):

> . . . it was just protecting the real me. So nobody could see. (DD30)

V22 also describes how he became rebellious in the face of the discord between his emerging gay identity and homophobia:

> . . . I spent most of my time alone . . . I watched a lot of TV . . . I had a lot of guilt. I ended up . . . smoking a lot of dope and becoming a bit rebellious and those sorts of things. . . . I mean it's partly about that dual life. (V22)

Having a dual life can become extremely complex, including inventing new names and constructing elaborate virtual identities:

> I started leading a bit of a double life then, in year ten. . . . Friday night going out with the girls and Saturday night goin' out with the boys. It was great you know [cynical] . . . once I started, work just got harder and harder, and I guess I found it too hard. . . . I had a straight set of friends, and my gay set of friends, and . . . even my gay friends didn't even know me as [C3 name]. I had a different name and all. I had this completely different identity, so that if anyone in the street met me and they called me [C3 pseudonym], I'd know straightaway who I was dealing with . . . in case I forgot. (C3)

The rift between identities seems to have been taken even further in the following extraordinary scenario involving V22:

> . . . meeting this guy, going off into the bushes with him . . . the only thing he really wanted was to be fucked . . . [he] eventually came while I was fucking him and . . . as soon as, you know, pretty well as soon as that was over . . . [he] pushed . . . pushed me away. Not . . . not violently . . . but you know pushed me away so I was out of him and he pulled up his pants and started abusing me saying. . . . "You disgusting poofter . . . I don't ever want to see you here again. If I see you here again I'll kill you" . . . literally within thirty seconds . . . of being fucked by me. It was quite astounding . . . it was probably . . . the most threatened I've ever felt. . . . I mean the time that he was abusing and stuff I really felt like he could kill me then and there. (V22)

The "most threatened I've ever felt" is a revealing statement considering V22 described previously how on another occasion he was attacked by a gang and received a broken arm.

The pressure to hide and renounce a homosexual identity, to devise a façade, to elaborate a false persona, and ultimately to lead dual lives with two identities is complex and not without cost. According to Herek, hiding sexual orientation creates a "painful discrepancy" between public and private identities (Herek, 1991: 74) that is difficult to sustain:

> . . . 'cause I've got a reasonable camouflage, nobody knew. I didn't really know myself. Sort of takes a bit of time for you to sort of realize in your own mind, it's a bit like a veneer . . . and as time goes the veneer wears thinner and thinner . . . I'd say the veneer was totally and utterly gone by the time I was in fourth year of Uni. (X24)

All gay men in this study had some experience with these strategies. None of these responses would have been necessary if being homosexual was socially acceptable.

Trying to Change

An alternative to concealment is to attempt to change one's sexual preference/identity. Many subjects tried to change unacceptable aspects of their sexuality, including trying to suppress sexual desire, trying to redirect desire toward heterosexual objects, trying to destroy one's homosexual side, or, in extreme cases, possibly even trying to destroy one's self.

A number of subjects suppressed their sexuality in an attempt to avoid homophobic targeting:

> I just didn't talk about it. It was just one of those things. Just been hidden. Maybe it's because I suppressed a lot of my feelings. . . . Because of the fear and everything . . . in high school. . . . So I had to suppress everything. (B2)

Contrary to the popular stereotype that homosexual men are promiscuous, in several cases, homophobia seems to have resulted in delayed and constrained sexual activity. For example, Y25 had his first sexual partner only a couple of months prior to the interview, despite having a gay identity since early high school and working in gay-related organizations for the years following school. O15 also gives an example of how sustained homophobic harassment can inhibit emotions and interfere with forming attachments:

> I sort of had this grand plan . . . because I was being hassled . . . at school, I wasn't happy. My only way to being happy was to be successful, was to achieve at school, and to build this . . . happy successful life that is portrayed on the television. . . . So I didn't want anything to stop that. . . . And, as far as I could see, any sort of sexual encounter would immediately stop that. So I just blocked it, in the most amazing . . . I don't know how common or uncommon it is, but that's what I did and I was very good at it . . . so what it became was . . . if I show any sort of emotion or anything to someone else, I'm in the most vulnerable situation. I'm setting myself up to fall. So that's not going to happen. . . . And that's the pattern that I've continued, for a very long time. And it's still very difficult to get over. (O15)

Suppression (as opposed to elimination) implies a temporary state, usually until circumstances change and expression can be safely resumed. In order to be successful at school, P16 "filed" his homosexual desires away:

The bottom drawer of the filing cabinet just couldn't stay shut. It had to be dealt with. But my problem was finding a way. (P16)

The metaphor of "filing away" his desires implies that he is systematically preserving the information for future reference. He did not use metaphors that suggest their permanent eradication.

Other subjects did attempt to eradicate their homosexual side. CC29 refers to his struggle not to be a "poofter" in the following quote:

I wasn't intentionally setting out to behave like a poofter; it just came naturally. . . . I was working harder than them, because it came naturally to them . . . to be stupid idiots and beat people against a brick wall. And I was trying hard, you know
. . . working harder at not being a poofter than they were and yet they were calling me a poof. (CC29)

He goes on to describe seeking treatment to cure his homosexuality from two separate health professionals:

S: They weren't trying to change me, I was asking to be changed. Both of them.
D: And they both agreed to go along with it?
S: Yeah, although the first one didn't get anywhere near that far in.
D: What sort of exercises was the second one doing? Was there anything?
S: Yeah, he recorded a story about me at the beach with some surfer further down the beach, and I had to try and relax instead of getting excited. And then he recorded a story about a woman, and I had to practice getting excited and more aroused. (CC29)

Such "professional" aversion therapy seems feeble compared to the intensive (in his case, unsuccessful) aversion therapy practiced on the school ground by peers.

In the next example, subject L12 describes contemplating medical treatments. The reasons his attempts didn't succeed are revealing:

I was going to go and see the doctor and ask him about it. But that would have meant I would have had to told [sic] him about it in the first place. And that was the thing that stopped me 'cause I didn't want to tell anyone . . . for ages I wanted to just find some sort of information on cures and drugs and things that could change you . . . and then, when I started "coming out" with it, I lost that urge because I liked being homosexual. (L12)

Self-Harm

Some respondents identified an association between homophobia and self-harming behavior, and while there is insufficient evidence in this study to draw any conclusions about the links between homophobia and suicide, it was raised by many subjects. Suicide and parasuicide are complex issues, and these terms will not be used without qualification. However, the reader should be aware of emerging literature that claims increasingly well-defined links between homophobia and suicide (Remafedi, 1994). On the other hand, while homophobia undoubtedly exerts considerable pressures on young men, there is no reason to believe that homosexuals automatically have a greater chance of psychiatric illness than others do. Garnets and colleagues have reported that "the lesbian and gay male community does not differ significantly in mental health from the heterosexual population. Obviously antigay victimization does not inevitably lead to psychological dysfunction" (Garnets, Herek, and Levy, 1993: 580). However, Ross found that gay men's life events do impact on mental health, which can be "amplified by stigmatization" (Ross, 1990). This project raises further possibilities: that early victimization targets "poofters" and "faggots," which is not the same as targeting homosexuals, and that homophobia produces psychological impact in homosexuals and nonhomosexuals alike. You will recall the evidence that homophobia has adverse effects on heterosexual men too (see the section titled "Limiting Opportunities," p. 164), and as we will see later, there is a surprising resilience among gay men who were victimized. As L12 says, he eventually lost the urge to have his sexual orientation "treated" because he came to like being homosexual.

In the first instance, there is a link with "substance use," in this case, associated with loneliness:

> . . . there's a lot of . . . lonely, yearning gay men out there who have chronic alcohol [problems] . . . that's people who aren't in the gay community, people who are afraid to get so far as a . . . gay community, end up being kind of . . . social misfits and even more lonely. (V22)

In the second example, resorting to alcohol is attributed to perceived mounting pressures to be heterosexual:

> . . . I couldn't handle it anymore, so I just I think I went drunk for about a year. . . . I think it was because both my sisters were married, had children. My brother got married, had kids, and all of a sudden the pressure was on me, 'cause my brothers only had daughters . . . and the pressure was on me to get married 'cause my dad wanted a "[grandson with the family surname]." (C3)

There is also a possibility that homophobia predisposes young men to risks such as HIV exposure. In the next account, "suicidal" ideation is linked to reduced concern about HIV. The trade-off is that restraint could give way to pleasure, which is at least one compensation for being gay and having a terminal illness:

> I can remember year eleven . . . when I was pretty much suicidal and I thought well if I just caught AIDS and died, well, pow, that would be the best way to go. . . . I could live for a couple of years and maybe have some fun but, it's like you're going to die. (AA27)

One subject also described how HIV risk was maximal prior to coming to terms with his homosexual side, but that his risk changed dramatically after he confronted that aspect of his identity:

> **D:** . . . you practiced unsafe sex frequently?
> **S:** Yes. All the time. Up until two years ago. All the time. . . . The agenda is that only gays get HIV/AIDS and I know that

not to be true now. Herpes only happened to people that deserve it. And most of the other things were curable. And if you have an STD you deserve it. And if a guy passes on an STD to a female it's acceptable . . . "the bitch deserved it."

D: And after this "coming-out" process, did those behaviors change?

S: [Affirmative response] Mmm, dramatically. (A1)

Other examples of suicidal ideation were also reported. The following example makes the link between homophobia and isolation.

S: . . . I have bad, very strong mood swings sometimes . . . and actually living on your own makes it worse because you tend to feel isolated. And I've sort of felt . . . like passive suicide . . . but the thing that really stopped me from ever doing it, I think, is the sense of it's a cop out. . . .

D: And is that then related to your sexuality?

S: Yeah. It has been. Very definitely . . . I think because basically it undermines your self-esteem. (X24)

In the next example, being dead or staging a death was considered a way of getting a clean slate to "start again":

. . . I can remember thinking that the easiest way for me to deal with not fitting in and with being different and . . . with what I would attach now as being gay, was to be dead. . . . Or for everyone who knew me to be dead so I could start again. (O15)

Several subjects described "suicide attempts" that were linked to difficulties with sexuality (although there is no way of knowing how far any of the acts described here were intended to go):

There's been a number of suicide attempts in my life. . . . The strongest one would definitely have been on my eighteenth birthday, which was . . . sexuality based. (A1)

A picture has emerged of C3 as a young man with serious problems related to dissonance about his homosexuality. This picture consolidates further with the following comments:

S: I've tried to kill myself many times over many years. [Ironic laugh] I've called it "roulette suicide."

D: Tell me about it if you can.

S: . . . I used to play games, like there's one hill that used to go out to the highway, and it was a really big hill. It was one way going each way, double yellow lines . . . so every morning, oh, as long as I can remember from the day that I got my license, I used to go round that hill every morning on the wrong side of the road . . . and just if a car came that would be it. It was a 60 K zone, so I used to hit it just about every mornin' doin' about eighty, ninety, a hundred K's. And just go over the top and it was more or less just a way to start the day, you know. If I didn't die this morning, well I wasn't meant to die. . . . 'Cause [laughs] I couldn't be who I wanted to be—this little faggot. I never had the guts to actually kill myself so I thought I'll get someone else to do it for me. What scares me is that I could've taken someone else with me [anxious laugh]. (C3)

A similar story was offered by L12, who also links his behavior with a homophobic view of his sexuality:

I was driving along in the car and I just shut my eyes and had my foot planted to the floor, [and] it was a straight road but I'd let go of the wheel and everything and I just "Let it go," and it felt like ages [that] I was sitting there. It felt like a really long time . . . at some point I just opened my eyes and I hit the brake, and I just grabbed the wheel. . . . I couldn't actually go through with it, crashing the car. . . . That was a pathetic, stupid, idiotic thing to do. They were the only two times really, that I'd tried to actually do something. . . . I didn't plan it but I was feeling really bad 'cause I knew I was gay and I'd just had enough of. My family didn't know, most of my friends, all of my friends didn't know. I was just having this really bad time with everything. (L12)

Rejecting Homophobia

Rejecting homophobia involves a capacity to question orthodox views and resist dominant culture. Themes that characterize these processes include resistance, defiance, and implicit and explicit acceptance of "difference." This section contrasts sharply with the previous one. While the negativity unearthed by this research becomes relentless at times, the strategies that flow from rejecting homophobia are more positive and provide some relief. As Peter Aggleton reminds us, "being gay is in many circumstances a positive and creative experience" (Aggleton, 1987: 108). The accounts in this section give some indications as to how that might be possible. The strategies recounted here, however, are risky. The price of resistance is exposure and intensified harassment.

Defiance features in a number of interviews. Even in primary school, the orthodoxy of the school-ground peer culture is open to question. CC29 previously recounted the dilemma of whether he should play cards with the girls or conform to expectations of the boys. In the following account, he defies peer expectations:

> **S:** . . . there was no reason why you shouldn't sit down and play cards with the girls and as much as people tried to tell me otherwise. . . . I suppose unless an adult tells me I'm not allowed, I'm going to go ahead and do it.
> **D:** So was there a sense of defiance there?
> **S:** Definitely! Yeah. (CC29)

Similarly, T20 attracted homophobia in high school when he started aerobics and became labeled as a "fairy in tights." In the next extract, he describes how, despite the costs, he challenged that label and defiantly continued aerobics:

> It hurt, because at that age you want to be accepted by your peers and you want everyone to like you. . . . You don't want to stand out, you don't want . . . to walk through the playground and have people shout things at you. You want to talk to people, you know. But, I just challenged it, and I didn't care, really. It was . . . just something that I wanted to do. I enjoyed it, so you know, do that. Live with it. (T20)

As well as questioning school-ground orthodoxy and standing firm, some boys are intentionally defiant and provocative in the face of homophobic pressure:

S: . . . in year eight, me and [male friend] decided we'd be the first two boys at [our] high school, to take sewing as a class. So that was quite interesting. That was actually good fun. . . .
D: You knew when you took something like that, that it would trigger another round of abuse?
S: Uh huh.
D: So why did you do it?
S: Oh it was kind of a taunt. A taunt, that sort of thing, you know? (Y25)

A similar stance was taken independently by Q17. Not only was he aware of the inflammatory position he was taking, but he also admits to enjoying being different.

. . . yet I sort of actually enjoyed being different. . . . And I knew that I could've not crocheted and avoided the problem or choose to crochet and be different. And I chose to crochet and be different. (Q17)

Provocative and defiant initiatives can take many forms. Answering back carries the risk of escalating harassment even to the point of violence. Notice how R18 neutralized the effect by making nonsense of the harassment:

. . . if they [the peer group] got a hint of . . . "poofter" in the air . . . one in particular would ask, "Oh, what do you do on weekends?" . . . "Do you go to the [bar name]?" . . . I think it was a hotel where the gay people hung out, but I don't know . . . but they would give up in the end because . . . I'd be so . . . sarcastic they wouldn't be able to get a proper answer out of me. . . . "Yeah, I love it there!" "Yeah, it's the best place in the world!" or . . . "The [bar name], isn't that an animal or something?" . . . Generally I was a lot more scathing than they were. (R18)

Sometimes defiance is made safer or easier with the support of another person. In a previous example, Y25 took sewing classes with a male friend. In the next example, DD30 describes how he and a friend, who was similarly marginalized, found strength in retaliating with clever retorts:

> . . . we made up these good things like . . . "Don't flatter yourself." . . . Just different things we'd always be able to throw back, because that stuff hurts. And I needed to say stuff back; I needed it. It was a real need because it hurt so much. (DD30)

Notice how responding to harassment seems to satisfy a need and is good for morale. Perhaps this is a trade-off for the extra risk that responding entails. Indeed, although "poofs" were stereotyped as soft, sometimes defiance did demand physical retaliation—even when violence is viewed as "ugly":

> I didn't actually initiate it . . . because of all of the violence that was happening and I saw a few fights and they got pretty scary, you know, they were pretty frightening. And so even though I'd been fairly violent before that, by this time I started to register that it just wasn't the thing to do. It was a really, really ugly thing. And so . . . somebody'd come up to me and call me a poof and they'd trip me or something . . . sometimes I'd just get so mad you know, I'd get so angry with it you know. And then we'd sort of start up a punch up. (DD30)

Rebelling was a means of defense against homophobia. DD30 relates how he felt his rebellion protected him against the homophobia of his sister:

> She laid heaps of homophobia on me. And I'm really glad that at that age I was really rebelling . . . and I didn't take her shit on. (DD30)

In the next quote, DD30 describes what rebellion means for him and how he defiantly relates it to his sexuality:

> And by this time I was really over the top. [Laughs] Like I had the daggiest clothes on you know, my hair was everywhere, I had it dyed different colors. Earrings all over my face . . . the more outrageous the better . . . 'cause it was like everybody was saying, "Don't do it. Don't do it because it's so poofy" . . . and so I did it, because I can do this whether you like it or not. (DD30)

But rebellion can also be mixed with concealment. Here C3 describes how he rebelled and took up a variety of social causes, providing they weren't causes that might have suggested that he was gay:

> . . . I used to like sticking it up the system . . . because I couldn't be who I wanted to be [gay], I thought okay, I'll be something else that I wasn't. So you got society here, I wanted to be over this side. Doing what I wanted to be, you know, which was the extreme. . . . I went to the other side and just became outrageous and went over the top, just with different things I did, especially with music, clothes rallies, and you know. Anything I could do to stuff up the system, but where people accepted it as far as, it's okay to be different as long as it's a "straight" different. So, it's okay to be . . . different from [the] norm as long as you're doin' somethin' that is a "cause"—that isn't toward the gay. (C3)

The suggestion that boys did have some supports appears to contradict earlier statements concerning the isolation associated with homophobia. While there were accounts of alliances between boys who were similarly marginalized, they usually both remained marginalized in relation to the rest of the school:

> **S:** . . . he was my art buddy, we were always in art together, and . . . he was always really camp, really, really camp, running around, laughing and kicking up his heels big time. . . . I think that's how he got his branding. But he didn't care; he was "out" about it.
> **D:** Do you think being friends with [name] made it easier or more difficult?
> **S:** No, harder.
> **D:** Harder?
> **S:** Harder. Definitely. (T20)

In addition, (homophobic) distance was still maintained between boys in those alliances despite the obvious comfort that they provided each other (see the section titled "Peer Groups," p. 98). Goffman observed that "it is in his affiliation with, or separation from, his more evi-

dently stigmatized fellows, that the individual's oscillation of identification is most sharply marked" (Goffman, 1963: 107). DD30 has
not remained in contact with his "friend" since leaving school. In
the case of DD30, V22 (each of whom had a loose association with
other "poofs" at school), and the friend of T20, their homosexuality
was not disclosed to each other until after completing high school.
In contrast, it is virtually compulsory for heterosexual school boys
to publicly attest (flaunt?) their heterosexuality.

For many, given time, the influence of homophobia eases and a
progressively stronger sense of their homosexual identity emerges,
particularly after leaving the secondary school environment:

> . . . in your own mind, there's a veneer . . . that you've got to
> present to yourself that you're straight. And I think as time
> goes on we get more and more exposure and you feel a stron-
> ger and stronger sense of identity. That veneer just wears thin
> until in the end, you just think this is bullshit and I'm wasting
> my life. (X24)

And many young gay men recognize the price of not being "themselves" and are prepared to sever important relationships in order to
reconcile their lives with their sense of identity:

> **S:** . . . you've got to be yourself and if that means other people
> don't cope with you, are hurt by it, fuck 'em. It's, when it
> comes to your sexuality, if it means you seclude yourself from
> your family, do that. Because . . . I think that's the best thing I
> ever did.
> **D:** Because if you don't, what happens?
> **S:** You'll lose your identity. And you will kill yourself. You'll
> develop shame, you'll develop guilt, you'll never have a prop-
> er relationship. (AA27)

Some descriptions illustrate remarkable determination undeterred
by savage homophobia:

> . . . doing the Mardi Gras thing . . . there was a couple that
> hadn't actually turned up yet. And so we were starting to think
> "Well, what's happened to them?" . . . And they actually turned

up at about one o'clock in the morning at the party and so we all said, "What the hell happened?" And they said they were actually standing outside their hotel . . . waiting for a cab and a bunch of guys just came along and started beating the shit out of them and one of them had his two front teeth knocked out and so they went back into the hotel, found a dentist, he got his teeth recapped, [and] came to the party. (Y25)

The resilience and "style" exhibited in the face of physical attack makes it seem that the victims view being attacked as a "routine" part of being gay.

"It is indicative of the strength of these young people that they all survived these crises and are now happy to identify themselves to us as homosexual" (Trenchard and Warren, quoted in Mac an Ghaill, 1994: 167). Participants made similar observations in the present interviews:

. . . knowing what he'd come through. Because I'd been there and I'd seen what he'd put up with . . . he hadn't hid it . . . well I don't even know if he knew he was gay then. . . . He tolerated people, I guess, and . . . did have to put up with quite a lot of shit. And then he'd obviously dealt with it himself and he's quite comfortable with it. (T20)

Some people are even able to "grow" through dealing with homophobia. DD30 remarks on personal growth that comes from confronting homophobia:

I think they can become very strong through their own experiences because a lot of homosexuals have really bad experiences and I think that a lot of people, a lot of homosexual men and women, they grow through that. (DD30)

Strength is also a feature of comments by V22. He pays tribute to the strength of some boys who were labeled, but he also acknowledges a downside:

. . . if you survive the whole experience of "coming out" it involves a hell of a lot more personal exploration . . . and insight than most men at least . . . if not most people . . . afford. And that in itself is a strength of personal conviction. I mean there are downsides because you know, most people don't survive it very well. (V22)

The flip side of growing due to the experiences of being gay and confronting homophobia was depicted as narrowness in heterosexual male development. Indeed, AA27 suggests that homophobic dynamics actually prevent men from growing because that would involve "exploring emotions" and "dealing with issues." We have already seen that that part of hegemonic heterosexuality seems to involve denying certain emotions:

> . . . you can't be "butch" if you're . . . exploring your emotions and dealing with your issues . . . for gay men, creativity is a result of things happening in the brain. You know, like stresses and pressures, and this is a way to get it out. Like, my flat mate, he's not a very verbal person, but I can tell what he's thinking, what he's feeling, by watching his paintings. (AA27)

AA27 is acknowledging a common stereotype that gay men are more creative. The aim of this thesis is not to verify or reject that proposition, but to consider what such observations might indicate about homophobia. O15 pursues a similar theme, but instead of attributing creative outpouring to accumulated homophobic pressures, he suggests that different perspectives resulting from homophobic marginalization offer insights that otherwise might not be available:

> . . . gay people have experienced so much more and [have] been forced to see things from so many different points of view. Whereas a lot of . . . heterosexual men particularly aren't forced to do that because they just sort of grow up so easily and slip into that dominant framework that . . . they don't have to see these other things in their lives, so they choose not to. (O15)

Some heterosexual subjects also acknowledge the possibility that homosexuals make important contributions as a result of being homosexual rather than despite it:

. . . I think that homosexuality is and always has been . . . an important part of society, a vibrant part of society . . . and I think to eradicate that wouldn't be good for society. (W23)

To suggest that experiencing marginality and dealing with homophobia can result in personal growth also suggests that being heterosexual can be constraining and restrictive. DD30 does not locate creativity intrinsically within homosexuality, but relates it to homosexuals being less restrained by convention:

. . . that's only because they [homosexuals] allow themselves to [be more artistic or creative]. They're in a minority group where they're outcasts from society and . . . they've got their own rules . . . they let themselves grow . . . they're not in this . . . structure of heterosexuality where they've got to stay in these boundaries. (DD30)

Finally, J10 proposes an additional dimension:

I think there's also something else, which is sort of like a spiritual thing. I think because we'll face our death without leaving any family behind us, I think gay men perhaps try and leave something else, and you know, excel in music and, I mean, their creative outlets and books or sculpture or clothes or that sort of stuff. (J10)

HOMOPHOBIA AND IDENTITY

The final part of this chapter explores the influence of homophobia on homosexual "self-concepts" and "identities." While many studies on homosexual identity formation implicitly acknowledge the influence of homophobia, most fail to explore its influence in detail. According to Troiden, "nearly all models view homosexual identity formation as taking place against a backdrop of stigma. The stigma surrounding homosexuality affects both the formation and expression of homosexual identities" (Troiden, 1993: 194; Martin, 1982). However, rather than attempt to describe homosexual identity formation as these studies generally do, the present work aims to identify and analyze pressures exerted by homophobia on identity formation (to explore the "backdrop of stigma," as Troiden puts it).

Devaluing Identity: "The Backdrop of Stigma"

An important factor in the process of forming a homosexual identity is the scarcity of positive role models:

> . . . up until this stage, I had never seen any gay culture, . . . never met or talked to another gay man. I had no idea how to get in touch or contact with that side of my sexuality or any other people. I felt very alone. (P16)

Perhaps not surprisingly, the absence of positive role models during identity formation contrasts sharply with the availability of a range of negative stereotypes. These include being criminals, communists, woman haters, and child molesters. In the following example, implicit parallels with serious crime can be seen when K11 is asked how he would feel if his son was homosexual:

> It would be a big shock. I would hope I would have brought my children up not to kill. . . . Yeah. Not to kill people and . . . maybe to be heterosexual. (K11)

And in P16's account of his "coming out" to his parents, his father's response relies on xenophobia and the threat of communism:

> He was convinced that I'd fallen in with the wrong set, the wrong Uni crowd. 'Cause this was all foreign to him, you know, all "reds under the bed" type activity. . . . I found it very frustrating 'cause I couldn't reason with him. . . . I couldn't apply any sort of rigor to our conversation. It was all reactionary. It was all uninformed. It was all ignorance. And I couldn't get him to understand. (P16)

Although masculinity is stereotypically associated with rationality and logic, accounts such as this reveal a resistance to logic when it comes to dealing with homosexuality. This further supports Halperin's observation that homophobia can persist and often assume a logically opposing position when the original justification is discredited (Halperin, 1995: 37-38).

Stereotypes for homosexuality often refer to homosexuals as being a "threat to children" or fail to distinguish homosexuality from pedophilia. This is another negative stereotype that impacts on identity formation, as A1 discovered:

> . . . my understanding of what a homosexual is, or was back then, was this person in a coat . . . a person that hangs around . . . schoolyards at night. . . . And [it] was almost like the boogyman type thing. And the boogyman lived under the house. . . . And the boogyman couldn't really do anything just scared people. Whereas the person you know, in the hat in the schoolyard at night, was a real person that could really hurt you. . . . It definitely wasn't me squeezed in fucking frocks! [Laughs] (A1)

A1's ironic humor functions by detaching his homosexuality from one (menacing) stereotype only to associate it with another (emasculated) one. While A1 has specific reasons for linking his ideas about homosexuality with childhood fears, X24 acknowledges that this stereotype is more widespread:

> I know with a lot of people that the distinction doesn't exist . . . they think pedophiles are gay. (X24)

Stereotypes of homosexuals also identify homosexuals as "woman haters." In the following quote, the irony is particularly acute:

> . . . you remember that guy that raped that young girl and put stones in her backpack and chucked her in the water? . . . Now that whole scenario was just hideous, and I heard a straight person say, "That fucking faggot." Like, how could that person have been a faggot? You know, it's like anything that . . . is not able to be coped with . . . by society is blamed on faggots. (A1)

At first it is puzzling how a brutal heterosexual rape can be attributed to a "faggot." A1 explains this by picking up on the consistent negativity that permits such attributions regardless of their lack of logic. However, there is another dimension that sustains this association: both faggots and rapists are thought to hate women.

Another complication of identity formation arises from internalizing homophobia. Internalized homophobia occurs when homophobia is endorsed at the same time that homosexuality is part of that person's identity (Shidlo, 1994; Ross, 1985, 1996). In a culture where homophobia is so widespread, it is likely that internalized homophobia is a problem for all gay men at some stage:

> . . . you go through stages where you try to deny the fact that that's what you are [gay] . . . if you sort of identify that with yourself you can feel quite self-destructive and so you don't feel particularly . . . pleasant toward these people that you identify as having characteristics in common with yourself. (X24)

This echoes statements by C3:

> I just started believing that being queer was wrong . . . and I was probably an instigator for a lot of the so-called, and I got a name for it now, "homophobia" around the school. (C3)

The next example describes the struggle between an emerging gay identity and internalized homophobia ("aversion to being gay"). Notice how the aim of not being gay is also stereotypical, but none of the stereotypes are sexual:

> I was trying to be more male. I wanted to wear a check shirt and wear jeans and be more masculine. And that was a lot of the stuff I was dealing with. . . . I would like to be more butch and play football . . . so my aversion to being gay was that, and also possibly the built-in persecution mechanisms that say I'm not a valued person if I was gay. 'Cause that's the word they use to ascribe to me—you're a faggot; you're a poofter. (Q17)

The dilemma that homophobia creates for an emerging gay identity becomes even more clear in the following discourse:

> **S:** I wanted to avoid *everything that would attach me to that,* because to me it only had the most *negative associations*

imaginable. So, the word, I never said the word, I would never read anything that had to do with it, just. . .
D: Which word's that?
S: You've already said it, the "P" word [poofter]. (O15)

O15 is now openly gay and facilitates gay community support groups for young men who are themselves coming to terms with their gay identities. Nevertheless, notice how O15 appears to struggle to say the "P word" as he recounts his experiences. You will recall in an earlier quote that O15 remarks how his homophobic childhood experiences are "still very difficult to get over."

"Coming out" is often described as part of gay identity formation. The "coming-out" process is relevant to this research because it appears to be constituted because of homophobia and, as such, testifies to the pervasiveness and power of homophobia. As Garnets and colleagues wrote, "coming out becomes a process of reclaiming disowned or devalued parts of the self, and developing an identity into which one's sexuality is well-integrated" (Garnets, Herek, and Levy, 1993: 583). A related phenomenon is the political strategy of "outing." While the rights and wrongs of outing do not concern this project, the power of outing as a political strategy resides entirely in its capacity to expose people as homosexual—an exposure that relies on homophobia for its impact. "Coming out" and "outing" refer to transferring knowledge into the public domain. In the public domain, this knowledge can become the subject of (homophobic) social scrutiny. The modern metaphor of "coming out" is further elaborated by providing a "closet" to come out of. Once again, the relevance of the "closet" for this research is that it is a place to hide and is constructed by homophobia (Sedgewick, 1990). "Coming out of the closet" was found to be a momentous process for people in this study. A1 describes his process of homosexual identity formation:

. . . when I made that big jump "out of the closet," as everyone says, it was horrendous. It caused me to have three weeks off work. It caused me to have one of those tantrums, you know, one of those childhood tantrums . . . the three-week period was basically indoors and not knowing what the fuck was going on. (A1)

At that stage, A1 equated homosexuals with "boogymen" who hurt children, and this affected his ability to come to terms with his own identity. Although at the time of the interview he was in a sexual relationship with a regular male partner, he was unhappy with sexual labels and rejected the term homosexual.

Foundations of Sexual Identity: Difference and Homophobia

Among the participants who identified as predominantly homosexual for this research, a recurring theme is the conjunction between childhood "difference" and adult homosexual identity. Other researchers have made similar observations (Gonsiorek and Rudolph, 1991: 166; Troiden, 1993: 197; Hockenberry and Billingham, 1987). On this matter, Gonsiorek and Rudolph write, "Children who will eventually be bisexual or homosexual often develop an awareness of being different at an early age" (Gonsiorek and Rudolph, 1991: 166). The present study also found evidence for this early "presexual" sense of difference by participants who are now gay. The data also suggest that this feeling of difference has a number of facets. In the first example, P16 emphasizes his early sense of difference:

I can't remember ever being an outcast, that sort of thing, I just felt really, really different. (P16)

P16 now reads this sense of difference as an early indicator of his sexual difference.

V22 provides another perspective on the same issue. In this case, it is his peers who detect and respond to his difference, but they don't define it as sexual difference either:

. . . it wasn't necessarily explicitly said that they were teasing me for being a pansy. They were teasing me for being different. (V22)

However, V22 links this retrospectively with his sexual difference:

> I was always very different from the rest of the family and I
> think in retrospect . . . I mean, certainly that had to do with
> sexuality. (V22)

Feeling different, initially from a nonsexual perspective, is also
expressed by Q17, who describes his own sense of difference, the
reaction of his peers to his difference, and how he uses his adult
sexual identity as a reference point:

> I do recall not being one of the boys. . . . I do recall being
> persecuted by them, like I was the "odd one out." For what-
> ever reason, I had no concept of it being an identity or sexual-
> ity, I just thought that I was the "odd one out." (Q17)

This sense of difference eventually assumes (or is reinterpreted
with) sexual dimensions. Troiden writes, "childhood perceptions of
self as different, crystallize into perceptions of self as sexually
different after the onset of adolescence" (Troiden, 1993: 200). "Although a sense of being different and set apart from same-sex age
mates is a persistent theme in the childhood experiences of lesbians
and gay males, research indicates that only a minority of gay males
(20 percent) and lesbians (20 percent) begin to see themselves as
sexually different before age twelve" (Troiden, 1993: 198). Accounts collected for this study contain similar "persistent" themes:

> I always thought I was different. All the way through child-
> hood. . . . But you . . . didn't really put your finger on any pulse
> till later. Then you sort of realized what gay and homosexual
> and poofter and all that sort of thing was supposed to have
> meant. But you didn't think that you were one . . . because up
> until that stage there was no sexual contact in any way. (B2)

The extension of this sense of difference to the adult sexual domain
adds another dimension to homophobia that seems to be more painful:

> . . . most of the time I felt . . . different. But not upsetting-
> different . . . not "Oh, my God, I'm different, I'm different!" I

just always felt different. It only got upsetting about the homo-sexuality side of it. (L12)

The importance of a childhood sense of "difference" is that ho-mophobia at this time is also asexual (even though it does have gendered dimensions) and it designates differences in boys. In other words, it seems as if homophobia bridges the gap between child-hood difference and adult homosexuality (Hockenberry and Bil-lingham, 1987). As we proceed, this picture becomes even more elaborate and contains the following elements: (1) early homopho-bia is asexual; (2) presexual homophobia uses boyhood/gendered/unmasculine difference as its frame of reference; (3) a persistent sense of childhood difference precedes homosexual identity forma-tion; (4) homophobic labeling was used by peers to designate differ-ent children who would later be homosexual; and (5) participants repeatedly reported that their peers seemed to know they were gay before they did. Taken together, these observations would appear to indicate that schoolchildren can predict sexual identity (at least for some people), and men experience a sense of déjà vu when they do become gay. This phenomenon is illustrated by B2 in the following quote:

Basically they [school peers] knew that I was [gay] before I did [laugh]. You know, I always got . . . 'cause I was different and I was fatter, I suppose I would come across fairly funny and I got picked on, called "poofter," and all that sort of thing. (B2)

B2 does not seem to acknowledge any incongruity between a "poofter," being "fatter," "different," coming across "fairly funny" as a child, and being gay as an adult. Notice the apparent continuity in B2's mind between having his homosexuality anticipated by peers and being different at school. In another account, B2 made a further reference to the same phenomenon, but this time, he refers to his own ability to anticipate the sexual orientation of a peer:

I've since met up with one of the guys I went to school with, and . . . he's gay, and he said, "Oh, you remember [name]?" and I said, "Yeah" and he said, "He's gay." And I said, "Well that was pretty obvious that he would be too." I said it's funny how everyone could work out what we were before we knew it. And he said the same thing. (B2)

So what generates this apparently smooth and logical continuity between childhood difference and adult homosexual identity—at least in people's minds? While there does appear to be a conjunction between childhood difference and adult sexual identity, it will be shown in Chapter 5 that (for this sample at least) there isn't an analogous relationship between childhood erotic practices and adult sexual identity. The main bridge between childhood difference and adult homosexual identity appears to be because both can provoke the label "poofter"—homophobia supplies the links. In reference to what younger children identify and label "poofter," T20 made this insightful overstatement about difference having homophobic connotations:

. . . they just think it's "alien central." (T20)

Being introduced to, and conversant in, homophobia prior to assuming an adult sexual identity means that people initially begin to understand homosexuality through homophobia—a situation that also applies to boys with emerging homosexual and heterosexual identities. In the next three extracts, it is possible to catch a glimpse of some defining moments when presexual homophobic frames of reference start to become homosexual identities. In the first extract, DD30 describes a formative moment when he was displaced from being the toughest boy in school to the second toughest and how that prompted him to redefine his identity:

. . . I was no longer the toughest; he was. So that was really challenging. And then it started, I dunno why, but I started to really concentrate on thinking, "Well, am I effeminate?" you know, "I must be effeminate if I'm no longer the toughest kid." . . . And I took that stuff on. (DD30)

In the mind of DD30, being the second toughest boy in the school equated with effeminacy and was the trigger for him to start questioning his identity. As DD30 goes on to explain, a homophobic concept of "effeminacy" underwrote his early understandings of what a homosexual was, and his experience of no longer being the toughest provided a link between his "self" and being homosexual. In contrast, the links between N14's sense of difference and his observation of someone else who was different led him to identify with that person and, ultimately, a homosexual identity:

> . . . one of the little boys who'd always been hassled, and you always saw his name up on toilet blocks. . . . he dressed up as Divine, and did a number in front of the school. Which I thought was the best thing I'd ever seen. Because this was the first person that I'd seen in drag, and I thought I want to do that one day. And I remember following in his footsteps then, discovering where he had been, what courses he had done, ended up getting a job in a library because he had worked in there with people. All voluntary, before and after school. And doing things he had done and wanting to know about him. And also being very interested, in the older boys who were labeled as the "poofters." (N14)

This case illustrates how identification was formed with another person based on his (presexual) homophobic labeling. Interestingly, N14 identified with this boy and studied him, but maintained a safe distance. N14 describes himself as being interested in boys who were different and that he was "attracted to their difference" rather than being attracted to them sexually.

Y25 has endured considerable homophobic targeting and it was during one of these attacks that he underwent a fundamental change —from being assailed with homophobic labeling to affirming his homosexual identity. He described this episode as "good" because it was during an attack that his homosexual identity crystallized:

> I started getting hassled almost immediately at high school, like even physical stirring, spitting on me, and that kind of thing . . . in a sense it was good. . . . I was walking down the track, which was this dirt track between [shopping plaza] and [suburb] High School. Which you did every afternoon, to get home, to catch a bus home . . . there were these boys the year above me that always hassled me . . . one of them just walked past me, slagged on me and called me a faggot and [it] was just

kind of like "Yeah! I am! That's it." . . . This was just walking through this track and this guy just sort of called me a poofter, and it was the last straw. I was kinda like, "I'm getting fed up now," and . . . I just thought to myself, you know, "I am! So what?". And it was like, "Oh, I am! Cool! That's fine" . . . this was all in my head and I just kept walking. (Y25)

Each of these cases offers insights into how these men approached their emerging homosexual identities initially from an asexual framework underwritten by homophobia. They also illustrate how homophobia can provide a bridge between early homophobic labeling imposed by peers and the formation of a homosexual identity. In each of these cases, it is as if the identity conformed to (was constructed by) the homophobic expectations of peers—particularly their homophobic understanding of difference.

So how can the apparent "predictive power" of childhood difference/homophobia for adult homosexuality be explained?

> . . . the little wuss, just usually tends to be[come] the queen after a few years for some reason. (AA27)

One possible explanation is that subjects retrospectively reinterpret their experiences into a sexual framework (Hockenberry and Billingham, 1987). That is, many boys have a sense of difference, many experience periodic homophobic labeling and many have childhood homoerotic experiences, but these are only invested with special significance in boys who later become homosexual. Thus, while people might claim to have always known they were gay and offer childhood experiences as evidence, they may simply be attributing unwarranted significance to experiences that many heterosexual men have also had.

A second possibility relies on essentialism. It may be that sexual preference is predetermined and that a range of differences signified by homophobia are a reflection of factors that determine sexual preference. This explanation is unsatisfying because it fails to account for the considerable historical and cross-cultural variability of homosexual stereotypes, identities, and homophobia.

The final possibility is that, in the absence of any other explanations for their difference, children who experience sustained feelings of difference, or who are labeled as different, may ultimately comprehend their difference using a framework that equates childhood difference with adult homosexuality. In other words, early homophobic labeling of difference, followed by the (homo) sexualization of homophobia, enables people to comprehend their difference in (homo) sexual terms, which thus underwrites modern gay identity formation. Thus, homosexual men may well have felt "different" from an early age, but not inherently gay. This accords with an earlier proposal that homophobia casts its shadow over eroticism and splits an initially "polymorphous" desire for intimacy along gender lines into polarized identities. In effect, homophobia precedes sexual identity, separates erotic practice, links difference with sexuality and thereby creates homosexual and heterosexual identities.

Whatever the ultimate explanation, homophobia plays an important role in homosexual identity formation. And, it remains the case that children learn about homophobia before they become aware of sexual identity, that homophobia targets difference in its presexual stages, and that boys initially come to understand homosexuality and heterosexuality through homophobia. Having formed a homosexual identity, it is notable that even in the face of homophobia, many gays steadfastly adhere to their difference and alternatives seem incomprehensible:

> ... the way that I like boys ... I can't imagine it any different, and I don't want to be any different. (AA27)

As Y25 comments when asked whether he could ever envisage changing his sexual orientation:

> **S:** God, I hope not!
> **D:** You hope not?
> **S:** I hope not! [Chuckle]
> **D:** ... why does that prospect frighten you so much?
> **S:** I suppose I'm quite enjoying being gay. So, you know, it doesn't seem natural to me ... to be in a straight relationship, whatsoever. (Y25)

Having taken possession of a tangible gay identity, these young men are no longer inexplicably different and isolated—now they belong.

When Self Is Other: Fluidity

This chapter has focused on the impact of homophobia, how homophobia defines the bounds of acceptability and transgression, and how homophobia contributes to fashioning the "self" and forming an identity. The present research identifies the importance of peer pressures in designating and regulating the bounds of acceptable boyhood masculinity and supports the findings of other researchers. For example, Mac an Ghaill writes, "sexual boundary maintenance, policing and control were definitive peer group cultural practices" (Mac an Ghaill, 1994: 101). DD30 provides his own description:

> There was a very clear-cut thing, you know, like boys or males don't do this and boys and males don't do that . . . wearing dresses, playing with dolls . . . you can't be too . . . emotional. (DD30)

In this final section however, we examine the converse: when boundaries are not observed. What happens to those who become homophobically labeled and therefore occupy the place and function of "other"? In theory, at least, for these people, "self" becomes "other" (and the divide between "self" and "other" becomes arbitrary, volatile, and miscible). If so, there would be significant implications for boundaries, which might lose their power and meaning.

Some boys experience sustained homophobic labeling and appear to cross boundaries regularly. This observation seems to match what other researchers refer to as fluidity. "Variability in the use of masculine and feminine behaviors indicates an important dimension to the experience of being gay, which is the experience of fluidity" (Pronger, 1990: 146). Fluidity is a feature of many of the accounts from gay men, but not those of heterosexual men, for whom fluid behaviors were generally seen as transgression. V22 illustrates this mixing of roles. He identifies the boundaries in relation to his "difference":

> . . . there was a fairly strict regime . . . of gender roles within
> the family . . . the boys . . . mowed the lawn, chopped the
> wood, did those sorts of things . . . and the girls cut veggies
> and cooked the dinner and did the housework . . . while I made
> fairy cakes [laughs]. I mean you can understand where . . .
> perhaps this sense of difference came from [laughs]. (V22)

Although he became defined by his transgression, the next quote
jokingly illustrates the fluid reality of V22's childhood and how his
(predominant) conforming elements can be overlooked in the face
of transgression:

> But, I mean, it was just terrible, I had to chop the wood, mow
> the lawn, and make the cakes. [laughs] (V22)

AA27 provides a similar account that emphasizes fluidity, being
both homophobically labeled (defined by his difference) and also
playing football, joining the "bikie gang," and being a "terror."

> I was never part of a particular group and I still don't. I just
> hopped from one [group to the next]. I'd go from playing
> skipsies with girls and then I'd go over and play footy with the
> boys and then I'd join a bikie gang and then go back and play
> skips and then I was a little terror. (AA27)

L12 and Y25 offered similar accounts.
   Another case in which boundaries appear to become indistinct is
between sexual desire (object) and gender identity (subject). CC29
describes a male schoolteacher whom he both desired and wanted to
be like:

> . . . he was exciting to me and gorgeous, and I wanted to be just
> like him when I grew up. (CC29)

For boys who become gay, while boundaries are sometimes painfully meaningful, they are not so meaningful that they can't be
crossed, and they are sometimes crossed defiantly. Several subjects
made statements that implied that the boundaries seemed arbitrary,
pointless, meaningless, unjustified, or unjust. Some of these were

reviewed earlier in this chapter and further examples from sports are contained in Chapter 5. Here is a view from DD30:

> . . . I thought it was pretty stupid [that] a lot of the kids . . . the reason that they were mucking around, hanging around the tough group and everything like that. It was like a real proving thing and I just couldn't get into that at all for some reason. . . . I'd usually go and stay off on my own, and if somebody asked me come and play handball, I'd usually go with them and, you know, just go with the flow. (DD30)

DD30 even uses the word "flow" to describe his style of involvement.

Others reported that conforming rigidly to the expectations of masculinity felt unnatural and the boundaries were restrictive and intrusive. Although P16 conformed successfully, he found the boundaries awkward:

> I used to find it too much of an effort to play the act, and I couldn't, carry on very well. It didn't come naturally to be. . . . I hate to use the socialized term "butch" and stuffing around and using bad language and being really rough and having my shirt hanging out . . . running around hitting each other really hard. (P16)

Recall that after P16 went to secondary school, he did emulate the standards of masculinity sufficiently and skillfully enough to become school captain—he was conversant in both domains. However, the skill by which these boundaries are negotiated is a key to whether the boy becomes an outcast or a school captain.

"Blatant" fluidity attracts homophobic labeling and is (by definition) transgressional and viewed as "bad":

> I think a lot of people see that as a really bad thing, because people aren't staying within that structure of boy meets girl, falls in love, and lives happily ever after. I think that they find that really threatening, because . . . they're not staying within that boundary . . . they're going about and doing their own thing. (DD30)

Meanwhile, from the perspective of those restrained by the boundaries, unfettered difference appears to be "opposite" rather than fluid. This is analogous to the earlier observation that boys are defined by their transgression—by their difference from others, not their more plentiful similarities. In this way, not conforming to hegemonic standards of masculinity can be credibly depicted as feminine, and homosexuals are positioned in opposition to masculinity rather than as variations similar to other masculinities. Similarly, designating homosexuals as opposite puts them in direct competition with femaleness, with all the attendant potential difficulties. The significance attached to the positioning of objects (male, female, homosexual) within this discursive field and normalizing them also appears to draw attention away from the processes that orchestrate this positioning. This may be one reason why the role of homophobia only gets passing recognition in other analyses in which the primary focus is gender or sexuality. As Foucault writes, power is tolerable when masked, and its "success is proportional to its ability to hide its own mechanisms" (Foucault, 1990: 86).

CONCLUSIONS

This chapter traces homophobic impact, how the "self" is fashioned in response, and how homophobia influences/underpins identity formation. It is clear that homophobia exerts its effects far beyond the immediacy of harassment and violence. The previous two chapters described how boys grow up in an environment saturated with homophobic references. Reviewing these examples, it is possible to identify different "species" of homophobia. These include "overt homophobia," such as homophobic harassment and violence; "implicit homophobia," which manifests in the way that people understand and explain social life and includes viewing certain activities as transgressive (boys dancing, being smart, or crying); "heterosexist homophobia," whereby heterosexuality is privileged over homosexuality instead of simply being seen as another way of relating ("I hadn't thought that homosexual relationships were as valid as heterosexual relationships." [S19]); and "silent" homophobia, whereby being "neutral" and remaining silent acknowledges both the existence and the power of homophobia and leaves its extensive operations unchallenged.

Examples of homophobia that do not explicitly relate to homosexuality were also explored and appear to be "presexual" or "asexual." These aspects emerge as extremely important. Rather than trying to establish a relationship between these different targets of homophobia by imputing some form of sexuality, their relationship is best understood as having derived their commonality from homophobia, and as being alienated (differentiated) from hegemonic masculinity. In other words, being a crybaby, being smart, avoiding team sports and being homosexual have nothing in common except for homophobia, which amalgamates them into a composite identity.

This chapter traces a number of transitions, all of which are characterized by a relatively unrestrained expression of certain behaviors prior to them becoming unacceptable, after which they abate. Furthermore, "rolling peer pressure" and homophobia were identified as having powerful roles in these processes:

> . . . out of . . . the attacks that were made in relation to sexuality in the schoolyard . . . some of them would have definitely become real homophobes . . . basically never to have to go through that allegation again. (A1)

Emerging from these processes is a picture of polymorphous, undifferentiated behaviors becoming increasingly constrained. This echoes Freud's "polymorphous perverse" formulation, which we will return to in the final chapter (Freud, 1977).

Boys who don't observe boundaries run a risk of becoming defined by their "transgressions" and of becoming targets for homophobia, regardless of their sexual orientation or whether they have yet formed their adult sexual identity. The agency of boys is influential in the management of these dynamics, and a variety of mechanisms is available to modulate their risks. By orchestrating the successive restriction of behaviors that are acceptably masculine and by stigmatizing fluidity as perverse and in opposition to hegemonic masculinity, it would appear that homophobia polarizes male sexuality and drives a wedge between what is homosexual and heterosexual. Perhaps the term should be "hegemonic homophobia." Simultaneously, behaviors that are acceptable to hegemonic masculinity are supervised and cultivated including toughness, emotional restraint, and compulsory heterosexuality (see Chapter 5). Homophobia contributes to this process because cultivating hypermasculine behaviors becomes a valued way of disassociating the "self" from homophobic stigma.

Homophobia is a contemporary regulator of the continual interplay between acceptable masculinity and what is unacceptable. Judging by observations about school subject choice, school performance, life patterns, harassment, violence, and risk taking, homophobia appears to take a considerable toll on boys and young men at both ends of the polarized sexual spectrum:

> At one end is the aggressive masculine bonding, in evidence when groups of boys disrupt classrooms, derogate girls and invade their play, and make fun of subordinated "weaker" boys. At the other extreme . . . boys who do not uphold the dominant notions of masculinity, who avoid the tough and aggressive, don't like sports, and are therefore vulnerable to ostracism, teasing, and being labeled "sissy," "nerd," or "fag." (Thorne, 1993: 168)

From this and other evidence, it is a small step to postulating how many modern-day men's health issues are, at least in part, orchestrated by homophobia. Being tough, restraining emotions, withholding intimacy, taking risks, and "proving one's self" have as much value as testimonies of masculinity as they are public gestures that have habitually arisen to evade homophobia.

Chapter 5

Regulating Male Intimacy

So far, most of this work has focused on nonsexual factors that can incite homophobia. In contrast, this chapter will examine the relationships between homophobia and intimacy.

Male-to-male contact occurs along a continuum that includes looking, talking, shaking hands, embracing, wrestling, and increasingly intimate physical contact, up to and including sexual intercourse. There is no obvious line to demarcate socially acceptable intimacy from that which invites homophobia. Further, whether a particular form of contact is considered transgressive varies historically and by its cultural context. For some cultures, embracing and kissing signify respect between men and are expected; in others, any contact beyond shaking hands is unacceptable. However, despite the arbitrary dividing line, mens' interactions are separated into homosocial and homosexual. Homosocial interactions are acceptable, encouraged, and carefully orchestrated, whereas homosexual contact is taboo, prohibited, and stringently policed (Britton, 1990). By imbuing certain types of male intimacy with deeply negative overtones, homophobia is the agent that delineates and enforces the boundary between acceptable (homosocial) and unacceptable (homosexual) contact.

In a term borrowed from Fredrik Barth, Barrie Thorne refers to the activities surrounding gender differences as "border work" (Thorne, 1993), and this seems to be an appropriate term for activities that define and maintain the boundaries between homoeroticism and the homosocial. A similar division also separates men's sexuality into homosexual and heterosexual, and this, too, operates by imbuing anything that is defined as homosexual with deeply negative connotations—this boundary, too, is delineated by homophobia. To explore the involvement of homophobia in regulating male intimacy, this chapter examines social situations that bring males together. These situations provide defined points along the arbitrary continuum of male-male contact, and they supply clear illustrations of homophobic dynamics when boundaries are encroached. Given that the words for acting like a poofter and being homosexual are deeply negative, everyday situations that encroach on the homo-sociosexual boundary would be expected to be highly regulated and codified (possibly even ritualized). The situations analyzed in this chapter include team sports, change rooms (locker rooms), sleeping together in boarding schools and school camps, and when males have intimate/erotic contact.

The homophobic split in otherwise seamless continua creates opportunities for paradox and "slipperiness" of labels. The deep negativity of homophobia, which aligns with one side of these arbitrary divisions, effectively places the resulting components in opposition—homosexual: heterosexual; homosexual: homosocial; acceptable: unacceptable. So while they appear to be opposite, they are actually derived from a continuum with an arbitrary dividing line, along which there is continual opportunity for flux and a need for codification. We have already seen how homophobic meanings and rationalizations can shift (sometimes becoming opposites) and the link that maintains continuity is the negativity of homophobia.

PHYSICAL ENGAGEMENT: SPORTS

Messner writes that sports offer young males "a way into a world of masculine values, rituals and relationships." (Messner, 1992: 8), and Pronger describes sports as an "apprenticeship in orthodox masculinity" (Pronger, 1990: 10). Male peer groups play important roles in sports. According to Messner, studies in the 1970s and 1980s showed that sports were "the single most important element of the peer-status system of U.S. adolescent males" (Messner, 1992: 24). In addition to the links between sports, masculinity, and peer status, Pronger identifies a third link with violence. He finds that far from teaching socially desirable skills, combative sports such as football can contribute to the development of aggressive behavior (Pronger, 1990: 22). Significantly, male peer groups, masculinity, and aggression were identified in earlier chapters as making important contributions to homophobia. Indeed, homophobia promotes aggression too—against boys who are homophobically labeled, helping to distance the aggressors from any suggestion of being a "poofter." This overlap between elements that characterize homophobia and those which characterize sports is striking and raises the possibility of important interrelationships between them. Perhaps, then, it is not so surprising that Messner writes that the extent of homophobia in sports is "staggering" (1992: 34). And, because sports emphasize "masculine" values, team sports pose difficulties for boys who are known as "poofters."

The suggestion that situations might become highly codified if they routinely bring males into close proximity has considerable support from the literature on sports. "For the boy who both seeks and fears closeness, the rule bound structure of organized sport promises to be a safe place in which to seek attachment with others, but it is an attachment in which clear boundaries, distance and separation from others are maintained" (Messner, 1992: 33). Messner's words "fears closeness" can be taken as a reference to homophobia because without homophobia there is nothing to fear when men are close. This tension between intimacy and homophobia is a recurring theme of modern writings on gender and sports, and the highly regulated and ritualized construction of sports suspends participants between their needs for intimacy and the imperatives of homophobia.

Sporting behaviors, similar to other social behaviors documented in Chapter 4, can be shown to undergo transitions according to boundaries and prohibitions encountered during childhood. Thorne writes that heterosexual meanings and homophobic insults pose strong barriers to boys and that "by fourth grade, definitions of acceptable masculine pursuit have settled around team sports; and playing with girls, especially in games like jump rope or gymnastics, is seen simultaneously as a sign of immaturity, being 'girlish' and being a 'fag' (Thorne, 1993: 134). The increasing gender segregation in play and sports is not surprising, nor is the following justification for this offered by BB28:

> . . . you don't play with them [girls] because, I mean, hell, you might get touched by one or something. (BB28)

Similarly, divisions increasingly emerge in play and sports between "the boys" and "poofters" and this is closely related to the school-ground "pecking order" and sporting status.

Sports and Peer Culture

Once differentiated along gender lines, boys' sports differentiate further, this time along status lines, and once again homophobia plays its role by distinguishing what is unacceptable. It was shown in Chapter 2 that there is a "pecking order" on the school ground where status is attached to physical dominance. This "pecking order" has a close relationship with sporting success (Kinney, 1993). Within sports, there is a hierarchy of prestige. At the top of the hierarchy is football (Australian Rules Football in the south and Rugby League or Union in the north). S19 describes how the most prestigious sports was rugby and how this was linked to boys' power:

> I mean, there's always a big power block in the "first fifteen" [the rugby team]. (S19)

In comparison, soccer was viewed as prestigious in some schools but not in others. The next two quotes illustrate this difference and highlight the arbitrary nature of peer standards of masculinity and the movable "goal posts" of homophobia. In the first case, T20 describes soccer as a popular boys' sports:

> In the playground, I remember, soccer was just huge. Everyone wanted to play soccer. . . . The boys wanted to play soccer, and girls weren't very prevalent at all. They were just there. But I think I was probably mixing a lot more with boys. I was playing soccer at lunchtime and at play lunch and at the big lunch we'd be playing soccer. That's all we'd care about. (T20)

In the second example, soccer has a very different reputation:

> **D:** And how would you have been described if you were interested in soccer instead of rugby?
> **S:** Oh, "girls' sports." (S19)

Soccer seems to have a more tenuous status than the other football codes in the Australian masculine psyche, which might be related to it being more characteristic of non-Anglo-Saxon populations and "alien" to Anglo-Saxon Australians.

Another example of the arbitrariness of masculine standards comes from comparisons between Pronger's descriptions of sports in Canada and the data collected for this project. Pronger observes how hockey has a reputation for being "truly violent" and "seriously masculine" (Pronger, 1990: 24). In contrast, on the schoolground culture of E5, hockey had a "sissy" reputation:

> There was a bit of, I suppose, the sissy factor, like, we didn't play football. We played hockey. (E5)

As a further refinement of the notion of sporting status, some sports, such as tennis, were safe for either sex:

> . . . you still weren't picked on for doing tennis. It was considered one of those sports that was . . . safe no matter what your sex was. (B2)

Just as "safety zones" and "danger zones" were identified on the school ground, there are dangerous and safe sports.

Three factors emerged as important for sporting status: being a participant; if the sports had a reputation for being "tough"; and if it was a team activity. Doing well in a tough, team sports affords the highest status. In contrast, some sports had a poor reputation and these were most frequently associated with homophobia. In the next quote, N14 describes how he felt pressured and found peer groups difficult because he didn't like sports:

> I was quite conscious of the fact that I didn't like sports. That was a pretty big thing at school. To be sort of "in," and one of the gang, you had to be quite competent at playing some form of handball, touch footy, soccer, or whatever. None of the "wussy" games like basketball. . . . (N14)

As he suggests, at the bottom of the hierarchy is anything with a homophobic association. In a previous quote, T20 described his infatuation with soccer. This only lasted until he started experiencing homophobic harassment, after which time he changed to other sports. In the next quote, he provides an example of a "low status" sport:

> . . . you can imagine what aerobics was. . . . I was a "fairy in tights" and a "fairy" "kicking up my heels" and that was just hideous. Despite the fact that I was doing what most of them were doing . . . the sprinting, the cross-country running, playing tennis, and everything like that, but the fact that I did aerobics, as well, that wasn't good. I was a dancer. (T20)

Even the term "kicking up my heels" is more than just an allusion to dance. This phrase has multiple meanings that rely on exploiting homophobic imagery because only girls wear "heels" and because "kicking up heels" is what girls do during intercourse when boys are "on top."

The association of sports with status provides opportunities for boys to dominate and to hold office in the school hierarchy. P16 describes how footballers are in a powerful position in the school:

> If you were the biggest and the best at football, you were the strongest and the most powerful in the boarding house. There was a direct correlation with the strongest and the most powerful boys [being] "first eighteen" football players and their authority and their physical powers were not questioned. (P16)

Schools were not above exploiting the masculine status associated with football to enhance their own public profiles (Connell, 1983). Both P16 and K11 expressed frustration that academic success was not as prestigious as football and that school authorities often contributed to the subordination of academic success:

> In years seven, eight, nine . . . it was the sports people who ruled because that's all people could see was sporting glory. Because academic glory wasn't such a big thing in those years. And so the first football team of the year, they'd stroll around and push everyone out of the way and do what they wanted to do. (K11)

Sporting success often had associations with other "character groups" (Kinney, 1993). One key interface was with academically inclined boys who were also good at sports, and another was between sports and bullies. In some accounts, high status was afforded to those who were successful at both academic and sporting pursuits. In others, this association was more equivocal. M13 illustrates this for his school:

> [the "sports-academic" group] hung around with each other, and they were academically gifted . . . they did quite well in their marks, they also were quite good in sports . . . more individual-based sports though. Not team sports, which the bullies in the groups used to be involved in. (M13)

It has already been noted that being academic and not being team oriented often occupy a relatively lower status, and in Chapter 2, both factors were shown to be susceptible to homophobic labeling. The previous quote reflects the subtleties of this relative positioning. These associations will become clearer as this chapter unfolds.

A second association is between sports and bullies (Boulton, 1995). Sports and bullying share the importance that boys attach to physicality and the power that stems from it. Q17 explains:

> . . . the people that play football, they was [sic] the cliques who ruled . . . being good at sports always automatically put you in either the clique group or the bully group. (Q17)

In some accounts the differentiation between sports and bullying was less clear, and this highlights the provisional nature of this classification and the overlap between bullying and sports:

> . . . the bullies were part of . . . the sporting group. So if fights did erupt it was probably because of the group that we'd associated with: sporting had the best bullies. (F6)

Sporting status was also equated with intolerance of individuality, and both were viewed as a product of group processes:

> [footballers] formed groups and once in groups they were unaccepting of people for *individual* qualities . . . physical achievements were very big. (R18)

Notice how this description confirms the importance of physicality and "self" against "otherness" formulations, where "self" is the group and "other" is the individual. This echoes how homophobia operates. The arrangement provides privilege and special dispensation for boys who have football status, and boys who don't have sporting status are vulnerable:

> . . . if you played football you got away with what you wanted . . . and if you weren't one of the footballers then anything about you could be used against you. (J10)

But this wasn't simply a "passive" process whereby boys who were good at sports were able to "bask" in their status. The hierarchy is based on physical dominance, which is enforced:

> They were always really big butch rugby guys . . . basically they were the ones that used to beat up all the ones that were a little bit different. (C3)

Here again, a relationship is suggested between sports and homophobia.

The dynamics illustrated in this section confirm the privileges and status associated with physical power, and they highlight the vulnerability of boys who are marginalized. The social geography of the school ground also reflects the associations between sports and power hierarchies, and the risks for those who are marginalized or who (privately) recognize their own vulnerability and want to avoid having it exposed:

> **S:** The bullies were more likely to be on the oval . . . and in the middle of the playground, rather than at the edge of the playground or near the buildings. They'd be away from the classroom.
> **D:** And where were you? Where were the areas that you inhabited?
> **S:** . . . near the buildings . . . the outskirts of the playground. (P16)

This description illustrates a catch-22 because of the risks of being exposed whether on the oval or by avoiding it. On balance, being removed from peer pressures appears safer.

Evidence of sports-related status and hierarchies suggests that football fulfills functions for schoolboys that extend beyond simply being a game (Connell, 1983):

> . . . there was a lot more to football than just the rules of the game . . . you were out there on the oval and . . . I just didn't think I'd be able to handle learning the rules and sticking up for myself and trying to keep up with the language, and trying to carve out. . . . That was the other thing they used to do, was to carve out a name for themselves as having a reputation for being, you know, he's good on the wing or he's faster or he's heavier or he's tough or all these things. . . . (CC29)

CC29's description shows that "the oval" is an important boys' cultural site. In this chapter, it is revealed as a site for contests and challenges. The oval is a "danger zone" for boys who are different, and in one example (N14) in the previous chapter (see p. 170) it was a site for homophobic punishment (being stripped, tied up and labeled a poofter). CC29 also describes how it is important to "carve out" a sporting reputation (based on physical criteria). This is one way of generating sporting status.

Another attraction of team sports seems to be competition, but competition can be a "cover story" for satisfying other needs, particularly legitimizing boys' closeness. In the next example, it is not competition on the sporting field, but competition in the swap-card stakes—an important sporting culture artifact:

> **D:** . . . tell me the qualities about sports that you think attracted all those other boys, including your brothers, to it?
> **S:** Competition, I think. Asserting themselves as males, particularly to the group. There was always the big competition of collecting the football cards. I'll never forget it, and I could never get it right. . . . I remember my main interest was eating the bubblegum! (N14)

The cultural imperative seems so strong that for most boys the bubblegum is superfluous—the product really being marketed (masculinity) is part of the packaging. This is another case of how arbitrary the standards of masculinity are. In the previous chapter,

CC29 came under pressure for playing cards because it was a girls' game.

Football also supplies the common ground and rules for legitimate male interaction. As Messner writes, "competitive activities such as sport, mediate men's relationships with each other in ways that allow them to develop a powerful bond while at the same time, preventing them from the development of intimacy" (Messner, 1992: 91). The common ground of sport is founded on teams and team membership. Z26 alludes to the importance of team membership for him, and he makes the observation that it was not the physical activity per se that attracted him:

> I suppose there must be something to do with the team, because I [have] never actually taken an interest in an individual sports, it's only ever been cricket or . . . in particular, in rugby. A good team is generally a team that's made of guys that get on really well. So there's got to be mateship there and I guess feeling part of a team has to be a part of it. (Z26)

O15 acknowledges the importance of teams to male culture, and suggests that for him, there was something about teams that he found difficult:

> [football] gives people something to talk about and something to aspire to and something that they can emulate as well. Something they can identify with and enjoy and there's all of that . . . you're part of a team and . . . you're drawn up with that . . . and I didn't want to be. (O15)

Sports culture can dominate school life, and in boarding school, especially, it is difficult to escape. P16 handled the dilemma differently:

> I don't think I had a choice [whether to play football] in that situation [boarding school]. I really didn't consider that I could do anything else. Whereas at home I could cocoon myself in the house and the family, I was there "living it" twenty-four hours a day. You couldn't escape the peer. You slept . . . ate, worked, lived, breathed . . . it was so much more difficult to be an individual there. (P16)

P16 echoes many of the participants who placed individuality in opposition to peer culture. He resigned himself to participating in team sports, which had the effect of transforming his status from "other" to "member:"

> I found that there was a hell of a lot more camaraderie and brotherly love and team spirit, when you were involved with the sports. You were part of the boys now. (P16)

Sports and Sexual Orientation

In addition to serving as an important source of status for boys, sports participation appears to be related to a boy's acceptance by his peers:

> . . . people that were good at sports, you know, had a much better chance of avoiding being an outcast. (U21)

In contrast, an uncomfortable relationship between sports and homosexuality was apparent in interviews from both homosexual and nonhomosexual participants. As Brian Pronger writes, "if team goals were simply athletic, then homosexual men and boys would probably have no problem identifying with them" (Pronger, 1990: 26). He adds "even gay men who were in fact fine athletes in individual sports would sometimes be the last picked for teams" (Pronger, 1990: 27). Pronger attributes these findings to an alienation of young gay males from the masculine standards on which sports are based: "this athletic ineptitude is probably a reflection of the indifference some homosexual boys feel toward sports because of its orthodox masculine leitmotif" (Pronger, 1990: 26). Significantly, classic (homophobic) explanations for young gay men's difficulties with sports, such as being too timid, weak, or incapable of playing sports, are not supported by this study: all participants were able-bodied and some young gay subjects had proven sporting abilities.

There was considerable evidence of disaffection with sports by young gay and bisexual men in this study. The following quote is from T20, who earlier reported a preoccupation with soccer at school ("that's all we'd care about"):

S: Hated it. Hated sport.

D: Hated sport?

S: Hated it with a passion!

D: And you're a gym teacher now?

S: Yep . . . I did nothing. I played no sport and I ate like a pig . . . I would do anything to get out of PE [physical education]. [I] forged notes, the works. Made up conditions. Everything, I just hated it. (T20)

In other cases, alienation was manifested by more of a frustrated rejection of the goals of sports, as CC29 articulates:

. . . I just used to think "What a stupid system is this!" . . . I just remember thinking that was really dumb. Not only did I have to learn all these rules, but while I was doing it . . . I wasn't going to be given any sympathy for any mistakes while I was learning. I had to be constantly proving myself and standing up for myself, and I just thought I could not be bothered. (CC29)

While the previous quote was relatively understated, many accounts by young gay men of their encounters with sports during adolescence were laced with strong wording, frustration, and hostility. In the following examples, as in others, a key word is "hate":

I hated, hated football. I hated all those contact sports that people used to play at lunchtimes. So I was more at home doing skipping or something like that, but of course that means that you're . . . a target for ridicule. (O15)

This antipathy contrasts with descriptions of how other males seemed "obsessed":

. . . when I got home, my brothers would all be watching it [football], and I used to hate it . . . because not knowing it or not being interested in it put you on the outer . . . I didn't see there was any point in doing it. I could never understand why so many people, adults in particular, were so obsessed by it. (N14)

Although T20 rediscovered an interest in sports after he left school, he is not alone in demonstrating a transition from an early sporting ability that later turned to alienation and hostility. DD30 describes how he was athletic in primary school:

> . . . I used to be really athletic when I was in public school. I used to do a lot of athletics. (DD30)

However, he also recounts a subsequent alienation and rejection of "high-status" sports, in this case, because of his fear of the associated violence:

> I started to take on women's sports, or what were considered women's sports, like volleyball, baseball, things like that. I started to take on those trying to get away from the real macho sports like football. . . . I always got really, really scared of that stuff. I always got really scared of the violence. . . . I wouldn't mind it if it was one on one with a person, but it was never the one on one. It was always with somebody else. (DD30)

AA27 also experienced alienation from sports in late high school, but in the next quote, he illustrates how rough play is part of boys' sports and how he willingly participated when he was younger:

> . . . we used to play it every lunchtime from . . . kindergarden . . . and somebody would stand on top of the hill and as soon as the teacher would come, it would be "Touch!" and as soon as the teacher was gone it was "Tackle!" So it would be like "king hits" and really violent. We used to go in after lunch and the jeans would be ripped and the shirt would have no buttons and from here to here there's grass stains. (AA27)

There are also several examples of the reverse situation, where boys experienced difficulties with sports, but with a change of circumstances they became participants:

> **D:** . . . how do you respond to this then? You could have done it [football] if you really wanted to?
> **S:** You're dead right, and I did later in life . . . I was "most improved under fourteen B." . . . It was something I made myself do because then I belonged. It was a social thing. (P16)

In the following example, R18 was able to shed much of his homophobic labeling when he proved his sporting ability:

> I think [they thought I was gay] just because I was . . . an outsider to them and maybe not masculine enough for them . . . it dropped off dramatically after year ten because I won the swimming championship and that gave me the status. That shocked the pants off everyone . . . it gave me sporting status. (R18)

In both of these cases, despite a "reversal of fortune" the subjects remained cynical about men's sports.

A possible explanation for the disaffection displayed by young gay and bisexual men toward sports in this study might be due to the "rough" nature of boys' sports. On the surface, this seems a credible explanation and there were a number of statements that alluded to sports being too violent. Here is one example:

> So in terms of . . . watching the game [football,] I loved it. . . . I mean, certainly if I'd have been a better player I might've wanted to play more. But my memory is pretty much that, you know, you get hurt. [Laughs] I didn't wanna get hurt. (V22)

However, like the "lack of ability" explanation for the sporting difficulties experienced by gay men, the "fear of violence" explanation is also not, in itself, consistent with all the evidence. Although V22 and DD30 both alluded to fearing the violence inherent in sports, AA27's statement describes how he frequently engaged in violent football and only became alienated later. Furthermore, being afraid of rough play in sports doesn't explain why heterosexual males do not appear to be alienated to the same extent. The next example illustrates that CC29's alienation from sports is not explained by his inability to "hold his own" on the sporting field:

> . . . one more thing about football, I do remember that there also seemed to be a big thing on trying to injure the other side or really tackle them hard and there didn't seem to be any rules about how hard was too hard. I was quite big and strong for my year and I felt like I could have pounded some of those other kids into the ground. But, I didn't have any rules as to when to stop and when not to. (CC29)

A closer examination of the interview transcripts reveals more sustainable explanations for the disaffection of young gay and bi-sexual males from sports. The first clue can be found in a preference expressed frequently by young gay men for solo sporting activities:

> ... I'd do running and sprinting and cross-country running and that sort of thing. But as far as up until then, all contact sport: no way! (T20)

In this statement, the physical capacity and an interest in certain sports is clear, as is T20's rejection of "contact sports." Preferring solo sports and avoiding team sports was also described by Q17, who explains that his preferences are not due to a general rejection of competition:

> I'd play at a competition any day—one that's not team sports. (Q17)

In addition to having a preference for solo sporting activities, some young gay males reported being rejected from certain team sports activities (Pronger, 1990). Boulton (1995) made similar observa-tions for boys who were bullied. CC29 illustrates team sport rejec-tion:

> I could go anywhere. And if they were playing soccer, I'd join in. And if they were playing a game I liked here on this particular day, I'd play there, and if it was hot and I wanted to go and sit somewhere and play cards, I'd do that. And I always felt welcome wherever I went . . . although I knew if I went down on a football day to the oval, I wouldn't be welcome. (CC29)

Notice the differentiation of soccer from football.

Q17 also complained that he was not welcome in team sports:

> ... the lack of camaraderie . . . being the one not wanted on the team that made me not keen to keep going with sport. (Q17)

He went on to report that even when he was involved in team sports, his involvement was superficial and he was still the "odd one out":

. . . if you were on the team and no one passes you a ball for forty-five minutes then, well why would you bother playing football? . . . I learned that playing football wasn't playing football, when you weren't one of the "in" people. (Q17)

Boys who are homophobically labeled can be put in a "no-win" situation:

D: But by not participating weren't you the odd one out?
S: Yeah, you lose both ways. (Q17)

The "no-win" effect of homophobia was also described by T20. His alienation from sports coincided with being homophobically labeled, and in the following quote, it is possible to get some idea of how strong this resistance is:

I hated it [football]. I absolutely hated it. And, if I was made to do it, I'd just be absolutely furious, because I had a temper at this stage. I just didn't want to do it . . . I wasn't doing any sports, I wasn't going to do sport. . . . Wasn't interested. Hated all the other guys that were doing sports because they were idiots and I had nothing in common with them. I didn't want to know about them . . . I didn't want to be part of that. . . . And then, as a result . . . the stigma bounced onto me, and the label stuck to me that because I wasn't going to do what they were doing, I was a poofter. (T20)

Homophobia can marginalize boys, and once marginalized, they attract further homophobia, which makes recovery from stigmatization difficult.

Disaffection with team sports, and teams in particular, echoes the difficulties that young gay men experience with peer groups in the schoolyard. This is not surprising given that sports teams are composed of school-ground peers. Moreover, as we have seen in the discussions on sporting status and physicality, sporting teams are most likely to represent the more homophobic elements of the school ground—and in a most immediate, concentrated, and physical form. The effect of collecting people into a team is similar to forming a peer group, and peer pressure makes team dynamics potent. R18 describes how boys change when they are on the football field:

> **S:** I didn't like it [football] because it was . . . rough-and-tumble. I had glasses . . . I felt different. The boys weren't nice when they got together on the football field . . . there was a lot less sports in it than there was group brawling.
> **D:** So you were able to see a change in boys between when they were by themselves in the playground and when they were all together on the football field?
> **S:** Oh, absolutely! Very much. (R18)

Team sports participation incurs the added hazard of proximity and physical contact with homophobic peers who can usually be avoided on the school-ground "safety zones." DD30 describes this dilemma:

> . . . because . . . it got more intense, the homophobia . . . I didn't get into sports. I just really hated sports and the one thing that really turned me off sports was that if you chose a sports, you could never ever be guaranteed which group. . . . So you might have somebody who's really hostile in that group. . . . Every six months you'd change your sport. And, I'd be really scared of what'd happen, you know, with this sport . . . I was scared of the hostility. Because by this time it started to get violent. (DD30)

The reasons for heightened levels of concern by "poofters" about being injured in team sports are clear. The fear of injury is not simply a result of ordinary fears of rough play, but of forcing school-ground differences together in an orchestrated show of aggression. The marginalized child realistically fears the unwinnable odds of being put among, and pitted against, the most powerful and homophobic elements of the school ground. It was a team that DD30 couldn't relate to, one that rejected him:

> . . . 95 percent of that football team doesn't like me because I'm considered gay . . . they were only calling me gay 'cause I

was doing things different to what they were. It wasn't necessarily because I was gay . . . on a football team with 95 percent
of people really hostile toward gays, I'd be just thrashed. They
probably would have beaten me to a pulp. (DD30)

For the young gay male, sports can be both a symbolic reenactment
and a real experience of homophobic attack:

I can remember other kids being chased, tackled, hurt in ball
games and footy, and stuff like that for being poofters. (N14)

These findings are consistent with studies on bullying that have
confirmed that team sports increase a victim's chances of coming
into contact with bullies, that victims were "significantly less likely
to participate in rule games," and that children who are unpopular
are consistently less likely to be chosen to be sporting team members (Boulton, 1995). Pronger has noticed that the alienation exhibited by young gay males is pronounced in more violent team sports
(Pronger, 1990: 24).

The intensity displayed by many young gay men in their descriptions of sports ("hated it with a passion!" [T20]) and the depth of
their resistance to team sports makes sense in light of these findings.
Many subjects quickly sensed the homophobic dangers inherent in
sports, and some took early steps to avoid any risk:

I started playing soccer . . . 'cause I enjoyed it, it wasn't
because I thought it was a masculine thing to do . . . and I
quickly gave that up when I . . . wasn't allowed to hurt myself.
That sounds really bizarre, but if I hurt myself, and I reacted to
it, I got, "Oh, you're a big wuss," and I got really pissed off
with that, and I left. (L12)

For L12, it appears that it was homophobia that hurt most, and
heeding the warning bells, he avoided further involvement:

I was among all these "testosterone heads" . . . who just
wanted to strive and be "men" and stuff like that, and it really
became uncomfortable 'cause that's not the way I . . . wanted
to be. (L12)

The next description shows the implicit connection between team sports and homophobic attack:

> I didn't like that whole idea of having a whole pack of people . . . grab me and try and drag me to the ground. [Laughs] To me that was like . . . the *most stupid* thing. I couldn't even conceive why we were even . . . especially when we were forced to do it. It's bad enough having to put up with it in the playground, but then when it came time for sports and we're forced to do it I really resented it. (O15)

Notice how he describes sports as being alone and being dragged to the ground by a pack. Also notice how O15 sees sports as "forcing" these incompatible playground elements together in a way that he feels is "stupid" and difficult to comprehend. Other accounts draw similar links. Notice how L12 contrasts his individual sporting interests with team sports, because team sports for him explicitly symbolize homophobia:

> I can't *stand* football. 'Cause it reminds me of acting just like, macho "bash each other round the head. . ." that big burly "let's kill them," tough kind of thing . . . it just really pisses me off. It's one of those things that makes me so angry. . . . I don't want to have to feel I have to prove something all the time 'cause if you don't do it to them, they're going to think, "Oh you. You're a real women's boy," "women's faggot" type of thing. . . . They always put pressure on you of some description to be a "man," and . . . football just reminds me of all that. I just hate it. (L12)

Sports are ripe with homophobic symbolism. The significance of the sports "oval" has already been mentioned and even the ball that both teams are pitting their strength against can symbolize the "poofter":

> Poofter could actually be used referring to the ball. (V22)

The Agency of Adults

Adults play important roles in maintaining the homophobic dynamics of boys' sports. It has already been mentioned how schools deliberately exploit the prestige associated with sports (Connell, 1989: 295), and many schools place enormous emphasis on sporting achievement:

> . . . right from day one was a massive sports culture at that joint . . . there was never really any recognition of academic achievement. We had a weekly boarders meeting and it would consist of praising sports teams. . . . I would latch onto and be friends with the very rare person who didn't like sports as well. And one of them remains my friend to this day . . . and we would sit there and roll our eyes and think, "Christ! Just listen to this crap." (P16)

Schools also seem to exploit sports as a means of controlling boys:

> . . . from my school's point of view . . . it [sports] was more about . . . structuring things. It was a way of controlling groups of young men. It was a way of forcing them to do things that you wanted them to do and being certain types of people. . . . I could never really buy it. (P16)

While the institutions provided the infrastructure in which homophobia could thrive, individual teachers often contributed explicit homophobia to sporting activities:

> . . . the sports's teacher saying "Hey! Poofters." or something choice, because people might have looked in the shower. . . . And, it wasn't the thing to do, and he had caught a kid trying to give someone a glance. (Q17)

DD30 also provides an example of how homophobia can be unspoken, but boys can "read" it from a teacher's innuendo:

> . . . he [sports teacher] couldn't handle homosexuality. And if he saw "it" in any of us, you know, just passing comments about . . . "Oh those shorts look like a" . . . you know, "They're very sissy" . . . you'd get the vibes and the general feeling. (DD30)

DD30 goes on to describe being hassled for wearing earrings to sport. The "cover story" that the teacher used is that they could be ripped out of his ears if the game was rough. However, it was obvious to the students that the argument was specious because the games were always mixed sex and female participants were not required to remove their earrings.

Sports also play an important role in family relationships, particularly between a father and son. In Messner's words, ". . . successful performance in sport is a key to successful emotional attachment with their fathers, and . . . conversely, failure to perform may destroy the tenuous bond between father and son" (Messner, 1992: 29). You might recall that R18 was alienated from sports until he became a swimming champion, and he attributes some of his sense of alienation to not forming a sporting bond with his father (see the sections titled "Education and Career" and "Family Membership," pp. 174-179). CC29 relates a similar story where he feels his early experiences with a football transgressed gender boundaries and had a special significance for his relationship with his father:

> I remember quite vividly sitting there on the carpet at the top of the stairs and being given this thing, playing with it, kicking it around for a while and thinking it was stupid and slippery and it wouldn't bounce properly. And then sitting on it and saying "I'm a mother bird," sitting on this football. . . . And I remember they all just turned and walked away. . . . I don't think anybody knew what to say and the girls probably might have laughed. And I think Mum might have had a little chuckle . . . this is a story that gets dragged out at family things . . . and I have a feeling Dad was a bit upset. (CC29)

In contrast, sometimes family members can rescue boys who are experiencing homophobia in sports. In the next example, DD30's lesbian sister and her girlfriend provide him with sorely needed support:

> I was sort of trying to get my sister to write me a note so I didn't have to go to sport cause I really didn't wanna go. And anyway they sort of sat down and [said] "Why don't you want to go to sport?" and she actually came with me. She drove me to sport and she told the teacher. She said, you know "There's kids hassling him [laughs] like give him a break." She's this

really really full on butch sort of really political dyke [laughs]
and [with] all of these kids [around], she stood there and
watched. She watched and made sure that nobody hassled me.
[Laughs] It was really funny. (DD30)

MANHOOD EXPOSED: THE CHANGE ROOMS

The sports change rooms (locker rooms) expose homophobic and
homophobically labeled elements of the school ground to each
other and bring them into close proximity. Change rooms are also
less open to public scrutiny, and the supervision of change rooms
can be limited by homophobia—by the risk for teachers of seeming
too interested. The exposure of boys that occurs in change rooms,
the proximity of disparate school elements, and the dictates of homophobia, all raise the possibility that change-room activities might
be codified and ritualized. As Messner reports, "conformity with
locker room culture was a way for both gay and heterosexual men
to construct their public masculinity" (Messner, 1992: 100).

Ritualizing Exposure

The importance attached to being exposed in the change rooms is
suggested by the following quote by V22:

> I remember some people being quite elaborate about not ex-
> posing themselves. And some people would go up to a toilet
> cubicle to change. (V22)

The word "elaborate" in this description seems to indicate important dynamics. The more personalized description provided by
DD30 demonstrates how intense this experience can be (depending
on who is there) and how vulnerable boys feel:

> . . . it's like "baring it all" basically. And it was like if I was in the
> situation where all of these homophobic people in my class were
> gonna be there . . . they could really rip me to shreds. . . . And it
> was just like . . . I can't let them . . . I can't be stripped down . . .
> I can't let them get to me. You know, the real me. (DD30)

The tensions inherent in the change-room environment appear to solicit several principal styles of change-room behavior. One style involves being talkative:

> I do remember with this bravado thing, that people seemed to be chattering away almost to pretend it wasn't happening. (V22)

The use of terms such as "bravado" is further evidence that negotiating the change rooms is not as straightforward as it superficially appears. T20 describes how uncomfortable the change rooms were from his perspective and he also describes two other styles of change-room behavior. One involves putting your "head down," getting changed, and leaving quickly. The other, exhibited by the "footy stars" and "in guys," appears to be related to the chatty bravado previously described, and involved joking and jeering—something that "lower status" boys probably couldn't get away with.

The importance of not being seen as loitering in the change rooms and of leaving as soon as possible is reiterated by Z26:

> There was always this heavy man-to-man sort of thing, you know? You had to be accepted as one of the boys. And I don't think any of the boys would have liked to [have] been caught being the last one out, for fear of the criticism they'd get after it. (Z26)

Anything that can be interpreted as taking too great an interest in change-room activities appears to be open to criticism:

> . . . anything that was other than just the pure, straight, normal get changed and be completely calm about it. Not hide yourself, but not look at anybody else. There . . . seemed to be a definite code of behavior in the bathrooms and afterward when people were out waiting, if someone had done something a little bit out of the ordinary, there would be "Did you see so-and-so doing that?" They wouldn't say, "He's a poof," but they'd say, "What do you think he was up to?" That was at primary school. I think at high school, they would have said, "Bloody poof!" (CC29)

Not surprisingly, homophobia emerges as an important element in most of the accounts of change-room dynamics and is another reason why young gay men experience difficulties with team sports even if they conceal their own sexuality. "The overt hostility towards gays that is displayed in casual locker room talk and the accepted use of antigay slurs by coaches and athletes make a gay athlete's acceptance contingent on his ability to convincingly pass as heterosexual. . . . He must constantly monitor how he is being perceived . . . . He must silently endure the expressions of contempt and hostility" (Griffin, 1995: 59). Ritualized expressions of "contempt and hostility" range from homophobic jokes to violence. An example of a commonplace homophobic "joke" is related by T20:

> . . . around year eight, year nine, there were always jokes in the change room . . . "Oh, don't bend over because what's-his-name will come and . . . fuck you up the arse," and things like that. . . . That was commonplace. That always came up. (T20)

Messner writes, "talk of 'queer bashing' is common in male locker rooms, a closeted gay athlete knows that to reveal the truth about his sexuality can be outright dangerous" (Messner, 1992: 35).

As might be predicted, homophobic jokes, comments, and accusations appear to be used to maintain distance between people while in the change rooms. In the next example, the role of homophobia in creating distance is described by U21:

> I remember . . . someone flicking a towel or having a play fight . . . with no clothes on. And another one pushing them away and saying "Ah, leave me alone" . . . and then "poofter" coming in there . . . as a way to . . . keep someone away from you. (U21)

A similar example uses a homophobic accusation to restore privacy in an occupied toilet:

> "Fag" at boarding school was very frequent. . . . In the showers, in the toilets, or anything like that, I mean, one of the ways that you'd check some of the toilets, because the locks sometimes didn't [function], we used to put our head over. If someone was on the thing you'd stand there and they'd go "You fag, get out of here!" (K11)

Styles of dealing with homophobic accusations were also invested with significance. Reacting strongly was likely to arouse further suspicions and intensify accusations. As a result responses required skill and composure to be successfully managed:

> **S:** . . . If you out-and-out denied it, the old "I think he does protest too much" would come into it. . . . And it would enable it. Instead of just a wild insult, it would enable the conversation—a rolling tirade—to occur.
> **D:** So it was important to disengage from it?
> **S:** Quickly, yes. And hope that it blows over as fast as possible. Again it was an unwritten, unspoken law that everyone just let it drop. Where everyone picked that up from I don't know. (K11)

Regulating the Gaze

How people use their eyes and where they look are important aspects of change-room practice: staring intensifies exposure and signifies an untoward interest in others. Looking has important homophobic implications and is highly codified. Notice how looking at the wall is a key part of Y25's memories of change-room behavior:

> . . . you sort of turn around and look at the wall and quickly put your clothes on and then you walk out. (Y25)

Trying not to look is not the same as not being interested in looking:

> I would have had to have been inquisitive to see what other blokes had . . . but at the same time, you would be conscious all the time of not trying to look. (Z26)

Z26 rated himself as heterosexual (see Appendixes), and his statement illustrates how change-room rituals are influential regardless of sexual orientation. W23 also rated himself as heterosexual, and in the following quote, the links between seeming too interested in another male body and the fear of homophobic labeling are clear:

I mean, even at that age [twelve], I would have had an awareness that you didn't really want to look too carefully at another
guy's body. .... I think because it would be perceived that you
were taking an interest in their body more than what was
appropriate. There would be a hint about your sexuality as a
result. (W23)

Instead of preventing looking, the combination of curiosity and
prohibition resulted in a range of stylized ways of looking without
attracting disapproval. First, quite simply, boys tried not to get caught
looking and became practiced at avoiding detection. Second, it was
important not to sustain the gaze in order to evade homophobia:

S: I always looked away [laughs] . . . well I mean, that'd make
you somewhat uncomfortable if someone's . . . staring at you.
D: Why?
S: . . . well again that brings homosexuality into it doesn't it?
Especially in an all-male school. (BB28)

Looking was also possible "from the corner of your eye," as X24
describes. Notice how he suggests that this would be acceptable, but
"anything more than that" was sufficient to invite homophobia:

S: . . . you'd look out the side of your eye and from the corner
of your eye . . . but you wouldn't do anything more than that.
D: Why not?
S: Oh I think . . . probably instantly cop . . . some kind of
poofter crap. (X24)

It was also possible to look in passing, providing you didn't stop to
look:

S: . . . you'd be looking around the room, but not looking at
anything in particular. Or if you did see somebody with their
pants off, which happened very rarely, you'd sort of glance by
and glance back. You would never stop and look. For fear of
either him catching you or someone else.
D: And what would happen if you were caught?
S: Oh, they'd call you a poof or something like that. (Z26)

In each of these cases, it is clear that the prohibitions on looking at other boys in the change room can be explained by people's fear of homophobia.

The following examples show this fear to be well-founded if boys were caught looking in an unacceptable fashion. Notice that none of these accounts relate to the fear of homosexuality, or of homosexuals, or of being approached by a homosexual. In the next quote, I9 describes his fear of homophobia:

> . . . you can really sense that there's this sort of homophobia. And if you're having a shower, a communal shower, and there are other guys naked, then you must be a homosexual or . . . if someone looks at you and they're naked, then they must be a homosexual. . . . So it happens here as well as in New Zealand and . . . it just seems to be this . . . male . . . fear of being accused of being homosexual. (I9)

In the next example, N14 ties the fear of homophobia to his fear of the football team, a key group implicated in enforcing homophobia. N14's fear of homophobia is also a fear of being caught looking. For him, a lot depends on how he uses his eyes:

> I . . . was always quite frightened of the footballers and that niche, the football niche, and I would never, ever contemplate coming into the change room where all the footballers were. Just in case . . . someone pointed out that I was a poofter . . . being caught looking . . . or my eyes lingering for too long. (N14)

The next example shows how the regulation of looking is a group code and how other members of the group play a role in policing and enforcing it. Being in the group domain makes being caught looking difficult to ignore. And being caught looking also implies that the person who did the catching was also looking. It is therefore in his interest to expose the "perpetrator" in order to circumvent any pressure on the other person to expose him!

> **S:** . . . usually the individual who'd be perved at, would be told, "John, fag!" "Pervo!" [or] whatever.
> **D:** So somebody else . . . would alert him?
> **S:** Yeah. Or somebody'd noticed. I mean you'd have to be absolutely stupid if you were caught perving on somebody. (K11)

Notice how the transgressive use of the gaze is implied by the use of the terms "perve" and "perving" (derived from pervert) to describe looking in these situations—a feature of several transcripts.

In special cases, the group can also relax homophobic codes and issue special dispensation to look. This will be examined later.

Physical Development

Although the gaze is restrained in change rooms and must be used with care, looking does occur, and a boy's appearance therefore has special significance. Physical development and masculine appearances are highly valued (Connell, 1983). Mac an Ghaill describes "the exchange value of the 'straight male body' as a form of high status physical capital in the competitive school marketplace" (Mac an Ghaill, 1994: 163). Being more developed and developing earlier is advantageous because in a culture that emphasizes masculine physicality, development affords status. Barrie Thorne has found that "boys who enter puberty early tend to have higher self-esteem and prestige, and a more positive body image, than other boys of the same age" (Thorne, 1993: 140). Conversely, being underdeveloped is devalued and can attract homophobia. "By junior high or middle school, some physically small and weak boys may be labeled 'wimps' and 'fags'; social hierarchies have a loose relationship with somatic type" (Thorne, 1993: 140). In a statement that echoes earlier findings, appearing different in the change rooms is sufficient to provoke homophobia:

> . . . referring back to showers and scenes like that, if anyone was looking different, that's probably where we'd get the connotation that they were a poofter. They looked different. (F6)

The reference points against which boys' physical appearances are judged rely on commonly held stereotyped dichotomies (footballers and faggots). P16 describes the homophobia that his heterosexual school friend experienced when he "failed" to fit the footballer model:

> . . . you just didn't have somebody in the "first eighteen" [top footballers] who would get that sort of tag. They don't get teased.

... My best friend from school was mercilessly teased for being a fag and . . . he wasn't your model of an Adonis. But he's probably the most heterosexual person I know, but back then that didn't matter. What mattered was your appearance. (P16)

Looking at somebody in the change room can imply more than just homosexual interest. If there is a discrepancy between the more mature development of the person being looked at, then fears of inadequacy can be imputed to the boy who is looking:

So if you're caught looking at someone that is more developed . . . people can work out that you're worried about this. Plus I remember being very worried that I would be the last person or the only one in the showers not . . . going through puberty, not growing hair. I remember that feeling very strongly. 'Cause you . . . don't want to be last at anything. (U21)

The anxieties associated with going through puberty later than peers is also illustrated by the following quote, which contrasts this with the "cred" (credibility/credentials) of going through puberty early:

Oh, Christ. I mean . . . one guy . . . didn't go through puberty till he was seventeen. And that was just terrifying. It was just hell . . . whereas I was pubescent by the time I got there. And I felt, well, this gives me some sort of "cred." (P16)

P16 was able to use the transition from primary school to high school to reposition himself as less "different" from his peers, and his early puberty may have helped him do this. N14 provides an illustration of this effect:

I started becoming a little bit popular because after school camp, which is right at the beginning of fifth class, people had realized that I had pubes, you see. (N14)

In addition to the development of secondary sexual characteristics, being bigger and taller also facilitated acceptance and afforded protection:

S: Definitely taller, yeah. Probably a bigger kid than most of the others, which is probably why you're accepted more.

D: So your size protected you a bit?
S: Yeah, definitely. (Z26)

Q17 describes how he'd "outgrown" many of his peers by year ten and how this protected him against physical homophobic attacks even though he continued to experience verbal homophobia.

Although boys feared being less developed than average, developing too early can also cause difficulties if it makes the boy noticeably different. In the next example, M13 was a "little bit embarrassed" by developing earlier than average, but there was no evidence that this was associated with the same lack of status as being less developed:

> . . . at fourteen odd years of age . . . I was fully developed, although I was quite lean. And other guys were fully developed but quite strong and muscular, and other kids hadn't even started. Just starting now . . . I was perhaps a little bit embarrassed about being developed. 'Cause I'd shot ahead of everyone else. (M13)

Occasionally, the standards implicit in homophobia can be conflicting and give rise to an ambiguous response. In the next case, the (antihomophobic) prestige of being physically mature is contrasted with the (homophobic) stigma of male intimacy:

> . . . where they'd sat around like in a spa and three or four had tried to masturbate at the same time. . . . And that was sort of a bit controversial. And no one quite knew whether that was okay or not because . . . it was doing something which was male . . . seemingly it was half okay, but then doing it in context of males and I remember some people used it as an insult and some people didn't really see it as an insult. (U21)

While the development of secondary sexual characteristics is a potential source of prestige, getting an erection in a nude all-male setting, similar to being caught looking, can be used to imply homosexual interest. This is the case in the next example, which illustrates how the fear of homophobia affects change-room practices:

> **S:** I was never round them [change rooms] long enough, 'cause I would get in and get out straightaway.

D: Why's that?

S: I didn't want to give myself away.

D: Well, how would you give yourself away?

S: By getting an erection, I suppose. Or by looking at someone. (R18)

Looking and getting an erection have a relationship, particularly in the "hands-off" environment of the change rooms. This relationship is illustrated in the next quote by AA27:

> I always used to get really worried about that because I was paranoid that I'd "crack a fat" from lookin' at everybody, but once I saw what they all had, I thought "You've got to be kidding. This is disgusting." Yeah, you couldn't really perve. (AA27)

Although considerable effort is put into appearing not to look, the fear of getting an erection in the change rooms adds to the evidence that people do look, and it has already been shown how the fear of exposure contributes to codification of change-room practices:

> I can also remember on a year-seven camp, this guy "cracked a fat" in the showers and the poor guy got ridiculed for ages . . . it was like "Nup. I'm not having a shower." So I didn't for the first two days and then I thought, "Yep, it's time to." So I didn't go down until about eleven o'clock at night. And I just dragged this "wuss" down with me and made him sit on the seat and wait for me. (AA27)

PUTTING THOSE FEARS TO BED: SLEEPING TOGETHER

Another setting that brings boys into close proximity is when they share living and sleeping arrangements. Two examples of shared arrangements will be considered here: the boarding house and the school camp. In a similar way to team sports and the change rooms, the boarding house and the school camp are subject to powerful homophobic codes. In both cases, the enforced cohabitation of boys in close quarters can lead to heightened homophobic tensions, particularly when vulnerable boys are confronted with powerful peer groups. Ordinarily, vulnerable boys can escape peer hostility by seeking safety zones and going home, but respite may not be possible in the confines of the camp or the boarding house, where tensions can persist around the clock and (for boarders) for years at a time. Homophobic tensions with groups of boys in cohabitation raise the possibility of ritualization as a means of managing these tensions. While some of these "rituals" are no more than routines that regulate tensions, "acting homophobic tensions out" is an attractive explanation for why newcomers and outsiders to single-sex institutions such as military camps and boarding schools can be "bastardized."

Boarder Police

The division between boarders and day boys creates an "us versus them" dynamic in a boys' school, and homophobia readily attaches to categories positioned as "them." In addition, boarders are more susceptible to homophobic labeling because of the homosexual connotations of groups of boys living and sleeping together in the boarding house:

> . . . cars used to drive past our boarding house and yell out "Poofters!" in the middle of the night. (P16)

Similarly, boys who attend an all-boys boarding school even if they are not boarders themselves, are more susceptible to homophobic labeling because of the stigma of association. In the next example, BB28 describes the hierarchy of homophobic labeling involved:

> . . . people who went to [boarding school] were always known as poofters . . . because they go to an all-boys school. So that was always a label that we had and . . . within the school itself, the boarders were labeled by the day boys as poofters. (BB28)

Despite the homophobic labeling that boarders experience (or perhaps because of it), some respondents report that the boarding house has a reputation for being less tolerant of difference:

The school was a much nicer place to be, much more tolerant of difference and much kinder . . . there weren't the outcasts and the violence at school that there were in the boarding house. (P16)

The intolerance of difference in boarding houses probably varies from place to place, but in view of the nearly universal way that peers embrace homophobic constructs, it would be surprising if homophobic tensions weren't universal in these settings. K11 describes how an unwritten code of privacy applies to boarders and that sensitive issues between boarders could be contained within the boarding house. The boarding house door defined the boundary between the public and private domains for boys who otherwise had very little privacy:

. . . even those people at boarding school that were genuinely disliked were protected by this barrier. (K11)

K11 also describes how within the homophobic context of the boarding house, homosexuality was constructed as a property of "outsiders":

. . . homosexuality was not something that was seriously considered . . . inside the boarding school . . . inside our own membership, so to speak. It was something that was discussed outside when we went out and some guys went out and went "poofter bashing." They never did it inside the school. They always did it to those individuals outside the school. (K11)

One explanation for homosexuality being assigned to the domain of the outside world is that the homophobic codes of the boarding house were effective in suppressing homoerotic activity between boarders, or rendering it invisible:

S: . . . I didn't hear of any [homosexual activity], though I do know now after I've left boarding school, that several of our boarders, were homosexual . . . practicing and believing, but were not prepared to admit it while they were at boarding school. . . .

D: What would have happened to them if they had admitted it?
S: Hypothetically? One of two things. They would have either been completely shunned and people would have been very nervous around them, especially when they went to have a shower, and they probably would have covered their body.
D: Or?
S: They would have got such a beating that they probably would have left the school. (K11)

The differentiation of homosexuality as a property of outsiders probably also reflects the principal positioning of homosexuality as "otherness." As will be shown later in this chapter, "in-house" homoerotic activities are described by other participants (P16, J10), but they take place according to definite codes that makes them difficult to catergorize as "homosexual."

Camp

Similar dynamics to those in the boarding house were also found in descriptions of the school camp. Camps can bring disparate elements into close proximity and there is no easy escape from homophobia:

I just hated being away with them, and when you're away on camp it's like you've got no escape . . . you're away and that's it. You just can't go home. (L12)

L12 attributes his adverse experiences to homophobic harassment (being pushed around and called a faggot) and for him, the school camp was an upsetting experience:

I went on the school camp, and I ended up bursting into tears halfway through the camp and going up to my Asian studies teacher . . . and I just said, "I've got to go home, I've got to go home." And she was like, "Tell me what's wrong, tell me what's wrong." And I said, "Look. I just don't fit in with anyone. I don't have any friends. I don't fit in with anyone, I hate it here, I just want to go home." (L12)

For some boys, the school camp was a source of anxiety because it was seen as increasing the risks of being homophobically labeled. It has already been shown that N14 experienced an increase in popularity when it became known at a school camp that he was developing secondary sexual characteristics earlier than many other boys. Despite this, N14 became extremely anxious about attending camps because of his fear of being exposed in the camp environment, which was noticeably homophobic:

> . . . after the first experience in fifth class, I never wanted to go [to school camp] in sixth class. And I got out of it 'cause I sort of begged my mother not to send me . . . after the first experience of being with the boys, being the only one with pubes. . . . I think I became aware that I was being aroused by these boys. Being together in a group, sleeping, I could never sleep in tents 'cause I'd just think about all the guys in the tent. We all had to sleep together, and then there was all the rumors going around about the [teachers] who were poofters. (N14)

Concerns about stepping out of line in a school camp and becoming homophobically stigmatized are realistic. In the next example, a boy who was previously popular lost his reputation in his hometown when he was homophobically labeled at a camp (not a school camp) with other boys:

> **S:** . . . a few guys went away camping and came back with the story that he was a "poof " . . . and when we went to the pool and stuff, we used to give him shit . . . when he jumped into the pool, everyone else would sort of get out that was 'round him. . . . Wrote "poof" on his back with sunscreen. . . Not really bashed up, but roughed around a bit.
> **D:** Okay. Before he went on the camping trip?
> **S:** He was fairly well liked. . . . He was just a normal person. See, I'm not really sure what happened on the camping trip. (D4)

A similar description was provided by V22 concerning a school camp. In this case, homophobia distinguishes between the stigma of being a "perpetrator" of homosexual activities and being "innocent":

> . . . it was year nine . . . or year ten . . . and I remember
> someone actually got caught having a roll around the grass
> with someone else . . . with two other people, that's right . . .
> that was [a] pretty hot topic at the time. Particularly, one of
> those guys was labeled a poof. . . . The way that they got found
> out was the second guy rejected him . . . and so he was seen as
> the poof because he had . . . approached another guy . . . the
> guy that made the approach, was pretty well ostracized for the
> rest of that year, and left school after that year. (V22)

The importance attached to the event is clear from expressions such
as this being a "hot topic" and how this episode left the "perpetrator" ostracized.

KNOWING WHEN TO GET OFF:
SEXUAL RESTRAINT AND TRANSGRESSION

Until now, the emphasis of this chapter has been on how the fear
of homophobia creates distance and restrains intimacy (Devlin and
Cowan, 1985). However, the homoerotic potential of sports, the
change rooms, the boarding house, and the camp is implicit in the
analysis: that homophobia does indeed have something to restrain:

> . . . well if you can walk about in public holding another guy's
> hand what's he going to do on the football field, you know? He
> could go in for a tackle and he'd be havin' a "free feel" as well.
> (E5)

Sporting venues and boarding houses often feature as sites for
homoerotic fantasies in the popular imagination, and evidence collected for this project did identify a range of homoerotic scenarios.
Finding homosexual and heterosexual subjects who have engaged
in homoerotic activities of some kind during childhood and adolescence appears to contradict earlier conclusions about the restraining
effects of homophobia. The picture is complicated further because
some homosexual subjects reported avoiding homoeroticism and
many homosexual subjects engaged in varying forms of heterosexual contact, including intercourse and marriage. There are also

theoretical problems with the validity of categories used to designate sexual preference and what the sexual orientation "ratings" mean (in the Appendixes of this project). However, this is not a major problem because the project is investigating homophobia and presumed status—rather than reifying/essentializing sexual preference—and findings are largely independent of the validity and accuracy of sexual identities: indeed, arguments in this work challenge those classifications. In addition, many of the examples to be examined occurred prior to adult sexual identity formation.

Closer scrutiny of cases where there is evidence of homoeroticism in childhood and adolescence helps to resolve these dilemmas. One consideration is that there is a distinction between acceptable homoeroticism and the discredited status of being a "poofter" (neither of which are [yet] perceived as homosexual). There is evidence for the controlling influence of male peer groups over homophobia when it relates to homoeroticism. Peer groups appear to be able to issue special dispensation for some homoerotic activities, providing these are conducted according to agreed-upon codes and sanctioned by the group. Although homophobia does not bring a complete halt to homoeroticism (without which the sexual dimension of homophobia would be meaningless), homophobia can be demonstrated to play a role in restraining and "ritualizing" homoerotic activities. In addition, a case will be made that under the influence of homophobia, undifferentiated childhood eroticism is subject to transitions analogous to those demonstrated in previous chapters (such as the disappearance of crying and learning to restrain "dressing up" behaviors). In this study, childhood (homo) eroticism initially appears to depend largely on opportunity and becomes increasingly subject to homophobic taboo; subsequently, adult homosexuality (as distinct from homoeroticism) emerges from under the weighty influence of school-ground homophobia.

Male-to-Male Intimacy Among Nonhomosexually Identifying Males

The starting point for this chapter was that male-male interactions take place along a spectrum of closeness. This is one reason why the definition of homoeroticism is not straightforward—because it depends on delineating the (shifting) divide between what is homosocial and what is homosexual. In addition, "homo-eroticism" is an adult term and, in the context of a boy's world, might misrepresent the undifferentiated state of childhood intimacy. Consequently, examples will be provided that demonstrate increasing intimacy leading to scenarios that, for adults, are unequivocally homoerotic.

On the surface, it doesn't seem homoerotic for a boy to put his arm around the shoulder of a male friend, but this will be used as a starting point for our exploration of homoeroticism. Rather than attempt to define homoeroticism, it is useful to allow homophobia to do this instead: if intimacy is sufficient to provoke homophobia, then the boundary that designates homoeroticism appears to have been encountered. In the following example, Z26 discusses how young boys often put their arms around their male friends. The key point illustrated by this extract is that after a certain age, this un-inhibited group activity becomes transgressive:

> You'd walk around with your arms around each other in the playground . . . you'd be in the middle with whole lines of boys with their arms around each other. But then if you got to a certain age and you saw that happening, straightaway they'd be poofs or pansies. (Z26)

The homophobic pressure on "innocent" actions such as this is clear, and V22 makes a similar observation where homophobia affects the stylization of this form of contact: arms around shoulders is initially acceptable, whereas arms around boys' waists never is. Later, both forms of contact become taboo except, as we will see, in special contexts such as sports.

The closer contact becomes, the more it is restrained by homo-phobia. However, instead of intimate contact being prohibited by homophobia, it often becomes highly stylized instead. As Kidd notes, "the only way many of us express fondness for other men is by teasing or mock fighting. . . . Anything more openly affectionate would be suspect" (Kidd, 1990: 40). In the following quote, wres-tling is offered as an example of how boys explore one another:

> I think the only exploration of other boys that I know of was actually when we had a wrestle . . . when you actually. . . . But

again, the question was more, "Is this guy stronger than me? Can I beat him if I had to? . . . Can he throw me over? Can he do this to me?" (K11)

K11 does not recall any experiences more intimate than this example, but it is interesting that he offered this one in a discussion of boys' intimacy.

Another example of how boys can legitimately explore is provided by Z26. This case is from late primary school around the time of puberty:

> . . . It was before I went to high school because I could remember sitting up in the library with three or four mates comparing pubic hair [Laugh]. (Z26)

Z26 describes how, in later adolescence, he was very homophobic, but this does not appear to be an issue in the previous example. In contrast, J10 provides the next description of his brother's activities:

> . . . I remember once walking into a room and [brother] quickly pulling up his pants and this other guy pulling up his pants. So I can remember that happening. And also the beach. We used to go up the beach every Christmas and [I remember] him doing things like that with another guy but I never [did]. (J10)

His brother's activities seem similar to the one described by Z26, except that the transgressive dimension only appears to become relevant when someone from outside the group (J10) becomes involved. Interestingly, while J10 is now open about his homosexuality to his family, and he was not involved in his brother's homoerotic activities, his brother now seems to be heterosexual.

The next examples illustrate a further degree of intimacy and a subsequent behavioral transition. H8 provides the following description from around the age of four:

> I . . . stuck my willie between my brother's butt cheeks and he stuck his between my sister's and we all stood in a line thinking it was all very hilarious. And called Mum and Dad in to

> have a look. . . . Basically, I think, she just had a bit of a giggle
> and said, "No, that's a bit naughty. You shouldn't really do that
> sort of thing" [chuckle]. (H8)

Two years later, after commencing school:

> . . . I just remember the girl and asking her if she wanted to see
> my willie, and she said yes. So I showed her and then immedi-
> ately felt really bad. . . . I'm fairly sure that if it had been a boy
> I wouldn't have done it. (H8)

However, H8 did have further experiences of intimacy with male
friends after this. The difference is that the next example takes place
in private and a feature of the interview is how both boys are alert
for the approach of others, particularly adults:

> . . . there was a big old bed with a big quilt on it and . . . we
> used to . . . play act and take our clothes off and jump under the
> doona . . . it was naughty because we had . . . a rude song . . .
> and it just felt nice. He had soft skin and I obviously had soft
> skin, so I don't even remember doing anything specifically
> with our penises. We'd sort of hug each other and wiggle and
> roll around a bit. . . . And, I can only remember being face to
> face . . . and I think we used to kiss . . . but from memory the
> penis didn't enter into it at all. I remember once, his mum
> came out and called for us, and we went, "Whoa!" and got
> dressed and ran out. (H8)

From an initially uninhibited public display with his brother, his later
experiences provide a neat illustration of increasingly restricted
male-male intimacy. At the time of the interview, H8 rated himself as
heterosexual.

A sequence provided by M13 also illustrates this process. He
engaged in genital contact with a boy at the age of nine or ten, when
he was old enough to appreciate homophobia. In the following
quote, the feelings and pressures associated with the memory of this
event begin to emerge:

> . . . for some reason, I've sort of glossed over it now. And I've
> put it right behind me. I haven't purposely tried to block it out

and say, "Oh, I can't remember, that was bad, that was bad," but I've never, ever mentioned it to anyone. No one knows about it, except of course him. (M13)

Notice how much of his account suggests that he is uncomfortable with this memory. Yet, at the time, M13 voluntarily participated and reached orgasm. In the following two statements, the pleasure associated with the event appears to have been replaced by homophobic stigma:

> . . . so the ideas that I had about sex were really based on boys did it with girls, and girls did it with boys. And all of a sudden when I had done this, I thought, "Oh, this is perverted." That's what I thought actually. . . . I thought, "Oh, this is . . . a very perverted thing to do." (M13)

Even though the episode occurred several years ago, M13 still regrets it, and there is a suggestion that his "purity" is compromised even now:

> . . . sometimes I wish it hadn't happened. I wish I'd developed purely heterosexually. (M13)

M13 rates himself as heterosexual, and since this experience, he has developed an aversion to intimate contact with other males, as this later comment shows:

> I just don't like the idea of another male physically involved with me. (M13)

The distinction between being sexually attracted to women and having an aversion to intimacy with men is relevant here. In this case, the account of the transition, from orgasm with another male to an aversion to male intimacy, is mainly characterized by descriptions of homophobic guilt.

This section has focused on homoeroticism and shows that it comes under increasing pressure from homophobia with age. Early engagement in intimate acts with other males is relatively uninhibited, but memories appear to be increasingly linked to homophobia.

A final example is provided by a subject who is now gay. During his adolescence, he had a number of sexual contacts with peers:

> Sex between boys, I feel, is rampant. Well at least I was. Dunno about everybody else, but I was . . . and [there were] little rules, you just can't talk about it; and you can't act like you enjoyed it too much, like it can't be completely satisfying, although I quite often was, it was like "Ahhh yeah!" . . . They're also the same rules that gay people in small towns get anyway. You can't talk about it and you can't show it, and you can't mince and stuff like that. Oh, fuck off! (AA27)

Notice how the sexual contacts were subject to certain codes that appear to be imposed by homophobia. AA27 also suggests that many of the people who participated appear to be heterosexual:

> **D:** . . . How many of them turned out to be gay, and how many turned out to be straight?
> **S:** I think I'm the only queen.
> **D:** Did they enjoy it?
> **S:** Oh God yeah! (AA27)

This section shows the role of homophobia in progressively re-stricting male intimacy as boys grow older (Devlin and Cowan, 1985). Initially, the capacity for intimacy appears to be "polymor-phous," whereas later the capacity to enjoy intimacy with other males becomes inhibited. While some heterosexual males reported engaging in childhood homoeroticism, others did not recall similar experiences. Similarly, although boys who are now gay partici-pated, some boys who would later be gay did not get involved. Furthermore, there appears to be no reason why an aversion to intimacy with men is a prerequisite for sexual attraction to women. This raises the possibility that instead of early patterns of male intimacy reflecting later sexual orientation, key influences on ho-moeroticism include the need for intimacy, available opportunities, and homophobia.

Sports Homoeroticism

> I suspect the reason a lot of guys like playing football is they like to be close to other males, and that's the only way the framework allows them to do it. (Q17)

The potential for homoeroticism in sports has surfaced several times in this chapter. Generally, the references have been in the negative sense, such as when Messner spoke of how sports "mediates" men's relationships by permitting powerful bonds while preventing intimacy (Messner, 1992: 91). In contrast, the data from this project include references to the homoerotic potential of sports and examples of homoeroticism. This raises questions about how powerful homophobia really is, whether its operations can be suspended, and whether it modifies the expression of homoeroticism.

Several subjects recognized the homoerotic potential of sports. We have seen that during childhood and when N14 was coming to terms with his emerging gay identity, he expressed a deep dislike for team sports. In the subsequent analysis of similar cases, it was possible to conclude that an important factor in this disaffection with team sports was the influence of homophobia. Now that he is a young adult, has left school, and has accepted his gay identity, N14's feelings have changed and he is now able to appreciate team sports:

> Whereas now I can sort of understand it [sports obsession], 'cause I'm quite interested in a number of different sports . . . [it's] nice watching the athletes' bodies. . . . There's an erotic side to it. Actually a lot of it's erotic, I think. (N14)

Even while playing football at school, AA27 had homoerotic experiences:

> I'd more often than not "crack a fat" [erection]. If we were in a scrum. . . . You know, it was "Wow boys!" . . . but I mean I continued to play because after a while, when you've got the ball in your hand, you can't be thinking about how much you'd like to "boof" so-and-so down the back there. It was like, "Oh, shit! I've got to run!" (AA27)

However, AA27's experience with sports was not unconditionally positive. He describes these experiences as "too close for comfort" and how he became less interested in football "when sex started coming into it." He finally gave up football when it became "too serious" and the homophobia more intense.

Despite homophobia, sports did provide a covert means for getting closer for some people. At school, P16's emerging homosexuality was unknown to anybody else. For him, a key source of pleasure during adolescence was to watch a male friend participate in athletics. However, because of homophobia this had to be kept "completely and utterly private":

> He never had any idea that I had a crush on him. And it continued for years and he was really good at athletics. I used to watch him run around the oval and . . . that was completely and utterly private. No one else knew. I used to carry it with me every day. (P16)

A similar description was provided by X24. He became involved in touch football in order to get "legitimately" closer to a friend, even though he wasn't interested in football:

> . . . what I did with this guy was that I couldn't give a shit about football, and just to be around him I got involved in the touch football competition and played touch football. (X24)

Homoeroticism in sports is not confined to boys who are now homosexual. Z26 describes how he traveled home nude from a "Grand Final" with the rest of his team (but there was nothing sexual):

> [male-male intimacy] never really interested me. I mean, we sat on the bus on the way home after the "Grand Final"—nude. A busload of men . . . but there was nothing sexual in it. Well, for me anyway . . . obviously I can't answer for the other blokes. (Z26)

Other accounts were not as reserved. P16 witnessed "mucking around" by the football team ("first eighteen"), which appears to have a homoerotic component:

... the only sexual experiences I had were ... looking at what
other people did, and occasionally you'd see someone carrying on. Like the first eighteen guys jumping in and out of bed
after lights out, mucking around. I remember they had the
vacuum cleaner out once and [someone] put his dick in it
[laughs]. (P16)

Similarly, J10 describes the scene at his first school "football" camp
at a seaside property:

... I remember the very first one I went to. It was just incredi-
ble. It was the first time I'd been exposed to so much sexuality,
you know, lots of guys sharing sleeping bags and streaking,
and you'd walk in a room and there'd be guys on the floor
together and so you'd close the door. I was a bit embarrassed
by it. I think I was just so shocked. (J10)

J10 describes having observed at least half of his peers engaging in
homoerotic behaviors at that camp during school year eight. The
situation changed in subsequent camps, which he describes as becoming very "girl oriented."

Differentiating Acceptable Homoeroticism

So how can earlier evidence concerning the extent and intensity
of homophobia be reconciled with the findings of homoeroticism
presented in the previous sections? As J10 observes:

... there was hypocrisy to it ... they were abusing the people
for the very same thing. For acts that they were doing themselves. (J10)

The explanation appears to lie partly with the differentiation of
male intimacy along homosocial and homoerotic lines during childhood. For a period of time, when peer groups are becoming increasingly influential, the term "poofter" is "presexual" and is not primarily deployed to target homoeroticism:

It would have been alright to take your clothes off and "jack
off" [masturbate] together and things like that, but that wasn't

what being a "poof" was. Being a "poof" was being girlie or
unpopular or something like that. (J10)

However, cases of homoeroticism also occurred at a time when
taboos against homosexuality were understood and firmly linked to
homophobia. In these cases, the "presexual" explanation is not
satisfactory. Two further possibilities suggest how male intimacy
can arise in apparent contradiction to the dictates of homophobia.
Both depend on the role that peer-group processes play in defining
and enforcing homophobic standards. Special dispensation for homoeroticism can be afforded, providing it occurs with peer approval
and according to established codes. Alternatively, homoeroticism is
possible if it takes place beyond the reach of peer-group scrutiny.
The data provide evidence for both of these possibilities.

Evidence for special dispensation for high-status boys to be involved in homoerotic "mucking around" appears in several accounts. In the following quote, P16 observes how homophobia is a
device for the exercise of power and how condoning intimacy was
arbitrated by those with power:

> . . . that term [faggot] was used by people in a position of power
> . . . and having said that . . . male-to-male intimacy was only
> really allowed and condoned among "the powers that be." (P16)

P16 illustrates how peer-based homophobia and peer-based in-
demnity work in concert to differentiate between acceptable, stylized intimacy and when it becomes unacceptable:

> . . . "mucking around" in the showers was okay, for big burly
> football players. Mucking around in the dorms, hopping in
>
> other beds, touching, grabbing, holding, wrestling was okay
> for them. 'Cause . . . it was done in a sort of exertive and
> physical type playacting. But if you were demure, pale
> skinned, [and] unmuscled and you did that, that's out—you
> copped it. (P16)

Being of higher status and stylizing the interaction so that it appears
consistent with the principles of "physicality" contribute to making
"mucking around" acceptable.

Stylized male-male contact recurs in other transcripts as an important part of the code of acceptable intimacy among powerful peer groups. CC29 provides a further illustration where "being brash" and having a legitimizing reason also indemnifies behaviors:

> . . . being brash about it and . . . having some sort of reason, whether it was just "we're going to have a look, that's why we're looking, to see what it looks like and have a laugh at it if it's too small or too big or too crooked," then that was okay, and anyone could get involved and there was no shame in it among the kids. Whereas if you were seen to be doing it furtively, there was something wrong with it. (CC29)

Being part of a group activity (rather than taking place outside the peer group) also makes behaviors acceptable, when ordinarily they would not be:

> . . . he was uncircumcised and he was probably a year or two more developed than us, and he had quite a long dangly curvy dick and we all gathered round to have a bit of a chuckle. And that was fine and there was no disgrace in that because we were all just looking at it. (CC29)

"Playacting," "horsing around," "carrying on," being "jovial," and not appearing serious also creates circumstances in which intimacy, including direct genital contact, is permissible:

> . . . they were quite happy to do it: carry on, grab genitalia in the shower, horse around, as long as it was playacting and seen to be sort of jovial and . . . you know, just "mucking around." It wouldn't have been if it was serious, like if it was any sort of tenderness or anything like that, that would have been out. (P16)

Boys being tender is another matter!

An important fear is that details of homoerotic "transgressions" might find their way into the public/peer domain. Therefore, another way of avoiding homophobia is to quarantine intimacy to situations that are divorced from peer scrutiny:

> . . . Because that was your biggest fear. Of gossip. As soon as somebody got told—whoosh! That was it! The whole school knew and then you were just laughed at. (AA27)

V22 also describes his awareness of the risks if (unauthorized) male intimacy became publicly known:

> I did quietly attempt to initiate sex with a couple of other guys during high school. . . . I didn't try very hard. I was always very conscious of backlash. (V22)

One way of quarantining this risk is to confine the experience to those involved. Under these conditions, it is in the interests of each party to preserve the confidence because all participants have something to lose:

> . . . if two boys were to do it, to "goose around" like that boy and I did in bed, that would never happen in front of anyone who wasn't involved. (CC29)

Another effect of homophobia, which often featured in transcripts of heterosexual and gay subjects, was to engage in homoeroticism away from school and with people who were not part of the school peer network. Typically, this was with "kissing cousins" and neighbors:

> Not between schoolkids. I think at that stage I was mucking around with my cousins . . . that's when it all started . . . late primary school, early high school period. But never at school; everyone was always too scared and aware that it wasn't the done thing. (N14)

Other participants provided similar descriptions.

These examples demonstrate ways that male-to-male intimacy can be, and was, experienced without risking homophobia. However, there are points at which transgression becomes intolerable to the peer group, and these boundaries seem to be very apparent to boys and are precisely mapped:

> . . . there's sort of specific boundaries or rules between the two . . . a cutoff point. . . . With mates . . . you will go this far . . .

and that's it. That's as far as we go. Sexuality goes beyond that. (Y25)

Many of the examples used thus far to illustrate homoeroticism include descriptions of the limits of acceptability. Lower-status boys, who lack peer dispensation, who are "demure," "pale skinned," and "unmuscled," or who are "furtive," "serious," or showing "any sort of tenderness," are at risk of homophobia for the same sorts of behaviors. Other examples delineating these boundaries include intimacy that is too obvious, open, and public; when a participant is identifiably homosexual or a "poofter"; and when intimacy is not orchestrated, sanctioned, or in accord with peer-group codes. In each of these cases, the appearance of homophobia is related to scenarios being blatantly "poofterly" or homosexual and escaping the usual social controls. When a situation becomes identifiably transgressive and threatens to escape group containment, then a homophobic response becomes a necessary maneuver to avoid culpability and to prevent homophobic stigma from spreading to implicate others.

The next example illustrates how boundaries can be transgressed when the perceived status of one participant changes—when he is identified as homosexual. In this case, an affectionate encounter is transformed into a hostile one:

> I was in a nightclub once where two footballers were getting a bit toddly, piddly, and one of them had his arm all around me and was playful and happy and eventually his girlfriend pointed out to him that I was a gay friend of a friend of theirs, and he got extremely . . . was ready to bash me to a pulp. (Q17)

Similarly, a romantic liaison with a woman in a bar is disrupted when one of the participants is alerted to its homoerotic dimension:

> . . . someone tapped me on the shoulder and said "You realize don't you, this woman is a man?" . . . there's some sort of guilt attached to it still. . . . I can deal with other people's homosexuality easily, but when it comes to being in a situation myself, it's not something I've told anyone else. (U21)

This experience revealed the hitherto hidden influence of the fear of homophobia and it had considerable impact on U21:

> There's something dirty about the conflict of . . . sitting there with somebody that's attractive, and [your] body is saying one thing and [your] mind is saying another. (U21)

Notice how the conflict for him was between his erotic desires, the "dirtiness" on discovering the homosexual component, and being observed by a knowing third party. U21 describes feeling "spun out" by the experience and was still embarrassed when he related the story for this project.

A slightly different perspective is illustrated in the next example. In this case, there is no third party and therefore no immediate risk of exposure. Here, a close friendship becomes challenged by three words:

> . . . my best friend about three months ago, a couple of days before he got married, and I was his best man . . . we were sitting on the beach late one night talking and he said, "I love you." And . . . my gut reaction, I suppose, when I think about it, is really, I love him. He's a person who I have a tremendous affection for and everything like that. . . . But . . . I was awkward with it. I was awkward with it; that's the only way you could describe it. And I think that's . . . an element of ingrained homophobia basically. (W23)

Despite the obvious heterosexual setting, these three words were the source of memorable anxiety.

These three cases illustrate how the unexpected appearance of homophobia can instantly destabilize a scenario, not by altering the basic elements, but with a sudden perceived change of status of one of the participants (Walker and Antaki, 1986). When BB28 learned that one of his friends was gay, he found himself "redefining" all of his friend's actions and words:

> . . . we redefined all his actions, all his words . . . simply because of that fact. Which you wouldn't do if I'm heterosexual; you don't redefine everything they say on that. (BB28)

BB28 found himself feeling "disgusted," but he also felt disturbed that he would feel that way:

> I was . . . in some ways disgusted by it, but then that was . . . my mind working. I'd interpret his action as disgusting, whereas it wasn't at all. But it still was an innate reaction to what he did. . . . I found it really disturbing that I'd actually feel that way. Because I always thought I was fairly liberal, and that I have to intellectually override what I'm feeling 'cause I want to feel nothing about it, you know, just normal . . . and yet I couldn't. (BB28)

Finally, AA27 found his childhood friendships transformed when he returned to his hometown with a "new" identity:

> . . . there are rules to these kind of things. You don't really enjoy it; you always prefer to do it with a girl; and you just don't talk about it. And then when I arrived there, I'm a queen and it's like "Oh God! Fuck!" And they just didn't cope with it. I can remember a guy that I "boofed" when I saw him last time in [country town], he put his head down and whooshed off the other way. (AA27)

In this case, the homoerotic component was not the primary problem, providing the rules were observed. AA27's transgression was to be too open. The fear of homophobia resulted in a fear of being associated with AA27 now that his stigmatized status was public.

Compulsory Heterosexuality

> I think it would be easier for a guy to approach a girl to try and develop a relationship, because in the eyes of everybody else that was normal. But if a man ever approached another man, or a woman approached a woman, straight away, buzzers and sirens would go off and something would be terribly wrong. (Z26)

Homophobia and the fear of homophobic labeling act in concert with heterosexism to create strong pressures to conform to heterosexual norms (Wells, 1991). The result is sometimes called "com-

pulsory heterosexuality" (Rich, 1980). The importance of presenting a heterosexual image has been noted in a variety of settings. For
example, Messner describes this in sports: "homophobia within
athletic masculine cultures tends to lock men—whether gay or not
—into narrowly defined heterosexual identities and relationships"
(Messner, 1992: 156). Similar pressures are identifiable in the interview data of this project:

> There's an intense societal pressure to have a girlfriend, to have a
> partner . . . and if you don't, then that immediately attracts
> attention and . . . puts question marks on your masculinity, your
> worth as a male, your attractiveness, and everything else. One of
> the key groups who won't have girlfriends will be people who
> are homosexual or leaning toward homosexual . . . so they're a
> natural target. (W23)

This quote illustrates "compulsory heterosexuality" and clarifies the
role played by homophobia. A study by Eliason found that choosing
to be heterosexual was partly related to rejecting a gay identity
(Eliason, 1995), and Wells found that heterosexual practices were
avoided if they were labeled homosexual (Wells, 1991). In the next
quote, U21 describes the pressure among his school peers to experience heterosexual intercourse and the fear of homophobia should he
not become actively and publicly heterosexual:

> . . . and the fear of being left behind I guess had . . . something
> to do with being labeled, you know, "poofter." (U21)

Pressures contributing to compulsory heterosexuality appear to
be reflected in the importance that young males attach to proving
one's heterosexuality. Instead of simply being heterosexual, it is
important to generate evidence of heterosexual activity for the scrutiny of peers and to denounce homosexuality. According to the
previous quotes, this has as much, if not more, to do with avoiding
being homophobically labeled as it does with being heterosexual. A
number of authors have observed how boys' heterosexual talk takes
the form of a repetitive, almost obsessive practice. "One of the main
functions of young men's sex talk was publicly to validate their
masculinity to their male friends. This collective peer identity af-

firmation often manifested itself in terms of highly ritualistic obsessive discourses" (Mac an Ghaill, 1994: 92). A similar observation was made by Z26:

> I think most of it's bravado. Most of it's showing off to the other blokes . . . trying to make out that you can do what he can do. . . . I think the interest . . . is not really in that particular girl. It's just that she starts developing boobs and stuff and you try [to] look down the top of her dress so you can see them or pull [her] dress up. I mean, we had a touch football team at high school, the start of high school called the "fanny grabbers." (Z26)

Similarly, while powerful codes restrain the use of boys' eyes when regarding other boys, powerful codes orchestrate the reverse for girls. This is illustrated in the next example, where the use of the gaze is clearly differentiated between the sexes:

> . . . if you could possibly get even a glimpse of the girls, you'd be in it and telling everyone straightaway. . . . But in the boys change room it was not accepted to be looking at each other. (Z26)

Notice how "telling everyone straightaway" is a feature of this description—there is no suggestion that these voyeuristic practices be done "on the sly" for purely personal reasons.

Wanting to have children also contributes to pressures to be heterosexual. For X24, the prospect of not having children made it more difficult to accept his gay identity:

> I think a way of coping with that sense of mortality is the fact that if you have children, you know that you're contributing to that sense of continuity . . . there's something of you that's gonna continue beyond the grave. And I found that very disturbing . . . if you don't have a family . . . there's that lack of continuity. . . . I found that very disturbing. (X24)

Likewise, the principal concern that S19 voiced in the event that his son was gay was a regret that he would not have grandchildren.

In addition to individual desires to have children, there are also pressures to have children as part of a contract to guarantee social continuity. This is reflected in concerns about guaranteeing "ever-lasting life" and fears of having no future:

> It's not natural; you can't keep progressing down the family chain with someone of your own sex. Where you can with . . . a female. (D4)

In addition, a fear emerges that everyone might turn homosexual and humanity would have no future:

> . . . if everyone started goin' for the same sex then you don't reproduce and you don't keep goin'. (D4)

These concerns are reminiscent of the issues considered in Chapter 1, that homosexuality is somehow conceived of as a transmissible condition, and potentially so irresistible that it has the capacity to threaten the human race:

> **S:** . . . men and women are designed to have sex together.
> **D:** Who says?
> **S:** Well, if you don't, the race dies out [laughs]. (H8)

Based purely on anatomical factors, can easily be concluded that two men are also suitably designed to have intercourse (even if not for reproduction).

It appears that becoming heterosexual involves obsessive public testimonies, close peer supervision, and time to get used to the idea of sex:

> . . . it was third grade, I was about eight years old . . . this friend came over and said, "I'm never going to get married." And I said, "Why not?" He said, "I've just been speaking to my older brother and he says that when you get married you have to put your willy up the . . . up the . . . the person you marry. So I'm never going to get married." And I remember at the time thinking blahhh . . . that's pretty horrible. (W23)

In another example, U21 did not enjoy his first heterosexual encounter:

> . . . it wasn't pleasant really . . . I remember more the feeling "I can't believe I'm doing this," rather than "Oh, this is nice." (U21)

He went on to describe his first encounter as an "out of body experience" and that it took practice before he was able to experience heterosexual desire. In the next quote, he describes his step-wise progression toward heterosexual intimacy:

> . . . each step was terrifying like . . . trying to break world records . . . you break a record but . . . all you can do then is to break another record . . . and each step was just as hard cause it was uncharted territory. (U21)

Peers regularly supervised their members' heterosexual development. "The male peer group tends to police its own members in terms of intimacy with females" (Messner, 1992: 98; Weisner and Wilson-Mitchell, 1990). For example, F6 described how his friends set out to organize his first sexual encounter for him:

> My friends set out to break my virginity for me. And I was always saying when the right one comes along I'll lose it . . . they were tellin' me there's never a right one and they then went on their way to . . . find me my first, so-called "victim" . . . so it was all planned meticulously. (F6)

In addition to having their heterosexual encounters organized, boys were quizzed afterward. This exerted pressure to display bravado, to overstate what occurred, and not to be caught lying. The pressure to appear successfully heterosexual was weighty and exacting. As Messner notes, "the need to prove one's manhood through sexual conquests of women was experienced as a burden by many young heterosexual males" (Messner, 1992: 99):

> . . . it was unclear as to how much you should tell either . . . you didn't know whether you were incriminating yourself or, you weren't sure what the right answers were . . . so it was like being in a . . . court case where you . . . have no legal advice. (U21)

In addition to implicit fears that homosexuality might be irresistibly attractive, it would appear that being heterosexual doesn't always come as "naturally" as is often assumed. "Becoming a man" is "something that boys (especially adolescent boys) work at" (Whitson, 1990: 22).

FRIENDSHIPS, RELATIONSHIPS, AND BEING HOMOSEXUALLY ACTIVE

Most of this chapter has focused on how homophobia infiltrates the lives of young males and influences how they relate, regardless of their eventual sexual orientation. However, homophobia has particular effects on the lives of men who become homosexual.

Homophobia has an important impact on the capacity for gay men to form friendships and relationships (Martin, 1982). In a previous section, we saw how finding that someone was gay caused people to "redefine" their relationships with them. The basis of a friendship is fundamentally altered and can interfere with it. When J10 and his male friend were judged by their peers to be getting too friendly, their peers reacted homophobically and took steps to disrupt the friendship:

> I can remember one of the other guys who I had been sort of friends with for years, became very angry and called me a poof and stopped having anything to do with me because of my friendship with [close male friend]. And a few people said I shouldn't be with him because the other boys were saying I shouldn't be. (J10)

His friend was also the subject of homophobic peer intervention, which included fighting:

> . . . He had a couple of friends from football who were quite angry at his friendship with me, and he got into a couple of fights about that. (J10)

In addition to peer intervention, homophobia can inhibit young gay men from opening up to others. O15 suffered considerable homophobia and marginalization during his school years. Here he relates how his confidence and his capacity for friendships and relationships was undermined for some time after leaving school:

> It certainly wasn't a fun time . . . it's only now, all these years later . . . before I actually could gain confidence again and talk to people and mix with different people. (O15)

In the next example, X24 is aware of the possibility that friends can react adversely to homosexuals; he responds by avoiding close friendships to escape awkward situations:

> . . . I just felt like what's the point in bloody . . . making the effort to invest time and effort into making friends, just to turn around and have them find out you're gay and then have some of them piss you off or . . . find that you've got a really funny relationship with someone 'cause they don't know how to handle it. So . . . with friends from school . . . I've let them just drift away, and I've really made no effort to maintain contact. (X24)

Although this approach could be criticized for being overly defensive and for not giving people enough credit or giving friendships enough value, the following quote demonstrates the basis for X24's fears. Even with "close" friends there is often an inevitable distance present:

> I've got a friend who's a [Christian denomination]. And he's one of the close friends from school I keep contact with, who I'd never tell . . . but you hear them going on about . . . how poofters should be killed and all this kind of business. (X24)

This account highlights another dilemma regularly confronting many gay men. How can they have a genuinely close friendship if they are hiding an important part of themselves? Alternatively, if they disclose, will their "friendship" be any more satisfactory? (Walker and Antaki, 1986).

Being Heterosexually Active: Just a Phase?

"Both lesbian women and gay men report doing a good deal of heterosexual dating in their adolescent years" (Anderson, 1995: 25). Presumably, many gay men and their female partners get considerable satisfaction from their sexual experiences, and it should not be assumed that gay men are incapable of heterosexual pleasure or that they have an aversion to contact with women. However, compulsory heterosexuality has important impacts on young gay men and their female partners.

Both O15 and V22 reported having heterosexual expectations of themselves, despite now being gay:

> ... my view was that I would marry and settle down. I wanted a girlfriend. I had crushes on . . . girls from time to time. But looking back on it, I don't think sex actually entered into any of that. (V22)

But, although V22 didn't describe any sexual arousal, some homosexual subjects did report heterosexual arousal:

> I also remember being quite aroused by naked women. . . . I remember particularly one summer when I was staying with my grandparents, they lived on a farm, and going into the tractor . . . service shop . . . they had pictures of naked women on the calendars. And I'd always be wanting to look at them 'cause I'd get an erection. (P16)

Furthermore, subjects in this study supplied descriptions of homosexuals experiencing heterosexual "phases," active heterosexual relationships, and marriage:

> I don't know whether this is normal or not, but it helps, when I'd just started . . . sort of becoming sexually active at all, I was interested in women and men. So I just concentrated on my girlfriend at the time. (L12)

In some cases, the dividing line between being homosexual and being heterosexual depends on how individual sexual practices are viewed. Certain practices are stigmatized by homophobia and are unacceptable. In the next description, N14 reflects on having mixed sexual experiences in young adulthood:

> I remember when I was . . . having sex with this woman on a particular spot on the beach down the coast, I was thinking "Oh my God. I've had sex with my [male] cousin on this spot," and

> doing a bit of comparison . . . it would have been in my earlier high school years . . . he would always initiate it. . . . And then I started to cotton on to the initiation thing, and I would start initiating it . . . it would have gone on for three or four years . . . it became more frequent and I remember, I freaked out when he got heavier with me, wanted to kiss me and have anal sex with me. And I sort of drew the line and said, "No, I don't want to do that. That's what gay people do." (N14)

Although N14 is now gay, kissing other men and having more intimate homosexual contact initially wasn't easy. As the previous quote shows, at that stage, he did not have a gay identity and "drew a line" beyond which lay homosexuality, and he wasn't homosexual unless he crossed that line.

The pressures to conform to "compulsory heterosexuality" were described by some subjects as confusing and painful. The next two cases describe the difficulties associated with the widening gap between (heterosexual) social roles and (homosexual) self-concept:

> at school . . . I was more or less pressured into being hetero . . . and that was just confusing and it hurt. (C3)

In the case of A1, the internal conflict between his homosexual feelings and having a girlfriend caused a dramatic reaction:

> . . . having a girlfriend for the first time . . . I just blew right out then . . . me having a tantrum in the middle of the fucking assembly and just chucking the biggest fucking wobbly. And no one could calm me down. . . . I can remember just being really confused. I couldn't understand . . . why I was going out with a girl when I'm a faggot. (A1)

Assumptions about the heterosexuality of males can also cause difficulties for women who are involved. While P16 was meticulous about not "leading his female friend on," he also buried his homosexuality. The result is that his important female friend could not understand why he didn't respond to her—and he couldn't tell her:

> . . . there was a girl who . . . got quite attached to me . . . and . . . no one had any idea that I was gay. I buried that very deep. . . . I

just . . . would find any excuse not to be alone with her, not to be intimate, any excuse at all. I would avoid any sort of physical contact yet would really cherish her company, [and] I couldn't get enough of it. However, I was very, very careful to avoid anything that . . . she would construe as me liking her in a physical sort of way. Of course that didn't work. She sort of . . . fell for me anyway and . . . it came to a head one day . . . she said, "Oh, why don't you wanna be. Why can't we be, you know, an item?" and I said, "I don't love you," and that just wrecked it. (P16)

Both parties ended up in an awkward and painful situation that sorely tested their friendship.

Two respondents (Q17 and B2) have been married, even though they now have gay identities and are divorced. In the case of Q17, it appears that he was unaware of his homosexuality at the time he married, and as we will see at the end of this chapter, he became increasingly and painfully aware of it during the marriage. A similar situation occurred for B2. Both Q17 and B2 suffered considerable homophobia at school, and this raises the possibility that these experiences postponed their realization of their homosexuality. This is B2's response when asked what would have happened if his homophobic school experiences had been different:

S: Marriage would never have happened, and contact with females would never have happened, I think.
D: So that's a "negative" side of things, but on the other side of the coin your former wife would have been able to get on with her life, I guess.
S: Mmm [agree]. Then again I helped her get along with her life the way it is.
D: Did you? Do you still see her?
S: Yes. [We're] still very good friends. (B2)

Homophobia and Becoming Homosexually Active

The relationships between commencing homoerotic activities and forming a gay identity are complex. In this study there were cases of homoerotic activity starting well before gay identity formation, and in others, gay identity formation occurred well in advance of becoming sexually active. In all of these cases, there is evidence for the influence of homophobia in bringing an end to childhood homoeroticism, in delaying acceptance of homosexual identity despite being sexually active, or in delaying sexual activity despite being gay.

Some gay men reported engaging in homoerotic activities early in childhood. For example, the case of CC29:

> . . . we had this whole role-play worked out that he would go to the door, open the door, say "Honey I'm home!", close the door and then come into bed, and we were going to be this couple that we knew. . . . And what did we do? I think we just played with each other's willies and that was about it, in the bed. And that would have been grade five. (CC29)

It is difficult to interpret these cases because childhood homoeroticism was reported both by gay and heterosexual subjects. This ambiguity becomes clearer in discussions with N14 about when his gay identity formed:

> **D:** But on the other hand you had "discovered" your cousins?
> **S:** I did. But did I discover homosexuality? Or . . . did I just put that down to experimentation of my sexuality? Not my homosexuality or my heterosexuality . . . just sexuality. (N14)

In the next example, J10 describes a transition period during which homophobia becomes associated with homoeroticism and homoeroticism is inhibited as a result:

> . . . that was my first contact with another guy . . . he was in Scouts with me . . . he just took off his clothes and got into my sleeping bag and we sort of rubbed against each other and he ejaculated. And I can remember thinking all the time this is wrong and I'll get a venereal disease. . . . The following Scout camp I wanted to sleep in a tent with him, and then I started to initiate it. I can remember this quite vividly because I took my clothes off and he didn't want to and he said I was a "poof." So that was probably the first time I was ever called one. (J10)

The evidence in this chapter suggests a useful distinction between the disappearance of childhood homo*erotic* activities, under the mounting pressures of homophobia, and the commencement of homo*sexual* activities in adults, associated with an emerging gay identity and shaped by homophobia.

The sexual dimension of homophobia is clearly understood when applied to postpubertal homosexual activities, but several subjects described being homosexually active but not *knowing* they were homosexual. Examples have already been given for N14 and Q17 and here is a comment by V22 that illustrates this point:

> Oh, I was having sex with guys for years before I knew I was gay [laughs]. (V22)

Homophobia appears to play a role in delaying adoption of a homosexual identity in some of these cases in spite of undeniable sexual activity. One such instance was when N14 described, earlier, refusing to kiss or have anal intercourse because "that's what gay people do."

For others, the commencement of sexual activity was delayed until after forming a homosexual identity. You will recall that Y25 decided he was gay in school year seven in the midst of an episode of homophobic abuse. Yet although he circulated in the gay community and worked for gay-related organizations for several years after leaving school, he didn't choose to have sex until age twenty-three. In some cases, this delay in sexual activity can be traced to the effects of homophobia. In C3's case, "if the teachers had laid all the facts on the table" and he hadn't become tied up with homophobic groups himself, he believes things would have been different:

> Well. I wouldn't have been running 'round hiding in dark corridors [Ironic laugh]. . . . like probably just would have come to terms with who I was; instead . . . I'm only just coming to terms with who I am now . . . twelve, thirteen years after I've left school. And that's wrong. It's something that I should have been able to come to terms with while I was at school, 'cause I missed out on probably the best part of my adolescence as far as doin' what I want to do. You know, my

brother's had the best time of his life fuckin' every girl in town [laugh]. . . . I haven't been able to do anything. (C3)

He expressed how resentful he was as a result:

. . . because you have to fit into the mold of "so-called" society . . . it just hurt me. And I feel that I've been robbed of the last fifteen years of my life. (C3)

Similar accounts were provided by T20 (who described homosexuality as "definitely too dangerous"), O15 ("as far as I could see any sort of [homo] sexual encounter would immediately stop [his idealized life]. So I just blocked it"), and L12:

I was so afraid of being told "You're a faggot," that I just went the opposite and I would totally . . . steer clear of all forms of sexual contact with anyone. Or physical contact like invading anyone else's space. (L12)

As R18 explains, homophobia at school affected his happiness:

. . . to the extent that I didn't really enjoy my childhood at school, and to the extent that I didn't learn about myself until much later on . . . so my development sexually I think and maturity has come later than a heterosexual person's would. But then I don't think a heterosexual has got a mature attitude toward a gay person unless they've been educated about it. I also think that I'm much stronger . . . having gone to my school. (R18)

Significantly, he goes on to add:

. . . I hereby declare this is not an ad for the school; it's a bad system. It's only purpose [was having] homophobic system and had I not had the strength in myself, then I couldn't have come out of it properly. . . . I'd have . . . come out homophobic myself. (R18)

Forming Homosexual Relationships

Homophobia complicates the way men find male sexual partners and form relationships. The strong pressures to hide a homosexual identity and to conceal homoerotic activities make establishing homosexual relationships difficult (Martin, 1982). While the most dramatic impact of homophobia occurs during adolescence, the pressure to be closeted starts very young. In an enactment of the "closet" metaphor, here is CC29's description of an event at the age of five to which he attaches homophobic significance:

> I remember the two of us going into the wardrobe and shutting the door and playing with each other's willies. . . . I'm sure Mum knew what was going on and she would walk past the cupboard and make a cough or make a noise . . . and we would stop and we would come out and we wouldn't do it again that afternoon. But even though nothing was said and we hadn't been caught, I do remember the first time it happened thinking, "Oh boy, that was lucky!" (CC29)

Homoerotic activities later in childhood become more difficult and are increasingly characterized by feelings of homophobic guilt:

> I remember a terrible feeling of guilt. Amazing guilt the next day, and for nothing. For absolutely nothing and this is weird, but I think it really was something that's stayed with me for such a long time . . . and I was just feeling so bad about it. And we did absolutely nothing, probably lasted about a minute, maybe not a minute, but not long at all, you know, a couple of minutes. And I must have been about . . . ten. (O15)

While homoeroticism was not prevented for the less inhibited of the gay men interviewed, it did become increasingly convoluted and unfulfilling. Previously, AA27 described how the constraints of homophobia meant that homoeroticism had to take place according to certain codes that he resented and found intrusive. One of those codes was that homoerotic experiences and feelings couldn't be discussed:

> **S:** But you could never talk about it, which kind of pissed me off a bit.
> **D:** Couldn't talk about it with who?
> **S:** With the person who just sucked your dick for half an hour,

but you can't actually mention it. . . . I hadn't told anybody or verbalized any of this until halfway through year ten.
D: You'd done quite a bit, but you actually hadn't ever spoken about it?
S: Yeah . . . and I wanted to; I really wanted to talk about it. (AA27)

Homophobia also contributes to the foreclosure of homosexual friendships and relationships. In the next example, the guilt associated with homoeroticism disrupts an important childhood friendship:

S: . . . when that boy and I were discovered, we were essentially separated. His parents were told and we basically didn't see each other . . . before that we were reasonably good friends.
D: And did you feel embarrassed to see him again or did you never see him again?
S: Yes . . . I wanted to forget the whole thing. (R18)

P16 describes how one of his first homosexual encounters was predicated on having to escape immediately after having sex:

I had to get back. I said, "Drive me back, I can't stay here!" you know, just like a vampire, you wake up and then you turn into a pumpkin or whatever. (P16)

After the need for intimacy is temporarily satisfied, residual guilt appears to undermine prospects of establishing an ongoing relationship.

Homophobia places sustained pressures on long-term relationships too, which can lead to them becoming unstable and terminating. You will recall that N14 drew the line at kissing, beyond which was considered "gay." The next example provides a clear illustration of the links with homophobia and with difficulties concerning his own homosexuality, even with an accepting partner:

. . . he and I had a relationship which was sexual, for over a year. . . . I ended up leaving him and . . . stopped the relationship because I decided I needed to have a girlfriend. . . . And I remember him being very confused because he had been brought up completely differently from the way I had been brought up, in that his upbringing was . . . a lot more open, he had a gay brother who lived at home with his lover [and] with his parents. His sister was in theater, his gay brother worked with his father, and everything was hunky-dory. And he and I used to sleep together in his room. His parents were next door and that was fine . . . it was no big deal. Whereas I had major problems with it, you know. . . . I wouldn't kiss him either. (N14)

A similar account was offered by CC29, who ended a two-year relationship to seek treatment for his homosexuality:

I was going out with this guy that I went out with for two years. So, I said to him, "I can't see you anymore; I'm going to a psychologist. I'm going to try and be straight, [so] don't, ring me or anything." (CC29)

Both N14 and CC29 were in stable homosexual relationships when they were interviewed.

Homophobia also influences relationship formation in other ways. While homophobia inhibited X24 from forming a direct relationship with his male friend, he found that he was able to get close by sharing his girlfriend:

. . . we had a very close female friend and he ended up going out with her . . . we would actually get very close together through her. (X24)

Occasionally, boys' early homosexual "relationships" occur in male prostitution because prostitution offers a way of earning a living (Strommen, 1993: 252). AA27 became homeless after having (homophobic) difficulties with his father, and he engaged in male prostitution while completing his secondary schooling:

I haven't [worked as a male prostitute] since I met [boyfriend], who I've been with since just before I turned eighteen. That's because he doesn't deal with it. He couldn't cope with it. But, if I needed money . . . well there it is. (AA27)

You will recall that the first time AA27 was paid for sex, he used steel wool to cleanse himself.

Social stigma against homosexuality also limits the places where people can meet and form homosexual relationships. Specific meeting places are usually only available in major urban centers. Often they are commercial bars that exclude young gay men who are "underage," which creates difficulties for people on low incomes and with no transport. One of the few alternatives are agreed-upon public meeting places or "beats." Traditionally, these have been covert and offer an ulterior motive:

> . . . to meet gay people you have go to a bar and meet them under an alcoholic environment, or you have to go to the toilet block and pick somebody up there. Otherwise, the odds of you finding the other 10 percent and meeting them at work and being able to safely find out who's who is unlikely. So you're already oppressed into a situation where you're in bars and you're in the toilet block, and that's all you're offered by society as a way of meeting other gay people. (Q17)

For several of the subjects in this study, meeting people in toilet blocks (public rest rooms) was the first point of contact with other homosexuals. These locations can be risky (as V22 described in Chapter 4) and seem unlikely venues for initiating a committed relationship:

> . . . there was someone in the very next cubicle, who was obviously keen . . . can't quite remember exactly what we did that first time, it must have been jerking off. . . . Didn't get to anywhere near the end, [because I was] too scared. I thought, "What the hell am I doing?" [and] ran out. So there was a lot of running out in the beginning and then [I] just started staying on for longer and longer. (CC29)

The combination of compulsory heterosexuality, restricted opportunities for meeting homosexual partners, and homophobia can powerfully shape peoples' lives. The next example illustrates the cumulative effect of these forces:

... It was definitely a compulsion. I would cry all the way to a "beat." ... It's something I couldn't control ... got a "blow job," cried all the way home. ... And [it] eventually became a scenario, of sexual things whilst I was married, which, because of my religious background, was extremely devastating and confusing and upsetting and there was two years of that before I finally separated from my wife. At which stage I still hadn't got a clue if I was gay or not. Because I wasn't actually asking the question. I was dealing with the issues of male bonding, intimacy. (Q17)

CONCLUSIONS

Homophobia has profound effects on the way men relate. Situations in which men come into close proximity with one another were analyzed: sports, change rooms, boarding houses, camps, and wherever there is intimacy and sex. The influences of homophobia are numerous and extensive—even to the point of elaborately codifying how men use their eyes and stylizing what aspects of "self" are available for public scrutiny. Furthermore, the effects of homophobia do not end with how men relate to one another. The contribution of homophobia to "compulsory heterosexuality" means that men's relationships with women are also substantially affected. For example, homophobia influences how peer groups approach heterosexual activities, the way that females fail to anticipate or accommodate the homosexuality of their male friends, and the formation of heterosexual relationships by men with emerging gay identities.

The evidence in this chapter also helps to delineate some important social boundaries that are defined by homophobia. By stigmatizing homosexuality, homophobia enables the separation of homosexuality from other social interactions and from other sexualities (Britton, 1990; San Miguel and Millham, 1976). This injects significance into the hetero-homosexual and the homosocio-sexual divisions. The weight of homophobic stigma associated with the homosexual components of these divisions places complex pressures on boys, particularly when these boundaries are approached in the presence of peer-group scrutiny. Boys become acutely aware of these boundaries; they are precisely mapped within peer culture, and there is a complex codification of behaviors in their vicinity.

Of all the highly codified activities of young men, team sports regularly attract intense interest. It was shown that team sports dominate the peer hierarchy in schools and that schools often prioritize prestigious sports over academic and other achievements. Male team sports are public events that are located along the limits of the homosocial divide (profoundly intimate, but not sexual) and they function to highlight those divisions, define masculinity and men's relations, and police them. The modern obsession with male team sports, the attention they receive, the rituals involved, and the funds invested, all appear to reflect the importance of team sports as dazzling rituals situated along the boundaries that define modern masculinity—and what is not. In contrast, team sports and the associated codes and rituals are deeply intimidating and alienating for boys who are homophobically labeled. For many of these boys, prestigious team sports are little more than officially sanctioned, ritualized homophobic traps, to be avoided at all costs.

Finally, there is potential for paradox to occur when homophobia arbitrarily disrupts the continuum of male-male relations and splits it into homosocial and homosexual poles. We have seen that codified intimate behaviors by high-status boys can escape transgressive labeling, while similar behaviors by marginalized boys will incite savage homophobia. In addition, some young men have gay identities well before becoming sexually active; others are homosexually active well before forming a gay identity; still others have frequent homoerotic experiences when younger and now identify as heterosexual; and several young gay men have had erotic and sexual relationships with women. Moreover, in the absence of homophobia, there is no reason why an aversion to male intimacy should be a prerequisite for preferring sex with women. Because of these and other findings, it can be concluded that rather than being *primarily* averse to homoerotic play, boys' interactions are extensively orchestrated by homophobic peer dynamics, the fear of homophobia, and the fear of homophobia escalating to incriminate others. In mens' spheres, the yardstick for what is acceptable is hegemonic masculinity, and what is unacceptable is marked by homophobia and enforced by the fear of homophobia.

Chapter 6

'On the Origins of the Sexual Species

At the close of the twentieth century, homophobia continues to be pervasive, deeply felt, intensely negative, and has complex ramifications. Paradoxically, the hundred-year Western preoccupation with homosexuality seems incongruous with prevalent stereotypes that depict homosexuals as an emasculated minority, and the extent of modern homophobia contrasts with advances in human rights and social justice elsewhere (Hendriks, Tielman, and van der Veen, 1993). To explore these observations and to understand homophobia better, the component processes involved in learning about homophobia and how homophobia is deployed were studied. It was found that boys invest homophobic terms with considerable significance prior to puberty, before forming an adult sexual identity and before fully understanding homosexuality. And although it doesn't target homosexuality per se during these formative years, homophobia is used intentionally, skillfully, and with substantial impact. An implication of this sequence of events is that a detailed knowledge of homophobia precedes, and therefore initially underwrites, boys' emerging understandings of adult sexual identities. These findings underpin some powerful insights into the significance of modern homophobia.

HOMOPHOBIC LOGIC: MOBILE DIFFERENCES AND CONSISTENT NEGATIVE BIAS

Homophobia has an extensive range of meanings, most of which are nonsexual. At different times in childhood, homophobia targets babyish, girlish, non-peer-oriented, nonphysical, and/or nonheterosexual characteristics. By analyzing these meanings, homophobia was shown to successfully target behaviors that are socially unacceptable for boys as they grow older. It was also possible to identify cases in which behaviors were modified and characteristics disappeared after particular homophobic meanings emerged to target them. A diverse range of behaviors were shown to be affected, most of which were expressed by many, if not all, boys when younger. Subsequently, boys who don't suppress them become vulnerable to sustained homophobia.

Homophobic meanings are reflected in the characteristics that homophobia targets—and which subsequently constitute the complex stereotypes commonly attributed to homosexuals. The meanings are cumulative and are invested into (mega)words such as poofter and faggot. These words are much more than simple references to homosexuality; they designate complicated composites of male otherness and are constructed by attributing deeply negative significance to their targets. An array of differences is united into these repositories of otherness, that consolidate in opposition to hegemonic masculinity. In other words, the orthodoxy of hegemonic masculinity prevails, in contrast to what is designated by homophobia as unmasculine, and which is demonized into a modern-day heretic known as a "poofter." Exactly why the homosexual has become the modern-day archetype for male otherness is unclear, but historical and cultural evidence reveals that this hasn't always been the case. Why this contemporary (but not last) version of heresy has come about will probably be explained by studies of personal, school-ground, and sociocultural histories.

The present research has implications for gender and sexuality theory. Homophobia appears to be a consequence of gender (the antithesis of orthodox masculinity), yet findings from this study confirm that being unmasculine is not the same as being feminine. Homophobia circumscribes males who are immature, loners, and academic as well as males who exhibit stereotyped effeminate (as distinct from feminine) characteristics. In Dollimore's words, "masculinity can be problematised, even feminised, so long as homosexuality remains its defining other" (Dollimore, 1991: 265), or in terms of the findings reported here—the targets of homophobia (not just homosexuality) are masculinity's defining other. Moreover, detailing what is targeted by homophobia exposes limits to the explanatory power of heterosexism, which cannot entirely account for many of the characteristics that homophobia targets. Evolving standards of masculinity do not simply draw on contrasts with girls or with heterosexuality, but on males who exhibit socially defined, homophobically targeted differences from their male *peers*.

The differences singled out by homophobia are definitive. While boys who are subjected to homophobic labeling are male and their similarities with other boys greatly outnumber their differences, those differences have sufficient social significance that boys are defined by them: the boy who is shy, cries, or who doesn't play football is a poofter. As a result, homophobia exerts weighty pressures on all boys (gay or not), and this gives rise to a further influential dynamic: boys are intimidated by poofter and faggot labels; boys *fear* homophobia. The fear of homophobia ("homophobiaphobia") haunts boyhood and profoundly influences how boys style and present themselves to others. Similar to homophobia and the diverse differences it targets, the fear of homophobia also antedates a mature knowledge of homosexuality and sexual identity and underwrites how they come to be understood.

The literal meanings associated with homophobia are multiple and changeable and this can generate paradox and contradiction. Other authors (e.g., Dollimore, 1991; Sedgwick, 1990; Weeks, 1985; Highwater, 1997) have also noted the slippages, paradoxes, and contradictions inherent in how homophobia and the "perversions" are formulated. For example, Dollimore refers to the "paradoxical perverse," which is simultaneously inherent and other, central and marginal (Dollimore, 1991), and Weeks reflects on these difficulties when he talks of sexuality as a "corridor of mirrors" (Weeks, 1985: 62). The evidence in Chapter 1 demonstrates how homosexuality can be portrayed as a premeditated crime, a congenital abnormality, and as if it were contagious (often in the same argument). Similarly, Halperin notes how homophobes can maintain the "integrity" of their homophobia simply by adopting another, sometimes opposite stance if their initial rationale is discredited (Halperin, 1995: 37-38). A number of similar examples of paradoxes, contradictions, and shifts in meaning were identified in this research.

The paradoxes and contradictions of homophobia complicate and undermine analyses that attempt to respond to the "logic" of arguments made by homophobes. The present research offers some insights into how and why this occurs. First, the rationalizations employed in homophobia are movable "decoys" that overlay and mask more fundamental underlying processes. Second, the chronological dimension of life histories helps to explain the apparent contradictions that arise when homophobic meanings change over time. For example, younger boys are poofters if they are too familiar with girls or, when they are older, if they are not close enough. Here, homophobia provides continuity while boys' relationships with girls shift: boys who don't act in accord with peer expectations are always poofters, initially because real boys shouldn't want to mix with girls (compulsory homosociality) and later because real boys must comply with "compulsory heterosexuality." Third, it was shown in Chapter 5 how male interactions are arbitrarily split by homophobia into stigmatized homosexual and valorized homosocial components. In this case, slippage and paradox are possible because the dichotomy that arises by stigmatizing certain forms of male intimacy is actually derived from a continuous spectrum with an arbitary, mobile boundary. Whether behavior is transgressive or not is determined by social conventions, a boy's status, and how he styles his "self" and his behavior—and these factors can change.

The internal logic of homophobia in all of these examples is its intractable negative bias and its role in rejecting otherness. While homophobic meanings slip and evolve, consistency is preserved because homophobia is a powerful stigma that continuously defines what is "out of bounds" for masculinity. Thus, homosexuality and homosociality can take on the appearance of logical opposites, even though they are part of a continuum of male interaction. Similarly, people who resort to alternative homophobic rationales after earlier ones are discredited maintain the "integrity" of their arguments by steadfastly maintaining their homophobic posture throughout. In addition, once oppositional dichotomies are formed, the homophobic components are available to be realigned with other negatively valued discourses (even if they contradict). For example, homosexuality can be realigned with being criminal, evil, degenerate, contagious, congenital, sick, sinful, treacherous, and unnatural despite many of these being mutually incompatible (e.g., willfully criminal and uncontrollably evil; congenital and contagious). Negativity constitutes the internal logic of homophobia—not the loosely adherent rationalizations that act as a foil and are often illogical, paradoxical, and prone to slippage.

BETWEEN SUPPRESSION AND EXPRESSION

A feature of homophobia during childhood and early adulthood is its involvement in renouncing certain stigmatized characteristics and behaviors. Heterosexual masculinity emerges as being substantially constituted by successive restrictions of behavior under the influence of homophobia. Dollimore describes the emergence of adult sexuality as "psychosexual development from the polymorphous perverse to normality which is less a process of growth and more one of restriction" (Dollimore, 1991: 176). Similarly, Freud wrote that "normal sexuality too depends on a reduction in the choice of an object" (Freud, 1977b: 375-376). A range of examples of homophobic restriction was documented in earlier chapters, and these support a general conclusion: homophobia contributes to the formation of masculine identity by targeting "unacceptable" behaviors. One important characteristic to be renounced (in the name of masculinity and to avoid homophobia) is immaturity; indeed, ultimately, childhood itself must be rejected in order to attain masculine status (Gilman, 1985: 213; Gilmore, 1990: 224; Schafer in Gilmore, 1990: 29). In Frosh's words, "masculinity constructs itself on the basis of a separation from that which the infant knows" (Frosh, 1994: 109).

Homophobia would be meaningless and the effort invested in renouncing, restricting, and eliminating unacceptable behaviors would be pointless if they weren't intrinsic and readily expressible. Further, the possibility that transgression is intrinsic to "normality" has been recognized by many scholars (Freud, 1977a: 87, 155; Dollimore, 1991; Foucault, 1990; Goffman, 1963: 127; Hocquenghem, 1993: 115). The way that homophobia uses stigma to excise characteristics and behaviors from a spectrum of related elements (pink from boys' clothing, crying from the public domain, tenderness from male friendships) helps to explain the intimate and somewhat arbitrary relationship between normality and transgression.

The present research documents a range of behaviors (crying, choice of clothing, etc.) that are considered normal until a certain age. Subsequently, they are considered transgressive and are used to characterize poofters and faggots. In this way, all boys experience various component behaviors that later become homophobically labeled, and all of them have an acute understanding and firsthand experience of homophobic stigma. While homophobia designates the "other," in a very practical and immediate sense, it simultaneously and repeatedly points to parts of the "self"—albeit parts that generally are quickly subdued. As Freud wrote, "there is indeed something innate lying behind the perversions . . . something innate in everyone" (Freud, 1977a: 87). That is not to say that being "a poofter" or "a faggot" is innate, nor is being "a homosexual" or "a heterosexual." But what is innate are the undifferentiated elements that might eventually be united by social forces and comprehended as a composite identity. So while masculinity is partly a process of restriction and renunciation, its counterpart "other" becomes progressively more elaborate and defined, and the residual elements of masculinity (such as "compulsory heterosexuality" and "hegemonic masculinity") are obsessively cultivated. As Gilmore has observed, "boys have to be encouraged, sometimes actually forced, by social sanctions to undertake efforts toward a culturally defined manhood, which by themselves they might not do" (Gilmore, 1990: 25).

Many boys express behaviors identified as "different" after an age at which the behaviors have become redefined as transgression. The labeling of these characteristics varies between cultures, but in the West, boys experience considerable pressures to target those differences with homophobia or be targeted themselves. The present research shows that boys are destined to suffer homophobia if they differ in ways that can't be explained otherwise (for example, by race, religion, or physical disability) or if they don't conform to peer-endorsed subculture(s).

Chapter 5 documents how some young gay men apparently knew they were "different" long before they thought of themselves as gay, and how peers seemed to know they were "gay" before they knew it themselves. This study has also shown that homophobia defines, tracks, and targets difference as boys develop, and it precedes and therefore underwrites boys' emerging understandings of homosexuality, heterosexuality, and sexual identity. Because of the groundwork laid by presexual homophobia, emerging adult sexual identities initially can only be conceptualized in terms of two intrinsically opposite categories of homosexual and heterosexual. The possibility then arises that boys whose childhood is characterized by sustained feelings of difference might come to conceive of their difference in (homo) sexual terms as their understanding of homophobia acquires homosexual connotations. Similarly, boys who have not experienced sustained homophobic marginalization will interpret their conformity in terms of a (hetero) sexual identity.

An objection to suggestions that childhood difference can ultimately lead a boy to think of himself as homosexual is that such arguments don't seem to account for the profound, physiologically authenticated and seemingly innate homosexual desires that gay men experience. However, modern AIDS research reminds us that homosexual desire is not the exclusive domain of gay men (Connell and Dowsett, 1992), and there are numerous examples in the present project of boys having homoerotic experiences who now call themselves heterosexual, others who had fulfilling heterosexual experiences who are now gay, and still others who were having homosexual sex long before they felt they were gay. As Freud said nearly 100 years ago, "it seems probable that the sexual instinct is at first independent of its sexual object; nor is its origin likely to be due to its object's attractions" (Freud, 1977a: 60). On these terms, homosexual desires, as with heterosexual ones, can feel authentic because they are authentic. Polymorphous desire can presumably adapt to increasingly restrictive, socially constructed sexual categories without desire having to be invented or perverted, but by becoming restricted and focused so that emerging identity and its sexual objects are in accord with each other.

Many boys experience undisciplined erotic play in childhood that homophobia later organizes and regulates. The retrospective significance that homosexual men attribute to childhood homoerotic experiences is probably an "illusion" because these experiences are not confined to men who are now gay. As Guy Hocquenghem notes, both homosexuality and heterosexuality "are the precarious outcomes of a desire that knows no name" (Hocquenghem, 1993: 75). On the other hand, while erotic experiences are initially polymorphous, being different during childhood has considerable significance and homophobia provides the bond that unites disparate boyhood differences (crying, being academic, not playing football, being girlish, being a loner) and eventually marries them to contemporary adult sexual identities. Evolving homophobia provides a mechanism to transform male difference into sexual otherness.

Homophobic stigma taints homoeroticism and differentiates it from what is social and sexual; it thereby detaches homosexuality from valorized homosocial and heterosexual elements. In that sense, homosexuality and heterosexuality are created by a single dynamic: the division between men brought about by homophobia. This division gives rise to a striking irony—any attempt to promote heterosexuality would simultaneously promote homosexuality by deepening that division; conversely, without homophobia, there would be no homosexuals (or heterosexuals). In effect, the "cause" of homosexuality is homophobia.

It is here that the theories of Freud and Foucault meet. Whereas Foucault emphasized the importance of expressing identities and of confessing to how power regulates people and their sexuality (Foucault, 1990: 33, 59, 116), Freud saw how society was shaped by "repressing" sexual desire (Dollimore, 1991: 106). Although these two propositions might seem incompatible, this project supports them both. Without expression, there would be nothing to know and to suppress, and the trumpeted twentieth-century sexual identities that are compulsively expressed and confessed are indeed formed by a process of restriction and suppression. The famous figure of 5 to 10 percent of men who are homosexual (Kinsey, Pommeroy, and Martin, 1948) is an essential symbol of modern Western sexual arrangements—as are visible poofters and homosexuals—without which there would be nothing recognizable to target and restrain.

Without the homophobic homosexual-heterosexual split, there is just eroticism—as in other periods of history, in other cultures, and during early childhood. But there wouldn't be a total deregulation of polymorphous desire if homophobia was to dissipate; other heresies and regulatory forms to manage difference/otherness would be invented (and were). A near precursor of the modern homosexual is the sodomite, "who was associated with a whole range of evils, including insurrection, heresy . . . and political treason . . . the sodomite indeed became the supreme instance of the demonized other" (Weeks, quoted in Hocquenghem, 1993: 35). The late twentieth-century preoccupation with pedophilia shows every sign of being the next metamorphosis in the crusade against "otherness."

TAMING POLYMORPHOUS PERVERSITY

Identifying a series of restrictions in the course of developing the masculine self inevitably raises questions about the "polymorphous perverse." This research did not find evidence for the existence of *the* polymorphous perverse as a cohesive entity, which, almost by definition, is undifferentiated and disorganized desire and not an entity at all. However, the present project demonstrates how relatively undisciplined and indulgent behaviors of early childhood can become increasingly governed by the external rules of masculinity/ homophobia, which impose a succession of restraints in the course of a boy's maturation.

Freud presumably thought that polymorphous perversity eventually became suppressed in both heterosexuals and homosexuals when he wrote that the "freedom to range equally over male and female objects—as it is found in childhood, in primitive states of society, and early periods in history, is the original basis from which, as a result of restriction in one direction or the other, both the normal and the inverted types develop" (Freud, 1977a: 57). However, this should not be taken to imply that the hetero- and homo-sexualities mirror each other and that heteroerotic desire is suppressed in homosexuals in the same way that homoerotic desire is suppressed in heterosexuals. Indeed, the persistent idea of fluidity discussed in the previous chapter raises the possibility that poly-morphous desire survives to some extent in homosexual settings. Hocquenghem suggests that there is a sense in which homosexuals have "failed" their sublimation, but he adds that this merely means a different way of conceiving social relations (Hocquenghem, 1993: 111). And in an echo of the work of Deleuze and Guattari, he writes, "'Queens' do not want to be either men or women: they carry the decoding of the fluxes of desire to its limit" (Hocquenghem, 1993: 144; Deleuze and Guattari, 1983/1972). "Homosexuality expresses an aspect of desire which is fundamentally polymorphous and un-defined, which appears nowhere else . . . it is more than just sexual activity between members of the same sex" (Weeks, quoted in Hocquenghem, 1993: 35). So while the sexual roles of heterosexual masculinity arise from restriction and are partly anatomically pre-configured, in a male homosexual setting, "male" and "female," "tops" and "bottoms," "insertive" and "receptive" are interchangeable roles, sometimes fluidly so.

Most important, this project found evidence that the concept of *the* polymorphous perverse is active in people's fears, where it is a counterpoint to the "order of things." Many homophobic discourses focus on what would happen if social restraints on homosexuality were surrendered—disorder, evil, chaos, and death. Fears of uncontrolled otherness are at the root of arguments against homosexuality, and prominent in fears about deregulating homosexuality are concerns about its capacity to have extensive, spreading effects—pollution, decay, contagion, corruption, sabotage, predation, recruitment. The possibility that homosexuality is communicable feeds powerful fears of being overwhelmed by perversity and of disrupting social and biological continuity. It implies that all males are susceptible—that the allure of masculinity threatens to overpower even the most heterosexual of men. Goffman acknowledged similar fearful assumptions when he wrote, "the tendency for stigma to spread from a stigmatized individual to his close connections provides a reason why such relations tend to be either avoided or to be terminated" (Goffman, 1963: 30). Perhaps *the* polymorphous perverse is too susceptible to becoming more than just a theoretical device; it is a focus for people's paranoid fears—after all, it is usually assumed that the polymorphous perverse is a reference to a marauding "other" and not to a former "self." But these fears must not be allowed to derail the central findings of this work: it is homophobia that is dangerous and is a source of considerable social and personal harm—not the risk of unleashing the polymorphous perverse, which isn't an entity, nor polymorphous desire, which can never be free. Homophobia is *the* "polymorphous prejudice"; it has chameleon rationales, but its intractable logic always derives from fearing and rejecting otherness. Without homophobia, there would be a shift in social and sexual arrangements, but not chaos.

HOMOPHOBIC PASSAGE: THE ORDERER OF THINGS

Homophobia climaxes at around the onset of sexual maturity, a point that is more likely to be defined by social practices than by actual physical maturity (Thorne, 1993: 147). The crescendo and (relative) decrescendo of homophobia on either side of this peak is an invariable feature of adolescence in this study. Yet, if homophobia were purely a prejudice against homosexuals, it might be expected to start around sexual maturity/sexual identity formation and be sustained. Instead, homophobia commences and crescendos prior to puberty and mostly prior to it acquiring homosexual connotations, and the decrescendo occurs during young adulthood at a time when young men are becoming increasingly familiar with adult sexuality. Other studies also suggest that homophobia moderates somewhat in early adulthood; for example, studies of antigay violence consistently show that it is committed by adolescents and young adults, but rarely later (see Chapter 1). These findings add weight to the emphasis placed here on peer-group dynamics and presexual forms of homophobia, and they suggest that sexualization of homophobia and increasing sexual maturity herald a stabilization and subsequent decrease in its intensity. As boys mature, become heterosexually active, leave their school-based peer groups, find female partners, and have a family, pressures to repeatedly affirm their masculine credentials subside.

Adults generally hold a narrow view that homophobia is an entrenched bias against homosexuals, despite its rich developmental history. However, with the homosexualization of homophobia, men aren't nearly as haunted by the mobile, polymorphous "otherness" of boyhood. In adulthood, homophobia's target acquires a fixed, knowable identity, with a sterile sexuality when it becomes embodied in the homosexual. According to Jeffrey Weeks, to name sexual identities "was to imprison" (Weeks, 1985: 93). The earlier role of peer-based homophobia in "containing" otherness largely comes to an end. Otherness is subsumed into the homosexual identity and becomes an object for social control. In the words of Guy Hocquenghem, homosexuality becomes "artificially trapped within the grid of 'civilisation'" (Hocquenghem, 1993: 35). In the present context, this might be better paraphrased as "polymorphous desire is trapped in the grid of a homophobic civilization where homo- and heterosexuality are its traps and homophobia its hunter."

The intensification of homophobia in the lead up to adolescence occurs at around that same time that boys realign their gender alliances and when homophobia also shifts its focus. Near when homophobia peaks, it is reoriented from policing boys' separation from girls (compulsory homosociality) to enforcing boys' interactions with girls (compulsory heterosexuality). In an interesting series that seems to add to this observation, Skrzipek (1978, 1981, 1982, 1983) reports how in the years nine to sixteen, boys' "preferences" change markedly. In one study (1978) a series of facial diagrams and physique silhouettes were shown to 6,202 people between the ages of four and thirty and they were asked which they preferred ("Welche Figur oder Abbildung gefällt dir/Ihnen am besten?"). These diagrams were varied to make them appear more male, female, or androgynous. Between the ages of four and nine, boys consistently expressed a preference for the male face/figure and after sixteen for the female face/figure. Between nine and sixteen, there was a distinct transition in their preferences from male to female. The meaning of "preference" is ambiguous in this study and it almost certainly differs at various ages, but the central point is the unequivocal shift in the answers boys gave.

These fairly radical shifts in boys' responses take place around the time that boys "come of age" and there are many parallels between the events described in the present project and the classic formulation of the "rites of passage" (Van Gennep, 1960/1908). Van Gennep described passage as a three-stage process of separation, transition, and incorporation into a new status, and he also identified social puberty rites, which are particularly relevant here. Puberty rites involve "separation from an asexual world followed by rites of incorporation into a sexual world" (Van Gennep, 1960: ix, 67). This has clear parallels with the presexual and homosexualized forms of homophobia previously described and which also undergo transition around this time. However, social puberty rites represent only a fragment of the processes described in this work, and the term "homophobic passage" has been coined to encompass these. Homophobic passage refers to the complex social processes extending from early boyhood to adulthood, during which homophobia starts, crescendos, peaks, and moderates and during which major shifts in homophobic meanings and corresponding reorganizations and restrictions of masculinity take place. It is the contention of this thesis that homophobic passage is a standard part of late twentieth-century Western male development and that it is historically specific. In Jeffrey Weeks's words, "the flux of desire is hooked, trapped and defined by historical processes" (Weeks, 1985: 157).

Sometimes the transitional periods of passage can become prolonged and semiautonomous (Metcalf and Huntington, 1991: 32). This appears to be the case for homophobic passage, which is long and elaborate and parallels the transitions involved in Western "coming of age." In Australia, universal education and extended youth dependency emerged in the interwar years, when the "specialised world of childhood" evolved, stretching from infancy to the teens (Gilding, 1991: 29). Lewis argues that initiation rituals, which regulate passage from childhood to "marriageable adult," are accomplished in modern societies "more or less" by schooling (Lewis, 1985: 131). Freud recognized the role that education plays in organizing boys' sexual impulses. He wrote that "the forces destined to retain the sexual instinct upon certain lines are built up in childhood, chiefly at the cost of perverse sexual impulses and with the assistance of education" (Freud, 1977a: 157). Likewise, he also wrote, "mental forces which are later to impede the course of the sexual instinct and, like dams, restrict its flow—disgust, feelings of shame and the claims of aesthetic moral ideals . . . construction of these dams is a product of education" (Freud, 1977a: 93). The organization of education was also implicated in studies by Mac an Ghaill, who found that student microculture was the site where adolescents "learnt the heterosexual codes that marked their rite of passage into manhood" (Mac an Ghaill, 1994: 53). The present study found that schooling (particularly school-ground peer groups) plays host to most of the key elements of homophobic passage, starting with *separation* from the family domain at the beginning of schooling, followed by *transition* in peer groups during the school years, and *incorporation* into adult male status soon after.

Rites associated with passage are often difficult to identify from within a culture. This is partly because rituals are often not recognized as such by participants, for whom they have specific purposes (La Fontaine quoted in Sabo and Panepinto, 1990: 124). For this reason, from a vantage point inside Western culture, there is a risk that important rituals, such as football, change-room practices, peer-group codes and homophobia itself (the quintessential modern male ritual complex), might appear mundane and utilitarian and their cultural and ritual importance is underestimated. Many of the rituals of homophobia are rituals of "boundary work," renunciation, and denial. Their influence extends right down to how men present and posture themselves so as to affirm their masculinity and evade homophobia. This study documents elaborate homophobic codes and repetitive practices and how homophobia permeates everyday life; how it radically influences boys' relationships; how it shapes self-concept; and how the self is styled and presented to others in response. The way men walk, how they use their eyes, how they apply sunscreen and use other cosmetics, how they move their wrists, how they talk, what clothes they wear, where they wear their earrings, who they mix with, what games they play, and their hair-styles are all prescribed in boyhood homophobic codes and rites.

Conversely, intense homophobia can be expected if renunciation is resisted. And in extreme cases, pressure to eliminate certain char-acteristics escalates to eliminating the individuals who exhibit them. Earlier chapters describe how adolescent boys invest "poofter bash-ing" discourses with considerable importance, and that antigay murders are often mutilating and involve more violence than would be required simply to kill the victim (reviewed in Chapter 1). There are also recurring accounts of self-destructive wishes and acts by young men toward their own homosexual impulses (Chapter 4). Death and homosexuality have extensive symbolic associations as well. These are echoed in the title of Leo Bersani's essay "Is the Rectum a Grave?" (Bersani, 1988, 1995), and they account for some of the enormous symbolic importance of the AIDS epidemic where symbolism and biology appear to conspire. Homosexual sex is nonprocreative, and fears of having no grandchildren, an end to the family line, the end of a race, and ultimately the end of the human race feature in discourses about deregulating homosexuality (Chapters 1, 3 and Highwater, 1997). The classic formulation of the rites of passage also features symbolic death followed by ritual rebirth into a new status (Van Gennep, 1960/1908; Metcalf and Huntington, 1991: 30).

In homophobic passage, the elements of childhood are success-ively eliminated in order to complete the transition to full hetero-sexual masculine status under the exacting supervision of the peer group; the child must die before he can become a father and be the source of ongoing life. These parallels between homophobic passage and the core beliefs of the Christian tradition are intriguing. (Perhaps homophobic passage is the historical successor of the ancient myth of Oedipus in more recent Christianized cultures; and the psychoanalytic successor between infancy and adulthood of the infant's earlier Oedipal struggle.) In any case, successively eliminating unacceptable characteristics, renouncing childhood and femininity, attacking and destroying habitual transgressors, and having self-destructive and suicidal impulses all appear to be tied to homophobia, and to making a successful transition from child to the definitive masculine status—the adult heterosexual male/father.

CONCLUSIONS

Homophobia is a mobile polymorphous prejudice that incorporates a range of meanings, many of which are nonsexual. This makes it difficult to assign a satisfactory name to homophobia. Boys learn about homophobia before they understand adult sexuality and sexual identity. This ordering effectively "dehomosexualizes" homophobia, but increases its developmental and social importance because the prominent prehomosexual phases set the scene for forthcoming sexual maturation: homophobia underwrites a boy's emerging understandings of adult sexuality and shapes his sexual identity because it comes first. Furthermore, homophobia casts its shadow over male intimacy and divides it into a homosexual/heterosexual dichotomy. In the process, it literally "causes" homosexuality and heterosexuality. Homophobia also divides male interactions into homosexual and homosocial components that restrain and split men's relationships and require extensive ritualization to maintain. These events contribute to what is called "homophobic passage": the way that homophobia shapes boys' development during the journey from childhood to becoming an adult. Homophobia has shifting and sometimes paradoxical meanings, but its true logic lies in its negative bias, its relationship with "otherness," and its antithesis to masculinity.

Appendix A

Methods

The studies reviewed in Chapter 1 indicate that homophobia is wide-spread, is found around the globe, is often deeply felt, and can have severe consequences. Chapter 1 also identifies a paradox: although the apparent principal target of homophobia is a small minority group (homosexuals) whose membership is stereotypically weak and emasculated, homosexuality attracts the intense (negative) interest of a surprising proportion of the population—rather than simple disinterest. But although studies confirm that antihomosexual bias is a significant problem, they have done so in the absence of adequate explanations. It has largely been left to speculation to account for what has been found. And while some academic disciplines have seen a growth in theoretical work concerning homophobia in recent years (for example, Sedgewick, 1990), the subject of the present research remains undertheorized. What are the origins of homophobia? How has it come about? How do people become biased? How is it transmitted? Why is it so pervasive? Why is it often so intensely cathected? These observations are the starting point for this research, which is principally concerned with searching for clues that provide insights into homophobia, to formulate reasons why it might exist, and to construct more satisfactory explanations.

To a large extent, the problems outlined here dictate the methodologies required for their elucidation. Hypothesis testing is best suited to scenarios for which there are well-developed theories; and while random samples, large numbers, and "snapshot" time frames are useful for epidemiological studies of homophobia, questions at the core of this research concern processes and meanings, which demand a different approach. Methods better suited to the issues that interest this project, include ones that utilize exploration and description; that document meanings and significances; that investigate how people conceptualize and justify their biases; that relate the findings together chronologically to identify developmental sequences and social processes; and that aim to generate new theories. Accordingly, the present work describes events and processes associated with antihomosexual bias and maps the processes involved in generating and expressing homophobia. Based on these findings, a set of theoretical propositions is developed concerning the "nature" of homophobia.

THE CHOICE OF METHODS

As a research tool, the detailed interview satisfies most of the methodological requirements of this project. By taking a detailed history of events and experiences, a profile of homophobic observations at different stages in a person's life can be compiled. Each interview is then analyzed individually and compared with others to identify similarities and differences.

A history, where the interview data are collected in chronological order, offers a useful primary structure for the interview. Collecting experiences and observations in historical order permits the analysis of processes. Two principal process elements are of interest here. The first is *developmental*. Its specific aim is to study how young people become homophobic. The second aspect is interrelated with the first. It concerns the identification and analysis of *social processes* underpinning anti-homosexual attitudes and events in everyday life. By compiling a profile of homophobic events, it is possible to identify some of the ways homophobia shapes the actions and identities of young men.

The detailed life history also has more utilitarian value. Taking a history, as far as possible in chronological order, provides a "neutral," less confrontational interview structure. This was considered particularly important considering the sensitive nature of the subject matter, namely, sexuality and sexual bias. It also provides for a more gradual "settling in" process early in the interview to improve the chances of extensive self-disclosure.

Using the history to structure the research also reduces the degree to which the ideas of the researcher might intrude into the data collected. Although it is not possible to completely eliminate this effect from any research, it is clearly an important issue in a study such as this, and it was considered important to attempt to minimize this effect as far as possible at the data collection stage. Although the primary structure of the interview is chronological, there were secondary structuring effects, such as comfort, trust, obtaining consent, finding a suitable venue, time restraints, and how the interviewer facilitates the interview process.

Finally, the interview is a methodology in which the researcher has considerable experience, and because of the potential sensitivities of the subject matter, this is an important consideration. Taking a sexual history and creating a setting where this process can be as comfortable, frank, and detailed as possible is one of the basic skills of health workers dealing with sexual issues. Being able to anticipate sensitivities and to organize the interview process accordingly is invaluable.

METHODOLOGICAL THEORY

Interviewing has a long history of being used as a research tool by many disciplines, including the humanities and the social and psychological sciences, and a considerable body of literature supports the use of interviewing for research. Important methodological developments came from the health sciences when Glaser and Strauss (1967) published their work *The Discovery of Grounded Theory*. The principal significance of this work is that it formulated the clinical interview and repackaged it as a legitimate research tool. In their formulation of *grounded theory*, Glaser and Strauss provided a scientific rationale for studies that relied on large amounts of qualitative data collected from relatively small numbers of subjects. Significantly, the validity of the methodology depends on recognizing an important paradigm shift: these methods are not easily amenable to classic hypothesis testing. In contrast, because they were less reliant on existing theory for the generation of hypotheses, qualitative studies provided a good basis for discovering and describing new phenomena, for studying processes, and for developing new theories. In addition, Glaser and Strauss argued that the theory that arose from this form of research had additional legitimacy because it was "grounded" in observation.

There is a close similarity between Glaser and Strauss's formulation and the clinical interviewing process. In the clinical interview, a single subject is progressively evaluated by collecting data through interviewing and observation. Starting with no theory about the patient's problem, the clinician uses past medical training and the clinical history to "sensitize" and "ground" the evaluation process. By increasingly focusing the questioning, a theory or theories about the patient's condition are progressively devised. From these, hypotheses are generated and tested by further questioning, examination, and, where indicated, laboratory investigations.

Since *The Discovery of Grounded Theory* was published, many studies have applied these methods. There is also a literature that develops the methodology further and integrates it into broader frameworks of qualitative research. In his book *New Strategies in Social Research*, Derek Layder (1993) elaborates some of these ideas further. Layder proposes an expansion of the scope of the research from that originally proposed. Glaser and Strauss were particularly interested in the study of microprocesses. In contrast, Layder formulates his developments in terms of a "research map" and expands the sources of data used for the research to include documents, interviews, and observation. The "research map" attempts to contextualize research findings by including five levels of analysis, each of which has an increasingly broad scope. These analytic levels are the self, situated activity, social settings, macrocontexts, and historical dimensions (Layder, 1993).

The expansion of the research process within the context of theory formulation is particularly pertinent to this project. One possibility, which this project uses as a starting point, is that homophobic phenomena have broad social significance. Given this possibility, then the methodology chosen for the study must be able to accommodate a detailed examination of context and investigate the validity of assumptions about the social significance of homophobia.

The historical dimension of Layder's theory is also of interest. There has been a rapid growth of inquiry into sexuality by the humanities in recent years, and some very significant contributions to sexuality theory are coming from historical research (for example, Foucault, 1990; Duberman, Vicinus, and Chauncey, 1991; Halperin, 1990). These theoretical advances in the humanities have had a powerful effect on informing this project, or as Glaser and Strauss would say, in providing the "sensitizing concepts" for the research. While the historical dimension is evident in Chapter 1, its influence is considerable but less explicit in the concluding chapters as well (even in the method of collecting data chronologically and taking a "history"). An important aspect of the histories for this research is found in the notion of reflexivity. The significant modern histories of sexuality are more than a recounting of events; they scrutinize the role that other disciplines played in those events, how those disciplines interpreted and contributed to those events and were affected themselves. For example, in addition to describing how professions such as psychoanalysis viewed sexuality, *Sexuality and Its Discontents* by Jeffrey Weeks (1985) also analyzed the political and historical dimensions of the concepts developed by psychoanalysis, that is to say, not just what psychoanalysis says about sexuality but what the approach to sexuality says about psychoanalysis. In being exposed to critical historical analyses of how disciplines have approached sexuality, the researcher has been sensitized to a "close reading" of how concepts are used by the research subjects as well as how concepts are utilized in the analysis conducted by the researcher.

SAMPLING

The classic sampling technique for studies using "grounded theory" methods is "theoretical sampling." Theoretical sampling involves intentionally selecting and revising the selection of a sample because of the importance of that selection for illustrating or checking a theory that emerges during the research. This method is neither blinded nor unbiased. In fact, it is deliberately "biased" because the intention is specifically to provide data to refine or refute certain propositions that the researcher is developing.

While theoretical sampling is a recommended technique for studies based on grounded theory principles, theoretical sampling is not well suited to this study so an alternate form of sampling was necessary. Theoretical sampling is unsuitable because it entails knowledge of certain characteristics of the sample in advance of each interview. In interviews concerning sexuality, it is usually not possible to have sufficient knowledge of the sample in advance (nor be confident of the reliability of the information). Also, participation in this study was voluntary and participants were not easily recruited, so the study could not afford the luxury of being too selective. Therefore, the study relied on certain inclusion and exclusion criteria established at the start, and the recruitment effort was deliberately broad to encourage diverse participation. Within those criteria, the sample could best be described as a convenience sample, with the analysis relying on retrospective scrutiny of what was captured. This proved to be a satisfactory technique that yielded an informative sample, as will be shown later when the characteristics of the research sample are examined.

For a number of reasons, this study focuses only on homophobia directed against males and it relies on the descriptions of male informants. While homophobia is also directed against women and by women against men, it was considered important not to assume that these experiences were the same as homophobia by males against males. This is an important distinction because sexuality is not symmetrical, and to conflate male and female homophobia would disadvantage both, whereas to study them as separate and different is beyond the capacity of this project.

It was decided to study homophobia as far as possible in "everyday life." This was considered feasible because homophobia is common and one aim of the research is to study the role it plays in the broader social fabric. Recruitment, therefore, did not focus on the violent end of the spectrum, where the analysis is vulnerable to being criticized as having no relevance beyond being a study of a small group of disturbed young men. While this does not relate to any rigid inclusion criteria, it serves to explain why this study did not specifically set out to recruit people who had engaged in homophobic violence.

In an attempt to ensure a reasonable degree of contemporary relevance, an approximate upper limit of thirty years of age was chosen for participants. Some were just above this age limit, but this was not discovered until the interview had commenced. Because this upper limit was arbitrary and only served as a guide, these subjects were not excluded from the study. A lower limit of eighteen years was chosen to avoid problems with parental consent and to focus the study on the observations of young adults who have completed their secondary schooling, in order to obtain a more complete developmental perspective. This lower limit was adhered to.

It was also decided to study young men who had spent most of their developmental years in English-speaking countries. This was to limit the interpretive difficulties that might arise because of cultural differences. In contrast, Australia is a multicultural society, and although most participants spent their formative years in Australia and New Zealand, their families came from a variety of ethnic backgrounds.

RECRUITMENT

A variety of recruitment techniques were employed to capture diverse perspectives on sexual development and homophobia. However, random sampling was neither possible nor appropriate. Instead, the aim was to construct a mosaic of observations, sufficient for the theoretical objectives of the project and without making unwarranted claims about the completeness of the picture nor drawing conclusions about the frequency of the observations at a population level. Certain legitimate maneuvers do allow the researcher to make conclusions about the broader relevance of the findings. The inclusion of epidemiology in Chapter 1 established homophobia as a widespread phenomenon and was specifically intended as one way of providing a link between the project and wider issues. Other links are discussed in the following material.

Subjects were recruited by advertising and by word of mouth. In mid-1995 an advertisement was placed in the "personals column" of the classified advertisements in the principal Canberra newspaper,* *The Canberra Times.* Key organizations were also contacted to assist with recruitment. Staff agreed to approach people accessing these organizations whom they

---

*The city of Canberra has a population of approximately 300,000. Although it is considerably smaller than most Australian state capital cities, it is the seat of the federal government and has been the national capital since 1927.

felt would be prepared to be interviewed, and "fliers" were placed in reception areas. Services that agreed to assist include the AIDS Council of the Australian Capital Territory and certain urban and rural public sexual health clinics.

Each interview identified the geographic area where the participant lived and the schools he attended, and a survey component at the end of the interview allowed the subject to rate his own sexual orientation. A preliminary analysis was conducted after each interview. Because of the potential methodological and theoretical importance of sexual orientation for the research, attention was paid to maintaining a balance between the sexual orientations of participants. When it was found that the sample was inclining more toward one end of the spectrum, renewed recruitment effort was directed at achieving a balance. Because of the desirability of keeping the accounts of the subjects independent of one another and collecting diverse, uncollaborated observations, the initial telephone contact with the project included a screening question to ensure that none of the participants had overlapping childhood or school histories. To this extent, *theoretical sampling* was involved in the study.

Participation was voluntary, and informed consent for a detailed interview on male sexuality was obtained from all participants. Consent was obtained to talk generally about sexuality and did not mention the term "homophobia" or similar terms. As it was thought that homophobia might be embedded in modern ideas about sexuality, it was considered that consent to an interview concerning male sexuality encompassed homophobia and was appropriate. The interviews concerning sexuality were retrospectively analyzed for evidence of homophobia rather than solely focusing on homophobia when they were conducted.

INTERVIEW STRUCTURE

The approach to interviewing and the procedures involved were based on those described by Minichiello and colleagues in their book *In-Depth Interviewing* (Minichiello et al., 1992).

Thirty detailed interviews were conducted. Each interview lasted for between three and four hours. The author conducted all interviews at a mutually agreed-upon safe and private site. Coffee, tea, and sweets were available. Interviews were tape-recorded in duplicate onto microcassettes with the informed consent of the participant.

The interview was carefully structured to maximize the chances of obtaining useful and meaningful accounts. It had five stages:

1. Introduction and informed consent
2. Settling in and the collection of background and demographic details
3. The chronological history
4. Specific questions and cross-checking interview findings
5. Completion of a supplementary questionnaire

The principal task of the interview was to obtain a meaningful sexual history (Component 3). The sexual history is at the core of the research process, and the interview was constructed around this outcome. Components 1 and 2 of the interview concerned administrative arrangements and provided a convenient "settling in" period. The main aims of "settling in" were to ensure privacy, comfort, and openness. Discussion at this stage was of a general nature and intended to be reassuring and nonthreatening.

The chronological history occupied most of the interview. It was important for the subject to feel that he could talk freely, with minimal intrusion of the ideas of the interviewer. It was paramount that ample material in the subject's own words was obtained during this phase in order to compile an adequate database for analysis. As far as possible, the interviewer attempted to facilitate discussion through techniques such as echoing and carefully judged silences. Guidance was offered by structural comments that encouraged the person to expand on particular points, to explain further, or to move along in the time frame. The interviewer has considerable experience in obtaining sexual histories in clinical settings, and this appeared to be an advantage because the interviews were lengthy and the data obtained from them are comprehensive.

Once the history was obtained, the interview moved into the final phases and there was a change in emphasis. The fourth phase was more directive and offered the researcher a defined opportunity to cross-check the subject's accounts and to use directed questioning to seek clarification and complete missing details. Finally, after the tape recorders had been turned off and while the researcher was packing the equipment away, the subject was asked to complete a questionnaire that included an "Attitudes Towards Lesbians and Gay Men" or ATLG Scale as described by Herek (1994). This time also provided an "off-the-record" opportunity for the subject to debrief.

Within a day of the interview, a preliminary analysis was performed. This involved making notes that summarized the key findings of the interview and any theoretical issues that these findings raised. These notes were incorporated into the analytical research log.

ANALYSIS: INTERPRETATION, VALIDITY, AND WIDER SIGNIFICANCE

Recordings were transcribed using standard word processing software. This version of the transcript was known as the "raw" version. Each raw version was printed and cross-checked for accuracy and transcription errors against the original tapes. The resulting version was known as the "corrected" version and is the primary data source for this analysis. A *precis* was made of each corrected transcript so that the resulting file contained material that gave a good representation of the material collected, but excluded material that was not considered relevant to the research. These "condensed" versions were further reduced to include only information that might be used as quotes in the analysis. Each of these collections of quotes was merged into combined files and a heading that identified the key points illustrated by the quotes was added to each fragment. These fragments were then printed and manually cut and reassembled so that data were collected into thematic groups according to the added headings. These groups were then used as the framework for this thesis and to provide a database for documenting the analysis.

A number of strategies have been employed to ensure the analysis is well argued and draws reasonable conclusions. First, the project design and the interview process have been structured to produce data that emphasize the descriptions and interpretations in the subject's own words. Nevertheless, it is recognized that one of the weaknesses of interviewing as a research tool, despite careful data collection, is that the process is susceptible to being influenced by project design and interview technique. The influence that the research process exercises over the results is a problem that is shared by all scientific research, qualitative and quantitative, and its control depends on the integrity of the researcher, the transparency of the analytic process, and academic peer review mechanisms. Accordingly, all data for this project were retained for further scrutiny until the project's completion. Wherever possible, detailed quotes are included to illustrate the arguments being made.

Second, the context of the data being analyzed should be taken into account during interpretation. The analysis of context in this project is guided by the arguments made by Layder (1993). Layder develops a "resource map" for social research that provides a framework that utilizes a sequentially widening perspective for the interpretation of data: self, situated activity, social setting, macrocontext, and historical dimension (Layder, 1993: 8, 72). This structure facilitates a thorough analysis that includes the consideration of context. The sequential widening of the analytic perspective is a principle employed in this research (and is reflected in the increasingly broad and theoretical perspective taken by each subsequent chapter). By broadening the analysis as Layder suggests, projects such as this have the capacity to include analyses of both the macro- and the microprocesses involved. The microview, best captured in the individual interviews and the individual variations described in the interviews, helps to delineate the role of human agency and personal interactions in homophobic processes. The macroview lays the foundations for drawing links between this research and its wider implications, although due regard must be given to avoid oversimplification and developing unwarranted "grand narratives."

Third, meanings and underlying dynamics would be uninterpretable except that they can be related to existing theory and literature, and the researcher attributes additional meaning from his own experience. The validity of this process depends on establishing a clear and well-argued link between the research findings and the literature. This project was an interdisciplinary project from the outset, and the analysis depends on drawing on a number of disciplines. Concepts have been borrowed from anthropology, psychoanalysis, historical studies, and other social sciences, including quantitative studies, and these are elaborated in the relevant chapters.

This project involved collecting accounts of some of the participants' earliest memories. However, the "accuracy" of memories is only a weakness if precise, literal memories are crucial to exploring the research question. This project places importance on the recounting of memorable, significant events and their general characteristics and residual impressions rather than on extracting details that are difficult to recover. How-ever, if those details are easily recovered and seem consistent with the account, they are accepted for analysis. It is recognized that any recounted memory is an interpretation of the original event—no matter how recent. This project is interested in those interpretations and how homophobic dynamics might be involved in them. The occurrence of recurrent similar descriptions across uncollaborated accounts gives the accounts increased significance that is drawn out in the analysis. This might be a reflection of shared social processes rather than a reflection of "accurate" recall of memories. When they involve what is arguably a homophobic perspective, these accounts of shared social processes are of primary concern to this project, whether the detail is recalled accurately or not. It is the homophobic perspective, how it may have arisen, and how it is justified that are of interest.

The recurrence of similar descriptions of homophobia in independent accounts raises the question of the wider significance of the project beyond the original sample. Because this is a small, nonrandom sample, statistical methods are not suited to predicting or testing generalizability.

Nevertheless, there is a striking similarity between the general features of the accounts of homophobic processes, which makes the question of the wider significance compelling. The sample is diverse in key features such as school attended, state of origin, adult sexual orientation, and socioeconomic and ethnic background. Yet the accounts of schoolyard practices, of the talk between boys, and of how boys who were "different" were approached had notable consistencies, and when related to the findings of other researchers, their claims to significance are strong.

As was mentioned earlier, several factors have been used to facilitate interpretation and to clarify generalizability. First, the analysis relates the findings of this research to the results of previous quantitative studies. This has a complementary effect: what other studies offer in numbers, this study complements with depth of detail and theoretical elaboration. Second, this study did not exclusively aim to recruit young men who had been involved in violent homophobic activities. Such a sample would have rendered the research vulnerable to being dismissed as a study of disturbed young men, with little wider importance. Third, in addition to providing accounts of their own experiences, all subjects in this study were asked to also give accounts of the experiences of others, particularly family and school peers. These accounts provide useful contextual information, but also substantially increase the data available, the people observed, and the power of the study. Finally, including the "ATLG Scale" (Herek, 1994) provides a further link to other research. This consists of a standardized series of questions concerning attitudes toward lesbians and gay men. The individual questions help to clarify attitudes to certain standardized issues, and the composite scores derived from the scales can be compared to studies of larger samples elsewhere.

The ATLG scores are in Appendix C because of their supplemental role in this work. The scale was developed on American populations and has not been extensively tested on Australians. Further, it was originally developed by Herek primarily to evaluate the attitudes of heterosexuals toward homosexual men and women, whereas in this study it was intentionally administered to all participants regardless of sexual orientation. The decision to administer the scale to all participants was based on some key theoretical points. It was decided not to limit it to people in the study who were exclusively heterosexual because of important theoretical uncertainties about the rigidity and stability of sexual orientation. The "sexual orientation scores" of the subjects of this study confirm how arbitrary this division is. The boundary between the negative attitudes of heterosexuals and those of people who are not heterosexual may be fairly arbitrary except that homophobia can be directed at one's self in the case of men who experience homosexual desire. As seen in Chapter 6, homosexual desire and homophobia may be present in all males but suppressed to varying degrees; therefore, a sharp distinction between external and internalized homophobia, or between heterosexual and homosexual, may well be more arbitrary than is commonly assumed. The final reason for including the study in Appendix C is because it contains questions that may not be phrased well for Australian participants. For example, most people were aware that lesbian activities are not subject to legal restraint in any Australian state, so the statement "State laws regulating private, consenting lesbian behavior should be loosened" is of limited use. Other questions would seem to be open to interpretation and are a little dated for more politicized younger people. For example, the statement "The idea of male homosexual marriages seems ridiculous to me" could be agreed to and scored "nine" both if a person was homophobic or if a person who is not biased against homosexuals thought that all marriage was ridiculous or wondered why gay men would want to participate in a system that was oppressing them. Nevertheless, the use of the ATLG Scale on Australian males who are not all exclusively heterosexual has produced some interesting and useful findings, but the capacity of the findings to be compared with other studies has limitations.

The ultimate outcome of this study is to make a significant contribution to the theoretical literature on homophobia. Interviews are used to discover and describe how this cluster of phenomena might operate and as a method of grounding the theoretical work in careful documentation and observation rather than being too speculative. The analysis uses the existing literature as an interpretive base, and, in turn, the analysis serves to provide an interpretive base from which to develop theory further. Theory is intended to yield as more evidence as comes to light, and because it is tentative, having an incomplete picture or lacking "proof" for some findings does not preclude substantial theoretical outcomes with general implications.

CONCLUSIONS

The methodology enables homophobia to be analyzed from several key perspectives. First, by identifying descriptions and themes that recur in independent accounts and by linking those findings to evidence from other sources, certain conclusions can be drawn about homophobia in general. Second, by identifying how individuals' descriptions vary in how they experienced and handled homophobic dynamics, a profile of the diversity of homophobia and of human agency in response to homophobia can be constructed. Third, collecting data in a chronological framework facilitated the interviews and provided sequential material that is useful for studying developmental events and social processes. Finally, while the descriptive data are a valuable outcome in their own right, they also provide powerful grounding for developing theory concerning homophobia. This relates to the primary aims of this research: to make a significant contribution to describing and explaining homophobia.

Appendix B

Sample

Thirty young men participated in detailed interviews for this study. The average age was twenty-six years, ranging from eighteen to thirty-three.

All participants were asked to rate their sexual orientation on a scale from one to nine, where one is exclusively heterosexual, nine is exclusively homosexual, and five is "symmetrically" bisexual. Scores for this item range from one to nine with a mean of 5.4. Eight people indicated that they are exclusively heterosexual and nine that they are exclusively gay, and three rated themselves in category five and are presumably "symmetrically bisexual." Of the ten remaining subjects, six rated themselves as inclined to be more homosexual and four as inclined to be more heterosexual.

Only three participants (D4, E5, I9) have never had any female or male friends, relatives, or close acquaintances reveal their homosexuality to them.

For confidentiality reasons, countries are mentioned in general terms, apart from Australia or New Zealand, which are named, but details of which state (or which island in the case of New Zealand) are omitted. Capital cities are not named, but because of the unique status of Canberra, which would make it easily identifiable, it is named. Moderate-sized towns with a population of between 10,000 to 30,000 people are described as "rural regional centers." Smaller towns generally have a population of considerably less than 10,000 and are referred to as "rural towns."

Twenty-seven subjects were born in Australia, two were born in New Zealand, and one was born in Britain. Thirty-seven of the subject's parents were born in Australia, five in New Zealand, three in Malta, three in England, two in Germany, two in Scotland, two in Portugal, and one each in Italy, Canada, France, Ukraine, Romania, and Denmark.

Nineteen subjects have parents who are married and still together. The mother of one subject died when the subject was age thirty-one. Three subjects had fathers who died when the subject was age six months, seven years, and eighteen years. Seven subjects had parents that separated or divorced when the subject was age one month, seven months, and six, eight, eight, fifteen, and twenty-eight years.

Fourteen subjects come from Anglican families, including two who attended Catholic secondary schools. Thirteen subjects are from Catholic families, including one who was charismatic and one whose other parent was Lutheran. Six have parents from other denominations, including Presbyterian, Fundamentalist, Methodist, Uniting, and Eastern Orthodox Christian. There was no representation of non-Christian organized religions in the sample.

Including the subjects, the average number of siblings in the family was 3.4. Two subjects are an "only child," nine come from a family with four or more siblings, and three are from families of eight siblings. The thirty male subjects of the study have forty-six brothers and twenty-seven sisters. The study was much more likely to recruit subjects who are either the oldest (16/30) or the youngest (14/30) of their siblings (this includes two who are the only child in the family and are therefore both the oldest and the youngest). Only two of the thirty are neither the oldest nor the youngest. The mean value for the sexual orientation score is 6.1 for those siblings who are the youngest, 4.5 for those who are the oldest, and 5.4 for the entire sample.

The highest level of education was recorded for each subject. One subject left school after year nine, five after year ten, nine after year twelve, and fourteen completed a university degree. Three completed a trade certificate, two of whom had also completed year twelve. The mean sexual orientation score of the six people who did not complete secondary school is 4.8. The mean sexual orientation score of the six people who completed a university degree is 5.8. Four subjects indicated that they were a school prefect or school captain: their sexual orientation scores were 9, 8, 2, and 1.

Ten subjects spent their primary and secondary school years in a rural environment, twelve in a capital city, and eight had mixed school years in both urban and rural settings. Twenty-one undertook at least some of their primary or secondary schooling in New South Wales, ten in the Australian Capital Territory, four in Victoria, three in Queensland, two in South Australia, three in New Zealand, two in Britain, one in the United States, and one in Denmark. In the latter three cases and one New Zealand case, the schooling outside Australia was a small minority of their school years. Ten subjects had their education in more than one state/territory/country. Twenty-three had at least some of their primary or secondary education at government schools, ten at Catholic schools, four at Anglican schools, and one at an "alternative" school. Except where specified, schools are mixed sex.

Eleven of the subjects are employed in professional positions, six are in unskilled positions, six are unemployed (some with some casual work), four are working in a trade, and three are full-time students.

Thirteen of the participants are not in a sexual relationship, nine consider themselves to be "in a relationship" with another male, and eight with a female. Nine of the participants live with friends, seven live with their male partners, six live alone, four with their female partners/wives, three with their parents, and one in a university hall of residence.

The political preferences were recorded for most subjects. Some subjects expressed a bias toward more than one party. The sample was biased toward the Labor party and being progressive. Fifteen subjects described themselves as "progressive," five as "moderate," two as "conservative," and two with no political interest. Sixteen expressed a bias toward Labor, ten as swinging, five toward the Democrats, two toward the Greens, and two toward the Liberal Party.

There were ten avenues that people used to access the project. More than thirty "access events" are recorded because some people learned of the project by more than one means, for example, first hearing of the project by "word of mouth" and then being further prompted to volunteer by seeing a "flier." Nine subjects volunteered after becoming aware of the project by word of mouth through "gay networks," ten though "health networks," one through "student networks," four through "professional networks" (not health professional), one through "gym networks," one through "tradesmen's networks." Four volunteered after seeing a "flier" advertising the project at "gay venues," one on a "work notice board," and one on the notice board of a "community hall." Four volunteered in response to an advertisement in *The Canberra Times* newspaper.

PARTICIPANT PROFILES

The following profiles introduce the participants, give an overview of key factors that structured their lives, and provide some context for the evidence used in this work. At the beginning of each profile, in parentheses, is age in years, sexual orientation score, ATLG Score, and ATG Score. The "sexual orientation score" is a self-assigned score where the participant ranks himself on a scale of between one and nine. A score of one indicates that the person currently rates himself as heterosexual, a score of five as "symmetrically bisexual," and a score of nine as "exclusively homosexual." There is no presumption that those orientations are fixed. The "ATLG Score" was obtained using the questions developed by Herek and reflects attitudes toward lesbians and gay men. A higher score reflects more negative attitudes, with a possible range of between 20 and 180. The "ATG Score" is a score derived from a subset of the questions concerning attitudes toward male homosexuality only. Again, a higher score reflects more negative attitudes, but the possible range is from 10 to 90. The mean ATLG Score is 36 and the mean male ATG Score is 21. For the reasons stated earlier, the ATLG scores are provided as guidelines only.

A1 (Age 26; Sexual Orientation 5; ATLG Score 44; ATG Score 18)

A1 is twenty-six years old and was born in Australia. He was brought up Catholic. His father migrated to Australia from central Europe. A1 is the youngest of three boys in his family. He had a complicated childhood. His mother left home when he was one month old. He was brought up partially by his father, whom he describes as authoritarian and who sexually assaulted him. He spent some time in several children's homes as a "ward of the state." He attended three primary schools and attended remedial classes in years five and six. After secondary school he had some further training in computer skills. He is currently unemployed and relies on casual cleaning work for his income, when available. A1 describes himself as stubborn but humanitarian. He has no affiliation with any political parties and is cynical about Australia's political institutions. He believes in the death penalty for murder and child abuse. He resists conventional labels concerning sexual orientation, arguing that sexuality is a small part of a person's life. He rated his sexual orientation as "five" or "bisexual" for this study. He accepted his capacity to experience same-sex desire less than two years ago. This was not easy. He currently lives in a sexual relationship with a male partner. One other male person also lives in the same house. A1 volunteered for this study after reading a flier distributed through gay community networks.

B2 (Age 32; Sexual Orientation 9; ATLG Score 40; ATG Score 22)

B2 is age thirty-two. He was born in a small rural town where he spent his primary years in a small government school with thirty pupils. He was brought up Anglican and is of Anglo-Scottish descent. Both parents remained together until his mother died six years ago. He has one brother who is five years younger. He attended a government secondary school to year nine and has not undertaken any further formal education. He traveled to a larger, nearby rural town for his three secondary school years and he boarded with his grandmother during the school week. Since leaving school, B2 has worked in light industry. He usually votes Labor, but claims to have no political opinions. B2 married when he was twenty and divorced when he was twenty-seven. B2 found out about the study by word of mouth through health professional networks.

C3 (Age 29; Sexual Orientation 7; ATLG Score 39; ATG Score 25)

C3 is twenty-nine and was born in the western suburbs of a state capital city. He was brought up Catholic and went through the Catholic school system, but he "denies all knowledge of being Catholic" now. He attended a parish primary school to fourth class and a Catholic boys' high school from fifth class to year ten, after which he left school. Politically he identifies as progressive with his allegiance split between Labor and the Democrats. His parents are Australian-born of Irish stock several generations removed. He is the youngest of four children. The two oldest siblings are girls and the next is a boy. He is prone to depression. He is currently living with a female partner, and they have been together for ten years. C3 volunteered for this study after reading a newspaper advertisement.

D4 (Age 29; Sexual Orientation 1; ATLG Score 100; ATG Score 71)

D4 is age twenty-nine, was born in Canberra, and has an Anglican background. At the age of seven he moved to a rural town to live with his grandparents following the death of his father. He rejoined his mother when she remarried and they moved to a state capital city where he attended state schools for the end of fifth class, sixth class, and year seven. He returned to Canberra to do years eight to twelve in a government secondary school. After school he completed a tradesman's certificate and he works in that trade. He has never been married, but he has had several significant relationships with women and was engage to be married to one of them. He says that he doesn't "really have a political view" but that he is more Labor oriented because of his family background. He has no brothers or sisters. D4 volunteered for this study in response to a newspaper advertisement.

E5 (Age 33; Sexual Orientation 2; ATLG Score 28; ATG Score 10)

E5 is thirty-three years old and was born and educated in a rural regional center. He has a brother and a sister who are twins and younger than him by one year. He describes his parents as "level working-class people." His parents are still together and he is closer to his mother than his father. His parents are Australian-born of English descent several generations back and Catholic. He now rarely attends church. He was educated at a Catholic primary school and a Catholic boys' secondary school where he completed year ten. Although the school was a boarding school, he was a day student. After finishing school at the age of seventeen, he enlisted in the Australian armed forces with the rank of "Private." He left after serving for three years in the tropics and has had a number of jobs since including laboring, building, and hotel and restaurant service. He currently lives with his girlfriend but has never been married. He has no party political preferences and is a "swinging voter." For four secondary years, he attended the same school as BB28, but they were separated by about fifteen years. E5 found out about the project by word of mouth through health professional networks.

F6 (Age 27; Sexual Orientation 1; ATLG Score 40; ATG Score 30)

F6 is age twenty-seven and has spent most of his life in a rural regional center. His parents are from different southern European countries. He was educated in the state primary and secondary school system and completed year ten. After leaving school he undertook a trade certificate and now works in that trade. He was brought up Catholic and still has religious beliefs, but he rarely attends church. He considers himself politically moderate to progressive and leans toward the Labor party. There are five children in his family, one girl and four boys. The girl is the second child and he is the fourth. He now lives alone in Canberra. He is engage to get married and has never been married before. F6 found out about the project by word of mouth through health professional networks.

G7 (Age 29; Sexual Orientation 3; ATLG Score 45; ATG Score 26)

G7 is twenty-nine. He was born in Britain and immigrated to Australia at the age of seven with his parents. In Australia, he lived in two capital cities and lived some time with his family on a small farm just outside one of those cities. He has two older brothers. His family is Anglican and his secondary schooling was at an Anglican boys' school. He completed year twelve but has undertaken no further formal education. He has no formal religious convictions. He describes himself as "progressive" but has no dominant party political affiliations. He is currently not working, although he considers himself a writer. In recent years he has discovered that cross-dressing helps him to write. He considers himself predominantly hetero-sexual. He married at the age of twenty-two. The marriage lasted for six years and he divorced two and a half years ago. G7 found out about the project through a newspaper advertisement.

H8 (Age 25; Sexual Orientation 1; ATLG Score 34; ATG Score 23)

H8 is twenty-five. He was born in Australia. He is the oldest of three children; the second sibling is his sister and the third his brother. His family is Anglican, but he describes himself currently as agnostic or athe-ist. One parent was born in North America and the other in Australia; they are still together and both are of Anglo-Saxon descent. His father served in the armed forces and was required to travel extensively. H8 spent his first three years on a farm in rural Australia; he spent the next three in an Australian capital city; the next two in Britain; the next two back in the Australian city; and from the age of ten in Canberra. He was educated in the government school system. H8 has a university degree, served in the armed forces, and now works as a public servant. He thinks of himself as politically progressive and voted "green" at the last election. He is married and has a daughter. H8 found out about the project through a newspaper advertisement.

I9 (Age 25; Sexual Orientation 5; ATLG Score 76; ATG Score 37)

I9 is twenty-five years old. He was born and grew up in a rural regional center in New Zealand. He is Anglican; both of his parents are of Anglo-Saxon descent and are still married and live together in New Zealand. His father is a tradesman who now has a management role. I9 attends church weekly. I9 has an identical twin brother and a younger brother. He was educated in the New Zealand state school system, has an honors degree, and is currently enrolled in doctoral studies in the physical sciences. He lives in a university hall of residence. He has never been married. He describes himself politically as between moderate and conservative. I9 found out about this project by word of mouth through university student networks.

J10 (Age 32; Sexual Orientation 9; ATLG Score 22; ATG Score 12)

J10 is age thirty-two and was born and grew up in a coastal Australian town that is a regional center. His parents are of Anglo-Scottish descent although they were born in Australia. His father was Presbyterian and his mother Anglican and they are married and live together. J10 has a non-identical twin brother and a younger sister. He was educated in an Anglican boy's boarding school as a day student. He has no formal religious beliefs but feels that people have their own spirit and spirituality. He has university qualifications and works as a health professional. J10 has a relationship with a male partner and they live together. In recent elections, J10 voted Labor. J10 found out about the project by word of mouth through gay community and health professional networks.

K11 (Age 26; Sexual Orientation 1; ATLG Score 39; ATG Score 21)

K11 is twenty-six years old and Catholic but has become an irregular churchgoer in the last six months. He is of Anglo-Irish-German descent, but his parents were born in Australia. His parents are married and still together. K11 is the eldest of five. He has three sisters and a brother. His brother is twelve years younger. K11 spent his primary school years in the public system in Canberra and went to a Catholic boy's boarding school in a state capital city. He was captain of the school rowing club. He is undertaking a university degree in science. He describes himself as politically progressive in financial areas, but more conservative in social and family issues. He is married. He used to be a Labor voter, but is looking to alternatives. K11 found out about this project when he saw a flier advertising the project on the notice board at work.

L12 (Age 19; Sexual Orientation 9; ATLG Score 23; ATG Score 11)

L12 is nineteen. He was born interstate but has spent most of his life in Canberra, apart from years three and four at primary school in a rural coastal town. He returned to Canberra to repeat year four and completed his schooling in the Canberra government school system. He lives with his parents, has recently successfully completed his year twelve, and has casual employment in a retail business. He is of Anglo-Irish descent, has two older brothers, and his father served in the armed forces. He is Anglican but he "doesn't practice religion." He says he is "very unopinionated" when it comes to politics. He has never been married but he has had both girlfriends and boyfriends. He found out about the project by word of mouth in gay community networks.

M13 (Age 26; Sexual Orientation 1; ATLG Score 64; ATG Score 46)

M13 is twenty-six and was an only child until the age of ten when his brother was born. He was born in Canberra to Southern European parents. His father was a laborer and his mother looked after the home. He has a Catholic background but attends church rarely. He attended two primary schools, a high school, and a secondary college in the Canberra government school system. He has a university economics degree and works as a public servant. He thinks of himself as politically moderate and usually votes Labor. He has recently also become interested in the Greens and the Democrats. He found out about the project from a flier on the notice board in a community hall.

N14 (Age 28; Sexual Orientation 9; ATLG Score 24; ATG Score 14)

N14 is twenty-eight. He was born to Southern European parents in the mid-outer suburbs of a state capital city where he lived until he moved to Canberra at the age of twenty. He is the youngest of five children. He has one sister. He attended the local Catholic primary school and Catholic secondary boys' school and completed year twelve. He was school prefect. He has a university arts degree and works as a public servant. He describes himself as a "recovering Catholic." He is "progressive" and in "favor of change," and usually votes Labor but is "having to reassess that." He has never been married and lives with his male partner. He found out about the project from a flier seen at the local AIDS Council.

O15 (Age 24; Sexual Orientation 9; ATLG Score 22; ATG Score 10)

O15 is twenty-four. His father is Scottish and his mother was born in Australia of Anglo-Saxon descent. He was born in a rural regional center, where he lived until the age of seven. At that age, he moved interstate with his family to a semirural coastal town where he lived until the age of eighteen. He has a brother who is three years younger and no other siblings. O15 attended two state primary schools and a state secondary school. At the age of eighteen, O15 moved to Canberra where he undertook a university economics degree. He works as a public servant. He has never been married, is not in a relationship, and lives with friends in a "group house." He has no significant religious background but attended the local Uniting Church Sunday School between years four and six of primary school. He describes himself as progressive with a leaning toward the Labor party. He found out about the project by word of mouth and a flier at the local AIDS Council.

P16 (Age 25; Sexual Orientation 8; ATLG Score 36; ATG Score 18)

P16 is age twenty-five. His mother and father are Australian born and still together. His father was a salesman, and his mother was a "traditional housewife." He was born in a small rural town where he lived until the age of twelve and attended the local state primary school to year six. He then went to secondary school at a Catholic boys' boarding school in the state capital city about two hours' drive from his hometown. He became school captain at that school. He has two younger brothers. P16 completed two university degrees, moved to Canberra, and works as a public servant. He has never been married, is not in a relationship, but shares a house with one other person. He describes himself as non-right wing and progressive. Although he doesn't usually vote along party lines, he leans toward the Labor party. He found out about the project by word of mouth through gay community and professional networks.

Q17 (Age 29; Sexual Orientation 8.5; ATLG Score 28; ATG Score 18)

Q17 is twenty-nine and was born in the mid-outer suburbs of a state capital city. His mother is English and his father was born in Eastern Europe. His father died when he was six months old. Q17 is the youngest of eight children. The two oldest were boys, followed by two girls, then two boys, and then a girl. Q17 was raised Catholic and went through a deeply religious "charismatic" period in his teens. Now he rarely attends church. He attended a mixed-sex Catholic school to year four and an all boys' Catholic school from fifth class onward. He moved to a rural mixed-sex high school in year twelve. He has completed a university degree in the health sciences and works in private enterprise in the health industry.

He was married and divorced. He now lives with a male partner, whom he has been with for twelve months. He describes himself as progressive and a swinging voter. He has voted Democrats and Labor recently. He found out about the project by word of mouth through health professional networks.

R18 (Age 23; Sexual Orientation 7.5; ATLG Score 20; ATG Score 10)

R18 is twenty-three. He was born in a state capital city where he still lives. His parents are Australian-born, Anglican, and of Anglo-Saxon descent. His mother is a businesswoman and his father teaches. He has one brother who is four years younger. R18 attended an Anglican boys' boarding school as a day student for primary and secondary school. This was split into several campuses: kindergarten, primary to year five, middle school to year nine, and senior school to year twelve. He is currently studying toward a university degree. He rarely attends church. He lives with friends, has never been married, has had girlfriends and has been in a relationship with a male partner for the last couple of years, although they do not live together. R18 thinks of himself as progressive, he comes from a Liberal voting family and voted Liberal at the last election. He found out about the project by word of mouth through health professional and gay community networks.

S19 (Age 30; Sexual Orientation 3; ATLG Score 21; ATG Score 11)

S19 is thirty and was born in a rural regional center in New Zealand. At the age of two he moved to a second town, which is also a regional center, and returned to the first town at the age of seven. He remained there until the age of seventeen when he moved to the main city on the island to attend university. Both parents were born in New Zealand and are of English, Scottish, and Irish descent. His father is a public figure and his mother manages the family home. His parents are married and still together. He has a younger brother and a younger sister. He was educated in the government school system, has completed year twelve, and has a university degree. He works as an administrator of a nongovernment welfare body. He lives with friends, has never been married, and has a current girlfriend. Although his parents are Protestant and regular churchgoers, he rarely attends church. S19 describes himself as progressive, a Labor voter, but is looking for alternatives. He volunteered for the project after hearing about it through professional networks.

T20 (Age 22; Sexual Orientation 5; ATLG Score 29; ATG Score 19)

T20 is twenty-two years old. He was born in Australia, is an "only child," and spent his childhood in a rural town. His parents are Australian born and Anglo-Saxon although his father has some Maori descent. His father is a policeman and his mother, an administrator. His parents divorced when he was fifteen and T20 lived with his mother. He was raised Anglican and attends church rarely. He attended one state primary and one state secondary school and completed year twelve. Both were mixed-sex schools. After school he moved to Canberra. He has casual employment at a gym and in retail. He lives alone and has a girlfriend of a couple of years, but has also had male partners prior to his current relationship. He describes himself as preferring Labor and the Democrats. He found out about this project by word of mouth through gymnasium networks.

U21 (Age 26; Sexual Orientation 1; ATLG Score 22; ATG Score 12)

U21 is twenty-six years old. He was born in a state capital city where he lived to the age of twenty-three. He then moved to Canberra to work in private enterprise. His mother is Australian-born and of Anglo-Saxon descent and manages the family home. His father was born in Northern Europe and is a businessman. Both are married and still together. U21 is the oldest of four boys. He is Anglican but rarely attends church. To year four, he attended a mixed-sex school and from year four, he attended a boys-only Anglican school. This was divided into a middle school campus and a senior school from years nine to twelve. He became school captain. He describes himself as "left socially" but "right economically" and a "swinging voter." He lives alone and has never married. U21 found out about the project by word of mouth through professional networks.

V22 (Age 30; Sexual Orientation 9; ATLG Score 29; ATG Score 19)

V22 is thirty and was born in a coastal town that is a rural regional center. His parents are Australian-born and of Anglo-Irish descent. His father, who died when V22 was eighteen, operated a taxi. His mother manages the home. He is the youngest of eight children, the second, fifth, and sixth are girls. He was raised Catholic but rarely attends church. He was educated at a mixed-sex Catholic primary school to year six, a Catholic boys' secondary school to year ten, and a mixed-sex secondary college for years eleven and twelve. At the age of eighteen he moved to a state capital city before he moved to Canberra at age twenty-three. He has a university degree. He works in the administration of a nongovernment welfare organization. He describes himself as politically "progressive" and "nonconservative," but expresses dissatisfaction with both major parties. He has never married and lives with a male partner of several years. He found out about the project through gay community and professional networks.

W23 (Age 29; Sexual Orientation 2; ATLG Score 27; ATG Score 15)

W23 is twenty-nine. He was born in a state capital city and lived there until the age of twenty-seven when he moved to Canberra to work. His parents are Anglo-Saxon and were born in Australia. W23 has one brother who is eight years older. He attended state mixed-sex infant school from kindergarten to year three, primary school from years three to six, and high school to year twelve. He became a prefect and school captain. He has two university honors degrees and is currently enrolled in a master's degree program. He works as a public servant. He describes himself as having been Catholic to the age of seventeen and since then "varied between being an agnostic to being an atheist." He thinks of himself as politically "progressive," "moderately left-wing," and a member of the Labor party. He has never married and lives with friends. W23 found out about the project by word of mouth through professional networks.

X24 (Age 23; Sexual Orientation 8; ATLG Score 30; ATG Score 20)

X24 is twenty-three. He was born in a state capital city and lived there until a year ago when he completed a university honors degree. His father is Catholic and immigrated to Australia from Western Europe, and his mother is a Protestant of Anglo-Saxon descent who was born in Australia. At the age of seven, his mother was diagnosed with cancer that required chemotherapy and radiotherapy treatment, which she survived. This was a difficult time for X24, and during this time, he was sent to Europe to live with his grandparents for four months. He has one brother who is six years younger. X24 went through two state primary schools and one state high school. He is enrolled in a higher degree program in science. X24 went to Sunday school as a child and thinks of himself as an atheist but he feels "everyone's got a spirituality." He claims to be politically conservative but this seems to be largely a reaction to his belief that Labor has treated his suburb (a traditional Labor area) with contempt. He has never married, lives alone, and is not in a relationship. He found out about the project by word of mouth in the gay community networks.

Y25 (Age 24; Sexual Orientation 9; ATLG Score 30; ATG Score 18)

Y25 is twenty-four. He was born in Canberra, where he has lived all of his life. His mother is from central Europe and works as a health professional. His father was born in Eastern Europe and raised Eastern Orthodox Christian. Y25 was raised atheist. His father was a public servant but is now exploring alternative lifestyles. His parents separated when Y25 was six. He has one brother who is five years older. Y25 attended a state primary school to year six and a state high school for years seven to nine. He experienced problems at that school and was transferred to an "alternative educational methods" school where he completed year twelve. He describes himself as politically moderate and leans toward Labor. He works in a clerical position in a nongovernment organization. He lives with friends and recently ended a relationship with another male. He found out about the project through fliers and word of mouth in gay community networks.

Z26 (Age 30; Sexual Orientation 1; ATLG Score 51; ATG Score 21)

Z26 is age thirty. He was born in a state capital city where he lived until the age of twenty-one. He then moved to a country town with his parents before moving to Canberra at the age of twenty-six. His parents are Australian-born, of Anglo-Saxon descent, and have recently separated. He has two older brothers and two older sisters. He attended two state primary schools and a state secondary school where he completed year ten. He has no further education, but works as a tradesman. He was brought up in a small, very strict Christian denomination, which he left at the age of sixteen. He describes himself as politically moderate and votes Liberal. He lives with two other males; he has never married, but he has a girlfriend. He volunteered for the project when he heard about it through his trade's network.

AA27 (Age 18; Sexual Orientation 9;
ATLG Score 20; ATG Score 10)

AA27 is eighteen. He was born in a rural town where he attended a single local state school from kindergarten to year eleven. His father is Scottish-born and a blue-collar worker, and his mother is Australian-born of Scottish parents and is "unemployed." He has an older brother and a younger sister. His childhood was quite poor financially. His parents divorced when he was in year three at school, and he lived with his mother until he was sixteen. In year eleven he moved to Canberra and initially lived with his father. Early in the year-twelve school year, he left because he and his father were incompatible. AA27 claims that his father gave him a choice of ending his gay life or leaving home. Gay friends, who functioned as his adoptive gay family, provided him with accommodation and this permitted him to complete his year-twelve studies. Due to his circumstances, the fees for the Catholic school he was attending were waived. His parents were nominally Anglican but he does not subscribe to any religion. He is dissatisfied with both major political parties and is interested in alternatives. He is not currently working, lives in government housing, and relies on a subsidy to undertake a course on business skills. He has never been married, shares accommodations, and currently has a male partner. He found out about this project by word of mouth through gay community networks.

BB28 (Age 18; Sexual Orientation 1;
ATLG Score 44; ATG Score 30)

BB28 is eighteen. He was born in a rural regional center and lived there all of his life except for twelve months at the age of sixteen, when he was an exchange student in Europe. His father is Australian-born and his mother was born in New Zealand to parents from Western Europe. He has a brother who is two years younger. His parents divorced when he was eight or nine and he lived with his mother on a farm until he was fourteen when he lived with his dad in town. BB28 attended a state infant's school for kindergarten and years one and two and a state primary school for grades three to six. His mother remarried when he was eleven. He attended a Catholic secondary boys' boarding school in the town as a day student. He has just completed his higher school certificate and is waiting to see whether he has been accepted into a university science degree course. He describes himself as progressive; he is a swinging voter but leans toward the "green vote." His grandparents were Anglican but he was not brought up with any religious convictions. He has never married and he lives with his mother and his stepfather. He volunteered for this project after hearing about it through health professional networks.

CC29 (Age 27; Sexual Orientation 8; ATLG Score 32; ATG Score 21)

CC29 is age twenty-seven. He was born in a state capital city where he lived until he completed a university degree. His parents are Australian-born, married, are still together, and are of Anglo-Irish descent. His father is an academic and his mother is a health worker. He has two older sisters. He attended one state primary school apart from spending first class in North America and six months of fifth year in New Zealand. CC29 regularly attended Sunday school and, later, church, from early in childhood until the age of twenty-five. His parents did not attend. At the age of twenty-five he ceased believing in Christianity, but he still believes in a less formal spirituality. He considers himself politically moderate, is "dissatisfied with the current system," and leans toward the Democrats. He has never married and lives with his male partner. He works in a health profession. He found out about this project through gay community networks.

DD30 (Age 24; Sexual Orientation 9; ATLG Score 20; ATG Score 10)

DD30 is twenty-four. He was born in a coastal, rural town where he still lives. His mother is Australian-born, Aboriginal, and Catholic. His father is Australian-born, Catholic, and of Anglo-Saxon descent. When DD30 was thirteen, his father spent time in prison for sexually assaulting him and several other male and female children in the town. Since then, he has been estranged from his father, but he still feels significant affection for him. DD30 is the youngest of eight children. The first four and the sixth siblings are girls. He attended the local state primary school and secondary school and completed year ten. His parents are Catholic but he is "not religious at all," although he has a sense of spirituality that links in with his Aboriginal identity. He describes himself as "in favor of change" and votes Labor. He has never married, is not in a relationship, and lives alone. He is currently unemployed. He volunteered for this project when he heard about it from health professional networks.

CONCLUSIONS

The sample recruited for this study is a convenience sample within the parameters of certain inclusion criteria. The subjects are all young males who spent most, if not all, of their childhood in Australia or New Zealand. They were recruited for interviews about male sexuality in general, and data about homophobia were subsequently extracted from those accounts. While there is no requirement to obtain a random sample, the study has benefited from obtaining a diverse range of participants. None had shared childhoods, and all but two attended different schools in five Australian states or New Zealand. The two who attended the same school for only part of their school career are separated in age by fifteen years. The older one left the school around eleven years before the younger one started. The study also exploited the additional power offered by using the informants as observers of their peers. This expanded the events and descriptions captured by this study considerably and enhanced the analysis.

Appendix C

ATLG Scores

Attitudes Toward Lesbians and Gay Men Scores

	A1	B2	C3	D4	E5	F6	G7	H8
ATG	18	22	25	71	10	30	26	23
ATL	26	18	14	29	18	10	19	11
ATLG	44	40	39	100	28	40	45	34

	I9	J10	K11	L12	M13	N14	O15	P16
ATG	37	12	21	11	46	14	10	18
ATL	39	10	18	12	18	10	12	18
ATLG	76	22	39	23	64	24	22	36

	Q17	R18	S19	T20	U21	V22	W23	X24
ATG	18	10	11	19	12	19	15	20
ATL	10	10	10	10	10	10	12	10
ATLG	28	20	21	29	22	29	27	30

	Y25	Z26	AA27	BB28	CC29	DD30	Mean
ATG	18	21	10	30	21	10	20.93
ATL	12	30	10	14	11	10	15.03
ATLG	30	51	20	44	32	20	35.97

Note: Scores are for attitudes toward male homosexuals (ATG), female homosexuals (ATL), and composite score (ATLG). Higher is more negatively biased (Herek, 1994).

Attitudes Toward Gay Men (ATG) Scores	**Mean Score**
1. Male homosexual couples should be allowed to adopt children the same as heterosexual couples.	7.53*
2. I think male homosexuals are disgusting.	2.07
3. Male homosexuals should not be allowed to teach in schools.	2.23
4. Male homosexuality is a perversion.	1.73
5. Just as in other species, male homosexuality is a natural expression of sexuality in human men.	7.87*
6. If a man has homosexual feelings, he should do everything he can to overcome them.	1.40
7. I would not be too upset if I learned that my son was a homosexual.	7.67*
8. Homosexual behavior between two men is just plain wrong.	1.87
9. The idea of male homosexual marriages seems ridiculous to me.	2.53
10. Male homosexuality is merely a different kind of lifestyle that should not be condemned.	7.83*

Note: Higher is more negatively biased; items marked with an asterisk are "reverse scored" (Herek, 1994).

Attitudes Toward Lesbians (ATL) Scores

1. Lesbians just can't fit into our society.   1.50

2. A woman's homosexuality should not be a cause for job discrimination in any situation.   8.27*

3. Female homosexuality is detrimental to society because it breaks down the natural divisions between the sexes.   1.77

4. State laws regulating private, consenting lesbian behavior should be loosened.   8.27*

5. Female homosexuality is a sin.   1.30

6. The growing number of lesbians indicates a decline in morals.   1.43

7. Female homosexuality, in itself, is no problem, but what society makes of it can be a problem.   8.27*

8. Female homosexuality is a threat to many of our basic social institutions.   1.57

9. Female homosexuality is an inferior form of sexuality.   1.13

10. Lesbians are sick.   1.13

Note: Higher is more negatively biased; items marked with an asterisk are "reverse scored" (Herek, 1994).

References

Chapter 1

Altman, D. (1992). AIDS and the discourses of sexuality. In *Rethinking Sex,* edited by R.W. Connell and G.W. Dowsett. Melbourne: Melbourne University Press, pp. 32-48.

American Psychiatric Association (1994). *Diagnostic and Statistical Manual of Mental Disorders.* Washington, DC: American Psychiatric Association.

Barstow. A.L. (1994). *Witchcraze: A New History of the European Witch Hunts.* London: Pandora.

Bennett. G. (1983) (Republished 1995). *Young and Gay: A Study of Gay Youth in Sydney,* Sydney: The Twenty-Ten Association.

Berrill. K.T. (1992). Antigay violence and victimisation in the United States: An overview. In *Hate Crimes: Confronting Violence Against Lesbians and Gay Men,* edited by G.M. Herek and K.T. Berrill. London: Sage.

Brown, L., ed. (1993). *The New Shorter Oxford English Dictionary.* Oxford: Clarendon Press.

Churchill, W. (1967). *Homosexual Behaviors Among Males.* Binghamton, NY: The Hawthorn Press.

Comstock, G.D. (1989). Developments—Sexual orientation and the law, *Harvard Law Review,* 102(7): 1541-1554.

Comstock, G.D. (1991). *Violence Against Lesbians and Gay Men.* New York: Columbia University Press.

Cox, G. (1994). *The Count and Counter Report.* Sydney: Lesbian and Gay Anti-Violence Project.

Davenport-Hines, R. (1991). *Sex, Death and Punishment.* London: Fontana.

Dollimore, J. (1991). *Sexual Dissidence.* Oxford: Clarendon Press.

Dover, K.J. (1989). *Greek Homosexuality.* Cambridge, MA: Harvard University Press.

Dowsett, G. (1994). *Sexual Contexts and Homosexually Active Men in Australia.* Canberra: Commonwealth Department of Human Services and Health.

Fyfe, B. (1983). "Homophobia" or homosexual bias reconsidered, *Archives of Sexual Behavior,* 12(6): 549-554.

Gay Men and Lesbians Against Discrimination (GLAD) (1994). *Not a Day Goes By: Report on the GLAD Survey Into Discrimination and Violence Against Lesbians and Gay Men in Victoria.* Melbourne: Gay Men and Lesbians Against Discrimination.

Gilding, M. (1991). *The Making and Breaking of the Australian Family.* Sydney: Allen and Unwin.

Godwin, J., J. Hamblin, D. Patterson, and D. Buchanan (1991). *The Australian HIV/AIDS Legal Guide*, Second Edition. Sydney: Australian Federation of AIDS Organisations.

Grau, G. (1995). *Hidden Holocaust?* London: Cassell.

Haaga, D.A.F. (1991). Homophobia? *Journal of Social Behavior and Personality*, 6(1): 171-174.

Haeberle, E.J. (1991). Swastica, pink triangle, and yellow star: The destruction of sexology and the persecution of homosexuals in Nazi Germany. In *Hidden from History*, edited by M.B. Duberman, M. Vicinus, and G. Chauncy Jr. London: Penguin Books, pp. 365-379.

Halperin, D.M. (1990). *One Hundred Years of Homosexuality*, New York: Routledge.

Halperin, D.M. (1991). Sex before sexuality: Pederasty, politics and power in classical Athens. In *Hidden from History*, edited by M.B. Duberman, M. Vicinus, and G. Chauncy Jr. London: Penguin Books, pp. 37-53.

Halperin, D.M. (1995). *Saint Foucault*. New York: Oxford University Press.

Halperin, D.M., J.J. Winkler, and F.I. Zeitlin, eds. (1990). *Before Sexuality*, Princeton, NJ: Princeton University Press..

Hansen, G.L. (1982). Androgyny, sex role orientation and homosexism, *Journal of Psychology*, 112(1): 39-45.

Heger, H. (1980). *Men with the Pink Triangle*. London: GMP Publishers.

Hendriks, A., R. Tielman, and E. van der Veen (1993). *The Third Pink Book: A Global View of Lesbian and Gay Liberation and Oppression*, Buffalo, NY: Prometheus Books.

Herdt, G.H. (1993). Ritualized Homosexual Behavior in the Male Cults of Melanesia, 1862-1983. In *Ritualised Homosexuality in Melanesia*, edited by G. Herdt. Berkley: University of California Press, pp. 1-81.

Herek, G.M. and K.T. Berrill (1992). *Hate Crimes: Confronting Violence Against Lesbians and Gay Men*. London: Sage.

Hester, M. (1992). *Lewd Women and Wicked Witches*. London: Routledge.

Higgins, P. (1993). *A Queer Reader*, London: Fourth Estate.

Hudson, W.W. and W.A. Rickets (1980). A strategy for the measurement of homophobia, *Journal of Homosexuality*, 5(4) (Summer): 357-372.

Karlinsky, S. (1991). Russia's gay literature: The impact of the October Revolution. In *Hidden from History*, edited by M.B. Duberman, M. Vicinus, and G. Chauncy Jr. London: Penguin Books.

Mac an Ghaill, M. (1994). *The Making of Men*. Buckingham: Open University Press.

Marshall, G., ed (1994). *The Concise Oxford Dictionary of Sociology*, Oxford: Oxford University Press.

Martin, A.D. (1982). Learning to hide: The socialization of the gay adolescent, *Adolescent Psychiatry*, 10: 52-65.

Morris, M. (1995). *Pink Triangle: The Gay Law Reform Debate in Tasmania*. Sydney: UNSW Press.

Neisen, J.H. (1990). Heterosexism: Redefining homophobia for the 1990's, *Journal of Gay and Lesbian Psychotherapy*, 1(3): 21-35.

New South Wales Attorney General's Department (1996). *Review of the "Homosexual Advance Defence."* Sydney: New South Wales Attorney General's Department.

Plant, R. (1986). *The Pink Triangle.* New York: Henry Holt Co.

Plummer, D. (1995). Homophobia and health: Unjust, antisocial, harmful and endemic, *Health Care Analysis*, 3(2): 150-156.

Pringle R. (1992). Absolute sex? Unpacking the sexuality/gender relationship. In *Rethinking Sex*, edited by R.W. Connell, and G.W. Dowsett. Melbourne: Melbourne University Press.

Sandroussi, J. and S. Thompson (1995). *Out of the Blue: A Police Survey of Violence and Harassment Against Gay Men and Lesbians.* Sydney: New South Wales Police Service.

Schatz, B. and K. O'Hanlan (1994). *Anti-gay Discrimination in Medicine: Results of a National Survey of Lesbian, Gay, and Bisexual Physicians.* San Francisco: American Association of Physicians for Human Rights.

Siedlecky, S. and D. Wyndham (1990). *Populate and Perish.* Sydney: Allen & Unwin.

Tomsen, S. (1993). The political contradictions of policing and countering anti-gay violence in New South Wales, *Current Issues in Criminal Justice*, 5(2): 209-215.

Tomsen, S. (1994). Hatred, murder and male honour: Gay homicides and the "homosexual panic defence," *Criminology Australia*, 6(2): 2-6.

Tomsen, S. (1997). Was Lombroso queer? Criminology, criminal justice and the heterosexual imaginary. In *Homophobic Violence*, edited by G. Mason and S. Tomsen. Sydney: Hawkins Press.

Weeks, J. (1985). *Sexuality and Its Discontents.* London: Routledge.

Weeks, J. (1991). *Against Nature.* London: Rivers Oram Press.

Weinberg, G. (1972). *Society and the Healthy Homosexual.* Boston: Alyson Publications.

World Health Organization (1992). *The ICD-10 Classification of Mental and Behavioral Disorders.* Geneva: World Health Organization.

Chapter 2

Bersani, L. (1988). Is the rectum a grave? In *AIDS: Cultural Analysis, Cultural Activism*, edited by D. Crimp. Cambridge, MA: MIT Press.

Brown, L, ed. (1993). *The New Shorter Oxford English Dictionary.* Oxford: Clarendon Press.

Clark, M. (1987). *The Great Divide: The Construction of Gender in the Primary School.* Canberra: Curriculum Development Centre.

Connell, R.W. (1983). *Which Way Is Up? Essays on Sex, Class and Culture.* Sydney: Allen & Unwin.

Connell, R.W. (1987). *Gender and Power.* Cambridge: Polity Press.

Connell, R.W. (1995). *Masculinities.* Sydney: Allen & Unwin.

Cox, G. (1994). *The Count and Counter Report.* Sydney: Lesbian and Gay Anti-Violence Project.

Davenport-Hines, R. (1991). *Sex, Death and Punishment.* London: Fontana.

Ficarotto, T.J. (1990). Racism, sexism and erotophobia: Attitudes of heterosexuals towards homosexuals, *Journal of Homosexuality,* 19(1): 111-116.

Goffman, E. (1963). *Stigma.* New York: Simon and Schuster.

Gonsiorek, J.C. (1993). Mental health issues of gay and lesbian adolescents. In *Psychological Perspectives on Lesbian and Gay Male Experiences,* edited by L.D. Garnets and D.C. Kimmel. New York: Columbia University Press, pp. 469-485.

Herek, G.M. (1994). Assessing heterosexuals' attitudes towards lesbians and gay men. In *Lesbian and Gay Psychology: Theory, Research and Clinical Applications,* edited by B. Greene and G.M. Herek. Thousand Oaks, CA: Sage Publications.

Jordan, E. (1995). Fighting boys and fantasy play: the construction of masculinity in the early years of school, *Gender and Education,* 7(1): 69-85.

Kinney, D.A. (1993). From nerds to normals: The recovery of identity among adolescents from middle school to high school, *Sociology of Education,* 66(1): 21-40.

Kurdek, L.A. (1988). Correlates of negative attitudes towards homosexuals in heterosexual college students, *Sex Roles,* 18(11/12): 727-738.

Layder, D. (1993). *New Strategies in Social Research.* Cambridge: Polity.

Lloyd, G. (1984). *The Man of Reason,* London: Routledge.

Mac an Ghaill M. (1994). *The Making of Men: Masculinities, Sexualities and Schooling.* Buckingham: Open University Press.

Messerschmidt, J.W. (1994). Schooling, masculinities and youth crime by white boys. In *Men, Masculinities and Crime: Just Doing Boys Business?,* edited by T. Newburn and E. A. Stanko. London: Routledge.

Messner, M.A. (1992). *Power at Play.* Boston: Beacon Press.

Messner, M.A. and D.F. Sabo, eds. (1990). *Sport, Men and the Gender Order.* Champaign, IL: Human Kinetics Books.

Minichiello, V., R. Aroni, E. Timewell, and L. Alexander (1990). *In-Depth Interviewing,* First Edition. Melbourne: Longman Cheshire.

Mooney, A., R. Creeser, and Blatchford, P. (1991). Children's views on teasing and fighting in junior schools, *Educational Research,* 33(2): 103-112.

Newburn, T., and E. A. Stanko, eds. (1994). *Just Boys Doing Business? Men, Masculinities and Crime,* London: Routledge.

Olweus, D. (1991). Bully-victim problems among school children. In *The Development and Treatment of Childhood Aggression,* edited by D. Pepler and K. Rubin. Hillsdale, NJ: Erlbaum Publishing, Hillsdale.

Olweus, D. (1993). *Bullying at school: What We Know and What We Can Do.* Oxford: Blackwell.

Opie, I. and P. Opie (1977). *The Lore and Language of Schoolchildren.* St. Albans, England: Paladin.

Parker, A. (1996). The construction of masculinity within boys' physical education, *Gender and Education,* 8(2): 141-157.

Pringle, R. (1992). Absolute sex? Unpacking the sexuality/gender relationship. In *Rethinking Sex,* edited by R.W. Connell and G.W. Dowsett. Melbourne: Melbourne University Press, pp. 76-101.

Rich, A. (1980). Compulsory heterosexuality and the lesbian existence, *Signs,* 5(4): 631-660.

Rigby, K. and P.T. Slee (1991). Bullying among Australian school children, *Journal of Social Psychology,* 131(5): 615-627.

Rofes, E. (1995). Making our schools safe for sissies. In *The Gay Teen: Educational Practice and Theory for Lesbian, Gay and Bisexual Adolescents,* edited by G. Unks. New York: Routledge, pp. 79-84.

Seltzer, R. (1992). The social location of those holding antihomosexual attitudes, *Sex Roles,* 26(9/10): 391-398.

Thorne, B. (1993). *Gender Play: Girls and Boys in School.* Buckingham: Open University Press.

Whitney, I. and P.K. Smith (1993). A survey of the nature and extent of bullying in junior/middle and secondary schools, *Educational Research,* 35(1): 3-25.

Willis, P.E. (1977). *Learning to Labour.* Farnborough: Saxon House.

Chapter 3

Bayer, R. (1987). *Homosexuality and American Psychiatry.* Princeton, NJ: Princeton University Press.

Biber, I. (1962). *Homosexuality: A Psychoanalytic Study of Male Homosexuals,* New York: Basic Books.

Boulton, M.J. (1995). Playground behaviour and peer interaction patterns of primary school boys classified as bullies, victims and not involved, *British Journal of Educational Psychology,* 65(2): 165-177.

Clark, M. (1987). *The Great Divide: The Construction of Gender in the Primary School.* Curriculum Development Centre, Commonwealth of Australia, Canberra.

Connell, R.W. (1983). *Which Way Is Up? Essays on Sex, Class and Culture.* Sydney: Allen & Unwin.

Connell, R.W. (1989). Cool guys, swots and wimps: The interplay of masculinity and education, *Oxford Review of Education,* 15(3): 291-303.

Cramer, D.W. and A.J. Roach (1988). Coming out to Mom and Dad: A study of gay males and their relationships with their parents, *Journal of Homosexuality,* 15(3/4): 79-91.

Davies, B. (1989). *Frogs and Snails and Feminist Tails.* Sydney: Allen & Unwin.

Galambos, N.L., D.M. Almeida, and A.C. Petersen (1990). Masculinity, femininity and sex role attitudes in early adolescence, *Child Development,* 61(6): 1905-1914.

Herek, G.M. (1994). Assessing heterosexuals' attitudes towards lesbians and gay men: A review of empirical research with the ATLG scale. In *Lesbian and Gay Psychology,* edited by B. Greene and G.M. Herek. Thousand Oaks, CA: Sage.

Holland, J., C. Ramazanoglu, and S. Scott (1993). *Wimp or Gladiator: Contradictions in Acquiring Masculine Sexuality.* London: Tufnell Press.

Jordan, E. (1995). Fighting boys and fantasy play: The construction of masculinity in the early years of school, *Gender and Education,* 7(1): 69-85.

Kinney, D.A. (1993). From nerds to normals: The recovery of identity among adolescents from middle school to high school, *Sociology of Education,* 66(1): 21-40.

Mac an Ghaill, M. (1994). *The Making of Men: Masculinities, Sexualities and Schooling.* Buckingham, England: Open University Press.

Martin, A.D. (1982). Learning to hide: The socialization of the gay adolescent, *Adolescent Psychiatry,* 10: 52-65.

Mooney, A., R. Creeser, and P. Blatchford (1991). Children's views on teasing and fighting in junior schools, *Educational Research,* 33(2): 103-112.

Netting, N. (1992). Sexuality in youth culture: Identity and change, *Adolescence,* 27(108): 961-976.

O'Conor, A. (1995). Who gets called queer in school? In *The Gay Teen: Educational Practice and Theory for Lesbian, Gay and Bisexual Youth,* edited by G. Unks. New York: Routledge.

Olweus, D. (1991). Bully-victim problems among school children. In *The Development and Treatment of Childhood Aggression,* edited by D. Pepler and K. Rubins. Hillsdale, NJ: Erlbaum Publishing.

Olweus, D. (1993). *Bullying at School: What We Know and What We Can Do.* Oxford: Blackwell.

Rigby, K. and P.T. Slee (1991). Bullying among Australian school children, *Journal of Social Psychology,* 13(5): 615-627.

Savin-Williams, R.C. (1989). Coming out to parents and self esteem among gay and lesbian youths. In *Homosexuality and the Family,* edited by F.W. Bozett. Binghamton, NY: Harrington Park Press.

Savin-Williams, R.C. (1994). Verbal and physical abuse as stressors in the lives of lesbian, gay male and bisexual youths: Associated with school problems, running away, substance abuse, prostitution and suicide, *Journal of Consulting and Clinical Psychology,* 62(2): 264-269.

Thorne, B. (1993). *Gender Play: Girls and Boys in School.* Buckingham: Open University Press.

West, C. and D. H. Zimmerman (1987). Doing gender, *Gender & Society,* 1(2): 125-151.

Whitney, I. and P.K. Smith (1993). A survey of the nature and extent of bullying in junior/middle and secondary schools, *Educational Research,* 35(1): 3-25.

Willis, P.E. (1977). *Learning to Labour.* Farnborough: Saxon House.

Yee, M. and R. Brown (1994). The development of gender differentiation in young children, *The British Journal of Social Psychology,* 33(2): 183-196.

Chapter 4

Aggleton, P. (1987). *Deviance.* London: Tavistock Press.

Anderson, D.A. (1995). Lesbian and gay adolescents: Social and developmental considerations. In *The Gay Teen: Educational Practice and Theory for Les-*

bian, Gay and Bisexual Adolescents, edited by G. Unks. New York: Routledge, pp. 17-28.

Connell, R.W. (1995). *Masculinities.* Sydney: Allen & Unwin.

Cramer, D.W. and A.J. Roach (1988). Coming out to Mom and Dad: A study of gay males and their relationships with their parents, *Journal of Homosexuality,* 15(3/4): 79-91.

Ernulf, K.E. and S.M. Innala (1987). The relationship between affective and cognitive components of homophobic reaction, *Archives of Sexual Behaviour,* 16(6): 501-509.

Foucault, M. (1990). *The History of Sexuality* (Volume 1). New York: Vintage Books.

Freud, S. (1977). *On Sexuality.* London: Penguin Books.

Garnets, L., G.M. Herek, and B. Levy (1993). Violence and victimization of lesbians and gay men: Mental health consequences. In *Psychological Perspectives on Lesbian and Gay Male Experiences,* edited by L.D. Garnetts and D.C. Kimmel. New York: Columbia University Press, pp. 579-597.

Goffman, E. (1963). *Stigma: Notes on the Management of Spoiled Identity* (1986 edition), New York: Simon and Schuster.

Gonsiorek, J.C. (1993). Mental health issues of gay and lesbian adolescents. In *Psychological Perspectives on Lesbian and Gay Male Experiences,* edited by L.D. Garnets and D.C. Kimmel. New York: Columbia University Press, pp. 469-485.

Gonsiorek, J.C. and J.R. Rudolph (1991). Homosexual identity: Coming out and other developmental events. In *Homosexuality: Research Implications for Public Policy,* edited by J.C. Gonsiorek and J.D. Weinrich. Newbury Park, CA: Sage, pp. 161-176.

Gray, C., P. Russell, and S. Blockley (1991). The effects upon helping behaviour of wearing pro-gay identification, *British Journal of Social Psychology,* 30(2): 171-178.

Halperin, D.M. (1995). *Saint Foucault.* New York: Oxford University Press.

Hazler, R.J., J.H. Hoover, and R. Oliver (1993). What do kids say about bullying? *Education Digest,* 58(7): 16-20.

Herek, G.M. (1984). Beyond homophobia: A social psychological perspective on attitudes towards lesbians and gay men, *Journal of Homosexuality,* 10(1/2): 1-21.

Herek, G.M. (1991). Stigma, prejudice and violence against lesbians and gay men. In *Homosexuality: Research Implications for Public Policy,* edited by J.C. Gonsiorek and J.D. Weinrich. Newbury Park, CA: Sage, pp. 60-80.

Herek, G.M. (1994). Assessing heterosexuals' attitudes toward lesbians and gay men. In *Lesbian and Gay Psychology,* edited by B. Greene and G.M. Herek. Thousand Oaks, CA: Sage, pp. 206-228.

Hockenberry, S.L. and R.E. Billingham (1987). Sexual orientation and boyhood gender conformity: Development of the boyhood gender conformity scale (BGCS), *Archives of Sexual Behaviour,* 16(6): 475-487.

Kurdek, L.A. (1988). Correlates of negative attitudes towards homosexuals in heterosexual college students, *Sex Roles,* 18(11/12): 727-738.

Mac an Ghaill, M. (1994). *The Making of Men: Masculinities, Sexualities and Schooling.* Buckingham: Open University Press.

Martin, A.D. (1982). Learning to hide: The socialization of the gay adolescent, *Adolescent Psychiatry,* 10: 52-65.

Mason, G. (1993). Violence against lesbians and gay men. *Violence Prevention Today, No. 2.* Canberra: Australian Institute of Criminology.

O'Conor, A. (1995). Who gets called queer at school?, In *The Gay Teen: Educational Practice and Theory for Lesbian, Gay and Bisexual Adolescents,* edited by G. Unks. New York: Routledge.

Pronger, B. (1990). Gay jocks: A phenomenology of gay men in athletics. In *Sport Men and the Gender Order,* edited by M.A. Messner and D.f. Sabo. Champaign, IL: Human Kinetics Books, pp. 141-152.

Remafedi, G., ed. (1994). *Death by Denial: Studies of Suicide in Gay and Lesbian Teenagers.* Boston: Alyson Publications.

Rigby, K. and P.T. Slee (1991). Bullying among Australian school children, *Journal of Social Psychology,* 13(5): 615-627.

Robinson, B.E., L.H. Walters and P. Skeen (1989). Response of parents to learning that their child is homosexual and concern over AIDS: A national study. In *Homosexuality and the Family,* edited by F. Bozett. Binghamton, NY: Harrington Park Press, pp. 59-80.

Rofes, E. (1995). Making our schools safe for sissies. In *The Gay Teen: Educational Practice and Theory for Lesbian, Gay and Bisexual Adolescents,* edited by G. Unks. New York: Routledge, pp. 79-84.

Ross, M.W. (1985). Actual and anticipated societal reaction to homosexuality and adjustment in two societies, *The Journal of Sex Research,* 21(1): 40-55.

Ross, M.W. (1990). The relationship between life events and mental health in homosexual men, *Journal of Clinical Psychology,* 46(4): 402-411.

Ross, M.W. (1996). Societal reaction to homosexuality. In *Preventing Heterosexism and Homophobia,* edited by E.D. Rothblum and L.A. Bond. Thousand Oaks, CA: Sage, pp. 205-218.

San Miguel, C.L. and J. Millham (1976). The role of cognitive and situational variables in aggression toward homosexuals, *Journal of Homosexuality,* 2(1): 11-27.

Savin-Williams, R.C. (1994). Verbal and physical abuse as stressors in the lives of lesbian, gay male and bisexual youths: associated with school problems, running away, substance abuse, prostitution and suicide, *Journal of Consulting and Clinical Psychology,* 62(2): 264-269.

Sedgewick, E.K. (1990). *The Epistemology of the Closet.* Berkeley: University of California Press.

Seltzer, R. (1992). The social location of those holding antihomosexual attitudes, *Sex Roles,* 26(9/10): 391-398.

Shidlo, A. (1994). Internalized homophobia. In *Lesbian and Gay Psychology,* edited by B. Greene and G.M. Herek. Thousand Oaks, CA: Sage, pp. 176-205.

Smith, P.K. (1991). The silent nightmare: Bullying and victimization in school peer groups, *The Psychologist,* 4(6): 243-247.

Smith, P.K. and S. Levan (1995). Perceptions and experiences of bullying in younger pupils, *British Journal of Educational Psychology,* 65(4): 489-500.

Strommen, E. (1993). "You're a what?": Family reactions to the disclosure of homosexuality. In *Psychological Perspectives on Lesbian and Gay Male Experiences,* edited by L.D. Garnets and D.C. Kimmel. New York: Columbia University Press, pp. 248-266.

Thorne, B. (1993). *Gender Play: Girls and Boys in School.* Buckingham, England: Open University Press.

Troiden, R.R. (1993). The formation of homosexual identities. In *Psychological Perspectives on Lesbian and Gay Male Experiences,* edited by L.D. Garnets and D.C. Kimmel. New York: Columbia University Press, pp. 191-217.

Wells, J.W. (1991). The effects of homophobia and sexism on heterosexual sexual relationships, *Journal of Sex Education and Therapy,* 17(3): 185-195.

Willis, P.E. (1977). *Learning to Labour.* Farnborough: Saxon House.

Working Party on the Review of the Homosexual Panic Defence (1996). *Review of the "Homosexual Panic Defence."* Sydney: Attorney General's Department.

Chapter 5

Anderson, D.A. (1995). Lesbian and gay adolescents: Social and developmental considerations. In *The Gay Teen: Educational Practice and Theory for Lesbian, Gay and Bisexual Adolescents,* edited by G. Unks. New York: Routledge, pp. 17-28.

Boulton (1995). Playground behaviour and peer interaction patterns of primary school boys classified as bullies, victims and not involved, *British Journal of Educational Psychology,* 65(2): 165-177.

Britton, D.M. (1990). Homophobia and homosociality: An analysis of boundary maintenance, *Sociological Quarterly,* 31(3): 423-439.

Connell, R.W. (1983). *Which Way Is Up? Essays on Sex, Class and Culture.* Sydney: Allen & Unwin.

Connell, R.W. (1989). Cool guys, swots and wimps: The interplay of masculinity and education, *Oxford Review of Education,* 15(3): 291-303.

Devlin, P.K. and G.A. Cowan (1985). Homophobia, perceived fathering, and male intimate relationships, *Journal of Personality Assessment,* 49(5): 467-473.

Eliason, M.J. (1995). Accounts of sexual identity formation in heterosexual students, *Sex Roles,* 32(11/12): 821-834.

Griffin, P. (1995). Homophobia in sport. In *The Gay Teen: Educational Practice and Theory for Lesbian, Gay and Bisexual Adolescents,* edited by G. Unks. New York: Routledge, pp. 53-65.

Kidd, B. (1990). The Men's Cultural Center: Sports and the dynamic of women's oppression/men's oppression. In *Sport, Men and the Gender Order,* edited by M.A. Messner and D.F. Sabo. Champaign, IL: Human Kinetics Books, pp. 31-43.

Kinney, D.A. (1993). From nerds to normals: The recovery of identity among adolescents from middle school to high school, *Sociology of Education,* 66(1): 21-40.

Mac an Ghaill, M. (1994). *The Making of Men: Masculinities, Sexualities and Schooling.* Buckingham: Open University Press.

Martin, A.D. (1982). Learning to hide: The socialisation of the gay adolescent, *Adolescent Psychiatry,* 10: 52-65.

Messner, M.A. (1992). *Power at Play.* Boston: Beacon Press.

Pronger, B. (1990). *The Arena of Masculinity.* London: GMP Publishers.

Rich, A. (1980). Compulsory heterosexuality and the lesbian existence, *Signs,* 5(4): 631-660.

San Miguel, C.L. and J. Millham (1976). The role of cognitive and situational variables in aggression toward homosexuals, *Journal of Homosexuality,* 2(1): 11-27.

Strommen, E. (1993). "You're a what?" Family reactions to the disclosure of homosexuality. In *Psychological Perspectives on Lesbian and Gay Male Experiences,* edited by L.D. Garnets and D.C. Kimmel. New York: Columbia University Press, pp. 248-266.

Thorne, B. (1993). *Gender Play: Girls and Boys in School,* Buckingham: Open University Press.

Walker, P. and C. Antaki (1986). Sexual orientation as a basis for categorisation in recall, *British Journal of Social Psychology,* 25(6): 337-339.

Weisner, T.S. and J.E. Wilson-Mitchell (1990). Nonconventional family lifestyles and sex typing in six year olds, *Child Development,* 61(6): 1915-1933.

Wells, J.W. (1991). The effects of homophobia and sexism on heterosexual sexual relationships, *Journal of Sex Education and Therapy,* 17(3): 185-195.

Whitson, D. (1990). Sport in the social construction of masculinity. In *Sport, Men and the Gender Order,* edited by M.A. Messner and D.F. Sabo. Champaign, IL: Human Kinetics Books, pp. 19-29.

Chapter 6

Bersani, L. (1988). Is the rectum a grave? In *AIDS: Cultural Analysis, Cultural Activism,* edited by D. Crimp. Cambridge: MIT Press.

Bersani, L. (1995). *Homos.* Cambridge: Harvard University Press,.

Connell, R.W. and G.W. Dowsett, eds. (1992). *Rethinking Sex,* Melbourne: Melbourne University Press.

Deleuze, G. and F. Guattari (1983). (1972 French Original). *Anti-Oedipus.* Minneapolis: University of Minnesota Press.

Dollimore, J. (1991). *Sexual Dissidence.* Oxford: Clarendon Press.

Foucault, M. (1990) (1978 English Translation). *The History of Sexuality* (Volume 1). New York: Vintage.

Freud, S. (1977a). *On Sexuality.* London: Penguin Books.

Freud, S. (1977b). *Case Histories II.* London: Penguin Books.

Frosh, S. (1994). *Sexual Difference.* London: Routledge

Gilding, M. (1991). *The Making and Breaking of the Australian Family.* Sydney: Allen & Unwin.

Gilman, S.L. (1985). *Difference and Pathology.* Ithaca: Cornell University Press.

Gilmore, D.D. (1990). *Manhood in the Making*. New Haven: Yale University Press.

Goffman, E. (1963). *Stigma*. New York: Simon and Schuster.

Halperin, D.M. (1995). *Saint Foucault*. New York: Oxford University Press.

Hendriks, A., R. Tielman, and E. van der Veen (1993). *The Third Pink Book: A Global View of Lesbian and Gay Liberation and Oppression*. Buffalo, NY: Prometheus Books.

Highwater, J. (1997). *The Mythology of Transgression: Homosexuality As Metaphor*. Oxford: Oxford University Press.

Hocquenghem, G. (1993). (French Original 1972). *Homosexual Desire*. Durham: Duke University Press.

Kinsey, A., W. Pommeroy, and C. Martin (1948). *Sexual Behavior in the Human Male*. New York: W.B. Saunders.

Lewis, I.M. (1985). *Social Anthropology in Perspective* (Second Edition). Cambridge: Cambridge University Press.

Mac an Ghaill M. (1994). *The Making of Men: Masculinities, Sexualities and Schooling*. Buckingham: Open University Press.

Metcalf, P. and R. Huntington (1991). *Celebrations of Death* (Second Edition). Cambridge: Cambridge University Press.

Sabo, D.F. and J. Panepinto (1990). Football ritual and the social reproduction of masculinity. In *Sport, Men and the Gender Order*, edited by M.A. Messner and D.F. Sabo. Champaign, IL: Human Kinetics Books, pp. 115-126.

Sedgwick, E.K. (1990). *The Epistemology of the Closet*. Berkeley: University of California Press.

Skrzipek von, K.H. (1978). Menschliche "Auslosermerkmale" beider Geschlechter I Attrappenwahluntersuchungen der Verhaltensentwicklung, *Homo,* 29: 75-88.

Skrzipek von, K.H. (1981). Menschliche "Auslosermerkmale" beider Geschlechter II, *Homo,* 32: 105-119.

Skrzipek von, K.H. (1982). Menschliche "Auslosermerkmale" beider Geschlechter III, *Homo,* 33: 1-12.

Skrzipek von, K.H. (1983). Stammesgeschichtliche Dispositionen der geschlechtsspezifischen Sozialisation des Kindes—eine experimentelle humanethologische Analyse, *Homo,* 34: 227-238.

Thorne, B. (1993). *Gender Play: Girls and Boys in School*. Buckingham: Open University Press.

Van Gennep (1960). (French Original 1908). *The Rites of Passage*. Chicago: University of Chicago Press.

Weeks, J. (1985). *Sexuality and Its Discontents*. London: Routledge.

Appendixes

Duberman, M.B., M. Vicinus, and G. Chauncey Jr. eds. (1991). *Hidden from History*. London: Penguin Books.

Foucault, M. (1990). *The History of Sexuality* (Volumes 1, 2, and 3). New York: Vintage Books.

Glaser, B. and A. Strauss (1967). *The Discovery of Grounded Theory.* Chicago: Aldine.

Halperin, D.M. (1990). *One Hundred Years of Homosexuality.* New York: Routledge.

Herek, G.M. (1994). Assessing heterosexuals' attitudes towards lesbians and gay men: A review of empirical research with the ATLG Scale. In *Lesbian and Gay Psychology*, edited by B. Greene and G.M. Herek. Thousand Oaks, CA: Sage, pp. 206-228.

Layder, D. (1993). *New Strategies in Social Research.* Cambridge: Polity.

Minichiello, V., R. Aroni, E. Timewell, and L. Alexander (1992). *In-Depth Interviewing,* First Edition. Melbourne: Longman Cheshire.

Sedgewick, E.K. (1990). *The Epistemology of the Closet.* Berkeley: University of California Press.

Weeks, J. (1985). *Sexuality and Its Discontents.* London: Routledge.

Index

Order Your Own Copy of
This Important Book for Your Personal Library!

ONE OF THE BOYS
Masculinity, Homophobia, and Modern Manhood

_____ in hardbound at $49.95 (ISBN: 1-56023-973-5)

_____ in softbound at $24.95 (ISBN: 1-56023-974-3)

COST OF BOOKS_____	☐ **BILL ME LATER:** ($5 service charge will be added)
	(Bill-me option is good on US/Canada/Mexico orders only;
OUTSIDE USA/CANADA/	not good to jobbers, wholesalers, or subscription agencies.)
MEXICO: ADD 20%_____	
	☐ Check here if billing address is different from
POSTAGE & HANDLING_____	shipping address and attach purchase order and
(US: $3.00 for first book & $1.25	billing address information.
for each additional book)	
Outside US: $4.75 for first book	
& $1.75 for each additional book)	Signature_____
SUBTOTAL_____	☐ **PAYMENT ENCLOSED: $**_____
IN CANADA: ADD 7% GST_____	☐ **PLEASE CHARGE TO MY CREDIT CARD.**
STATE TAX_____	☐ Visa ☐ MasterCard ☐ AmEx ☐ Discover
(NY, OH & MN residents, please	☐ Diners Club
add appropriate local sales tax)	Account #_____
FINAL TOTAL_____	Exp. Date_____
(If paying in Canadian funds,	
convert using the current	Signature_____
exchange rate. UNESCO	
coupons welcome.)	

Prices in US dollars and subject to change without notice.

NAME _____

INSTITUTION _____

ADDRESS _____

CITY _____

STATE/ZIP _____

COUNTRY _____ COUNTY (NY residents only) _____

TEL _____ FAX _____

E-MAIL_____

May we use your e-mail address for confirmations and other types of information? ☐ Yes   ☐ No

Order From Your Local Bookstore or Directly From
The Haworth Press, Inc.
10 Alice Street, Binghamton, New York 13904-1580 • USA
TELEPHONE: 1-800-HAWORTH (1-800-429-6784) / Outside US/Canada: (607) 722-5857
FAX: 1-800-895-0582 / Outside US/Canada: (607) 772-6362
E-mail: getinfo@haworthpressinc.com
PLEASE PHOTOCOPY THIS FORM FOR YOUR PERSONAL USE.

BOF96